SHAHEED BHAGAT SINGH

SHAHEED BHAGAT SINGH
Unique Martyr in Freedom Movement

OMESH SAIGAL

GYAN PUBLISHING HOUSE
New Delhi-110002

Shaheed Bhagat Singh
Unique Martyr in Freedom Movement
(Biography, Political Science, History)
Rs. 790

ISBN : 81-212-0796-7

Published in 2002 in India by
Gyan Publishing House
5, Ansari Road, Darya Ganj
New Delhi - 110002
Phones : 3282060, 3261060, Fax : (011) 3285914

E-mail: gyanbook@vsnl.com

Website: http://www.gyanbooks.com

Lassertypesetting at: A.A. Computer
Printed at : Mehra Offset Press

Contents

Preface 9

Introduction 11

1. **Nation in those Days** 15

Central Council; Structure of Central Council; Promulgation of their Views; Pamphlets of Naujawan Bharat Sabha; Uniting Peasants.

2. **Revolution in Blood** 31

Early Career; Ajit Singh; His Uncle: Ajit Singh; Bhagat Singh is Born; Revolutionary Family; Sh. Arjun Singh and Sh. Kishan Singh; Influence of Yashpal; Career of his Father; Contemporary Patriots; Personality of Bhagat Singh.

3. **Early Career** 43

Influence of Parents; Impact of First World War; Father and Son; Bhagat Meets Comrade; Formation of HRA; Revolutionary Groups Unite; The Tribunal.

4. **An Eventful Youth** 51

Influence of Teachers; Impact of Chhabildas; National Dramatic Club; Service to Motherland; College Education; Final Step in Life; Deep Study; Labour Revolution; Exponent of New Age; Gopinath Saha Attains Martyrdom; Revolutionary Activities; New Phase of Life.

5. **The Bomb Incident** 87

The Jolly Event; Revival of Central Assembly Plans; Sukudev Instigates Bhagat Singh; Bomb Dropped.

6. **Trials of Bombing Case Hunger Strike** 105

Utopian Non-Violence; Our Intentions; What is Revolution?; The Plot at Lahore.

7. **Pronouncement of Verdict** 121

Views of Jury; The Punjab Kesari; Views of Sinha; Advice of Chattar Singh; Khudi Ram; Death and Reaction; Bhagat Singh in Communist Eye; Impact of Soviet Union; Views of Sohan Singh Josh.

8. Proceedings in Privy Council **137**
Opening of Petition; Views of Pritt; Assessment of Existing Legislation; Reaction of Pritt; Chamier and Mitchell.

9. The National Martyr **159**
Kuka's An Inspiring Chap; The Nayi Hawa; Indians Abroad; Aftermath of Jallianwala Bagh.

10. Could Gandhi Have Saved Bhagat Singh? **191**
Gandhi and Irwin; the Viceroy; Reaction of Subhas Bose; Views of Emerson; Views of D.P. Das; Delhi Pact; Gandhi's Responsibility.

11. Judging the Revolutionaries **201**
Role of Young Patriots; Gandhi's View; Personality; As a Student; Refusal to Commute; Lord Irwins Speaks; Comparing Gandhi and Bhagat Singh.

12. Bhagat Singh and his Comrades **221**
Chandrashekhar Azad; Bhagavaticharan Vohra; Rajguru; Sukhdev; Jatindranath Das; B.K. Dutt; Bejoykumar Sinha; Yashpal; Kamalnath Tiwari; Shiv Verma; Women Revolutionaries.

13. Left Wing Opposition and Role of Subhas Chandra Bose **233**
Demands for Better Treatment; Jatin Das; The Agreement; The Karachi Congress; Patel as President; Bose's Assessment; Police Atrocities; Views on Amnesty; Critical of Gandhi; Atmosphere in Delhi; Search for Better Order; Socialist Republic; Appeal to Workers; Praise for Bhagat Singh; Critical of Executions; Blunder of Congress; Views on Gandhi-Irwin Pact.

Appendices

1. The Government Advocate's Speech **261**

2. Jinnah's Speech in the Central Legislative Assembly on September 12 and 14, 1929 **269**

3. Text of Statement of Bhagat Singh and B.K. Dutt in the Assembly Bomb Case **285**

4. Government Order on the Classification of Prisoners and Undertrials. **291**

5. **Petition dated 20th September, 1930 by Sardar Kishan Singh to the Special Tribunal** **297**

6. **Gandhi-Irwin Pact S. 481/31- Political Home Department** **301**

Bibliography **307**

Index **311**

Preface

The role of Bhagat Singh is most significant in the history of Indian nationalism and freedom movement. Having deep connections with a patriotic family, young Bhagat Singh was greatly influenced by his father and uncle Ajit Singh. At that point of time, Lahore was the suitable headquarters of revolutionary activities. As a student, Bhagat Singh was greatly impressed by his devoted and sincere teachers who taught the students much more than the routine courses and their teachings had deep bearing on anti-Raj stance.

Under the revolutionary banner of the HSRA the young revolutionaries planned their programme well under the leadership of Bhagat Singh who proved to be a very sincere guide.

The manufacturing of bombs, using them against the administrative machinery of the *Raj,* to retaliate in a severe way—all these factors were responsible for gearing up their plans. When Lala Lajpat Rai and the processionists were lathi charged at Lahore, and Lala died after a few weeks, the revolutionaries made up their minds to wreak revenge and meticulously planned to murder J.A. Scott, the Senior Superintendant of Police, Lahore. Instead another young police officer, Saunders, was shot dead.

Throwing the bomb in the Central Assembly was a daring and fearless action by the revolutionaries. Bhagat Singh and his associates were arrested and were lodged in solitary cells at Lahore. The law of the *Raj* took its course and ultimately the judgments and appeals went against them. Bhagat Singh, Rajguru and Sukhdev were hanged on 23 March 1931.

Thirteen chapters, an Introduction and six appendices have weaved the romantic career of young revolutionaries, particularly Bhagat Singh, Rajguru and Sukhdev. The story comes to an end with the final hanging of this brave and fearless trio who have become a significant part of history. The controvery raised with Gandhi's role has also been depicted. The Bibliography is fairly exhaustive in contents.

The work would be useful for teachers, social scientists, scholars, political leaders and students in India and abroad.

Omesh Saigal

Introduction

'Lives of great men all remind us, we can make our lives sublime; and thus departing leave behind us, footprints in the sands of time.' It is not just about one 'great man' that we will read here, Bhagat Singh, but a whole lot of other 'great men' who either inspired him or were inspired by him. Seen in the background of the insipid fare that the leaders and self professed 'great men' of today dish out to us, it is difficult to believe that the people about whom you are about to read also trod the same earth that we are privileged to walk on.

India's struggle for independence was singular in its own right. It could not have been achieved without great sacrifices, sanguine love for the Motherland and the zeal to emancipate her from bondage of foreign rule by thousands and thousands of our countrymen. Any man with a heart would have vowed to avenge the Imperial British. This book solely dedicates its cause to a national martyr 'Bhagat Singh', who was incredible in his endeavours and infused in many the urge to fight for the cause of freedom. It also takes into account not just his life in detail, but that of his companions and his followers as well.

The need of the hour was a mass movement ; mass awakening, whether involving violence or nonviolence. Gandhiji,'the father of the nation' urged people to follow nonviolence but could not convince all his countrymen. As a result the Naujawan Bharat Sabha was formed in March 1926 at the suggestion of Dr. Satyapal to educate young men, especially the student community of the educational institutes located at Lahore.

This Sabha worked to lessen the communal distance between different communities of India, and to evoke anti-British feelings in the hearts of these men. The Sabha was a well organised association and held the first provincial conference at Amritsar on 13th April amidst a large gathering. It declared clearly that it was to establish in India an

Independent Socialist republic of the workers and peasants by all possible means. This Sabha had its roots in revolutionary thoughts and violence and its aims and objectives were promulgated in easy language to make them understandable to all. The police also vowed to treat these revolutionary ideas and their originators very harshly and did so.

Amidst a revolutionary fervour was born a great revolutionary, Bhagat Singh in 1907 in a family with revolutionary background. This was a time when people had already started sensing the end of British rule. Father Kishan Singh, uncle Ajit Singh, uncle Subaran Singh who were knowledged and great revolutionaries were to influence Bhagat Singh's life to some extent as we see in the book. Bhagat Singh grew up on stories of exploits of his uncle and his father. The Ghadar movement also left a deep impact on his mind. Kartar Singh Sarabha, hanged when he was only nineteen after conviction in the Lahore conspiracy case, became his idol. His feeling against the British imperialism was the manifestation of the brutalities of the British that he either witnessed or came to know about. The massacre at Jallianwala Bagh on April 13,1919, drove him to Amritsar where he kissed the earth soaked and sanctified with blood of the martyrs and brought back home a little of the blood-soaked soil. He had decided by then that he would devote himself to the cause of the nation, and thus always negated his father's incessant appeals to get married.

During the non-cooperation movement of 1921, boycott of councils, courts, schools and, colleges was only too common. Bhagat Singh also left DAV college and, after much hardship he got enrolled in the National College at Lahore. Since he was in the 9th standard then he first had to pass his matriculation at a short notice of 2 months. In this college he widened his knowledge and the implications of the struggle for independence. In order to propagate patriotic ideas among the people this young man set up a 'National dramatic club' and staged plays like 'Bharat Durdasha' and 'Chandra Gupta' in which Bhagat himself was the protagonist.

The coming together of Bhagat Singh and Azad was a great event in the revolutionary movement. Neither Bhagat Singh could have become what he was without Azad, nor could Azad attain the eminence that he achieved. Some others those got involved with him were Sukhdev, Raj Guru, Jatindra Nath Das, B.K. Dutt, and some others, and they uplifted our struggle for independence.

Then came the shocking murder of the A.S.P, Saunders, which put the British empire on a state of convulsion. The police implicated Bhagat

Singh, but he had vanished into thin air, i.e., he had shaved off his beard and moustache and could not be recognised and thus evaded the police. At that time he hatched the plans to rock the British rule once again—by dropping a bomb in the Central Assembly. Some oppressive bills were before the Assembly and the Government was adamantly backing them through into the statute book. This issue was to be utilized to arouse the Nation ; through a bomb. Sukhdev, another ardent revolutionary complicated matters at this juncture which left no option for Bhagat Singh but to get arrested after dropping the bombs in the Central Assembly and also to prove that he was more devoted than those misconceptions Sukhdev had been trying to create. Bhagat Singh chose although amongst dissent from comrades Batukeshwar Dutt for this bombing assignment. The plan was hatched in great detail. To make it most effective it was decided to drop the bombs at the psychological moment when the announcement of the viceregal approval would be made. And as soon as George Schuster had informed the house, H.E. the Viceroy by dint of his special powers had okayed the bill, Bhagat Singh and Dutt stood up. Bhagat Singh took a step forward and dropped a bomb behind Schuster. Then Dutt moved a step and dropped the second bomb. They didn't try to escape but raised slogans expouding the cause of revolution and offered themselves to be arrested. All this happened on the 8th of April 1928.

On the 7th of May 1929 the hearing of the case started in the court of Mr. Pool, inside Delhi Prison. Later on, this case was transferred to the court of Mr. Middleton. Their trial had been difficult given the fact they used the courtroom as a launching pad for their ideological missiles. They utilized every little occasion to issue a statement. The whole country was moved by their action and they were considered National heroes. They also observed hunger strikes which developed into an all-India affair. 30th June was celebrated throughout India as Bhagat Singh day.

The revolution was not a simple movement serving the cause of the revolutionary ideals only. These revolutionary groups made sure to make it a mass movement. Most of them were erudites through simple language they reached the masses, In this simple language, only they wrote and publicised the objectives of the revolutionary groups. This was well received by the masses and was also fuelled by British atrocities. It would not be less if we say that they had been pivotal in taking the whole country together, peasants, workers and all else into the struggle for independence.

Mahatma Gandhi, on the other hand strongly favoured non-violent means of overthrowing the British. The 'Satyagraha', 'Non cooperation', movements all symbolise his ideals. Although he believed in non-violence towards the mid-late phase of the Independence struggle people gave vent to their support for violence and as an outcome occurred many incidents like Chauri Chaura. But it was impossible for the whole Indian peoples to come out in open as they were too intimidated by British oppression.

Gandhiji's role in Bhagat Singh's trial seems a little awkward as opines Mr. D.P. Das, who had delved into the archives. Gandhiji's talk with Lord Irwin, the then-Viceroy speaks of an ambiguous stand taken by Gandhiji. Other writers give different opinions. Gandhiji did not even pursue the great momentum he could easily have thrusted on the National movement by giving credence and support to the sacrifices of Bhagat Singh and others.

Bhagat Singh was hanged at 7.33 in the evening on the 23rd March along with Sukhdev and Raj Guru. This awkward timing was chosen to maintain secrecy which otherwise was morning in other cases. Under cover of the night a collective pyre was prepared. After sometime, the half burnt bodies were thrown into the waters of Sutlez. However people came to know about all this and the whole country went into strikes and protests. Although people of all castes and races were united, the British succeeded here too in manoeuvreing communal riots. This highlighted the vulnerability of Indian people.

Bhagat Singh was more than a symbol. He was a visionary with a dream, the madness of a spinoza, the halo of a superhuman. He was neither a dead mental principle nor an empty political view. Bhagat Singh was a symbol of bravery and courage. As the time passed even Mahatma Gandhi praised him and his comrades without reservation saying, "It is impossible to assess his courage. Hanging has placed a crown of bravery on these young men. We must appreciate their sacrifice, bravery and unbounded courage".

"A gaint who stole the spark of the angels to kindle the forest fires, Bhagat Singh symbolises a new idealism that set everybody thinking, a new surge and thunder whose music led the slaves to Salvation".

Although the introduction gives some idea of the man and patriot that was Bhagat Singh, only a complete reading will give the reader an idea of the trying times of the country and the actual parameters and conditions that contributed to the making of Bhagat Singh as a national symbol of martydom.

1

Nation in those Days

The prominent part played by the young revolutionaries in 1920s is most significant and remarkable as this period depicts the trying phases of our freedom struggle. The revolutionary spirit caught the imagination of the masses as well as their political ideology received impetus and encouragement from the deeds and writings of earlier heroes and the important historic events which saw light as a result of early revolutionary activities.

The revolutionaries of this period were influenced tremendously by the deeds of patriots like Rash Behari Bose and Sachindranath Sanyal. The Hardinge Bomb Case, the *Ghadr* Movement, the Manipuri Conspiracy, the First Lahore Conspiracy Case and other political events had a great impact on the working of their young impressionable minds. The other important factor which influenced their views was the inauguration of the first Non-Cooperation Movement launched by Mahatma Gandhi. In this kind of non-violent *satyagraha*, many young men like Bhagat Singh, Sukhdev, Jatin Das, Chandrashekhar Azad, Bhagwati Charan Vohra, Yashpal, Jogesh Chandra Chatterjee and Dr. Gaya Prasad jumped in along with numerous other *satyagrahis*. They abandoned their homes, schools and colleges and courted arrests at the call of Gandhi. But the sudden annulment of the movement, following the gruesome events of Chauri Chaura and perpetration of violence at other places perplexed these youngmen and their faith in Gandhi's methods was shaken.

The rise of communal hatred further heightened and the orgy of communal riots and an atmosphere poisoned by mutual communal hatred further increased their frustration. These idealist youth could not comprehend anything unjust with Chauri Chaura. They could also not appreciate a conception of politics and morality which would fall a powerful popular movement with a single blow. The two alternatives offered, parliamentary politics of the Swarajists or the so-called constructive programme of the Nochangers and the one offered by Gandhi, were equally unacceptable to them. Their search for alternatives led them to socialism on the one hand and revolutionary terrorism on the other. They embraced both, as had been done half a century earlier by the Revolutionary Russian youth.[1] In mid-twenties, there was strong revolutionary fervour amongst the young men which necessitated that they work under the banner of one organised and well-disciplined forum. The *Naujawan Bharat Sabha* was formed in March 1926 at the suggestion of Dr. Satyapal to educate young men, especially the student community of the educational institutions situated at Lahore.

The programme of the Sabha comprised debates on moral, literacy and social subjects ; the popularisation of swadeshi goods, the inception of a sense of brotherhood, simple living and physical fitness and the orientation of interest in Indian languages and civilisation.[2]

Jai Dev Gupta, an active worker of the *Naujawan Bharat Sabha* reminisced thus : 'Bhagat Singh did not believe in God or in any religion. Why? After going through history, we found that Christians carried out crusades, Muslims executed *Jehads* only in the name of same God. But, because the other was not following the same faith, he must be killed. What was this? Was this God's volition? He concluded that in order to remove the physical slavery, we must do away with the mental slavery and it was the most efficient weapon in the armoury of our rulers—the British. Whenever they wanted to disturb the communal harmony for their own ends, they would instigate different religious heads against each other and create communal frenzy on large scale. Those who ruled us were successful in implementing their policy of 'divide and rule'. All clashes were there only in the name of God. So when this wall of God would be removed among communities, then those watertight compartments, artificially created, would vanish and humanity would prevail all over. He replaced God with humanity and religion by service to humanity. So this must be taught to the people if we had to emancipate them from the mental slavery.

'This was one of the main planks of the *Naujawan Bharat Sabha.* And to practise this, arranged community dinners, lunches in which all sorts of people would arrive. Hindus, Muslims, Sikhs, *Chamars*, *Bhangis* and everybody would cook. They would give *Jhatka* meat to the Muslims and *Halal* for the Sikhs. In order to remove that feeling, these meals were freely arranged. Secondly, lectures were delivered by the persons against their own religion. A Muslim or a Hindu or an Arya Samajist would speak against his own religion to the audience. So that the listeners might have some idea about the reality of God. In order to eliminate physical slavery, removal of mental slavery was necessary. Consequently, Bhagat Singh bade goodbye to this creation and became an out and out atheist.

'... The platform of *Naujawan Bharat Sabha* was utilized to create hatred or some sort of ill-feeling against the British and prepared the country for final assault in due course . . . The story of Kartar Singh Sarabha's life was also propagated from the platform. His photographs were exhibited with projected slides. So the *Naujawan Bharat Sabha,* on the one hand, wanted to preach non-existence of God and removal of mental slavery, on the other, they wanted to enthuse nationalism by highlighting the heroic deeds and sacrifices of such revolutionaries. In this way, capable youths were screened out for secret revolutionary work.'[3]

As a result *Naujawan Bharat Sabha* was a platform meant for open-discussion and expression of their opinion, anti-*Raj* in substance. Amongst them, suitable, reliable, sincere and trustworthy youngmen were bestowed with performing various kinds of jobs while maintaining strict secrecy and saving their own skin from the clutches of C.I.D. and other agencies of police. The rules and regulations of the Hindustan Republican Association were clearly enshrined in the form of a manifesto. Its object was to establish a Federal Republic of the United States of India for an organized and armed revolution. The final form of the constitution was to be framed and declared by the representatives of the people at the time when they would win that capability. The fundamental principle of the Republic was universal suffrage and the abolition or all systems which made any kind of exploitation of man by man possible.

Central Council

The governing body of the Association was a Central Council (reference-constitution of revolutionary party-page 264 appendix I) which consisted of the representatives of all the provinces of India. All the decisions of this Council were to be arrived at by unanimous consent and it was vested with absolute powers. The main functions of the Council were to supervise, adjust and coordinate the myriads of activities in the different provinces. The Council was also required to direct charge of the work which was carried in the countries outside India. In the provinces, this organisation took its roots on firm footing. A committee consisting of five persons represented five different departments of the Association in each province and they required to regulate all the activities of the Association in the province. The decisions were to be unanimous.

Structure of Central Council

Every provincial organisation had the following departments. These were propaganda, collection of men, collection of funds, collection and storage of arms and ammunition, and foreign connections. The propaganda was to be carried out systematically and the media was to be based on an open and a secret press ; through public platforms ; through a system of organized *kathas* and through magic lantern slides. Funds were to be collected by means of voluntary subscriptions and occasional use of force was acknowledged. It was incumbent to arm each and every member of the Association, but all such arms and ammunitions were to be stored at different centres and were to be used according to the direction and advice of the Provincial Committee only.

The district organiser was required to start branches of the Association in every nook and corner of his district. And for this he was to keep himself well acquainted with different public bodies and institutions of the district. Besides, the district organisers were to see that the members of the Association were aptly divided into separate groups and they maintained perfect secrecy of their endeavours in their respective areas. The district organiser was to be a tactful and an intelligent person to manoevre people of different temperament ; he was to be well-conversant with the social, economic and political conditions of the people; he was required to be courageous, fearless, imbued with the spirit of self-sacrifice and above all, he would have full faith in his mission. The activities of the Association were both public and private.

The aims of the Association were to incept social organisations and learned bodies like clubs, libraries, *sewa samities* and the like ; to start labour and peasant organisation and exercise our control over the labourers in the different factories, the railways and in the coal-fields ; to begin a weekly paper in every province, to give publicity to the idea of an independent Indian Republic and to publish booklets and pamphlets to enlighten the public about the course of events and the current of thought as was prevalent in the countries outside India.

Further, it was supposed to publish such literature as could not easily be published openly ; to circulate such literature ; to collect funds ; to send suitable men to foreign countries where they might get military or scientific experts to take charge of arms and ammunition factories at the time of open rebellion ; to import arms and ammunition and also to manufacture them, as far as possible, with in the country ; to remain in close touch and to cooperate with the Indian revolutionaries outside India and to get the members of this Association enlisted into this army. The membership was open only to those persons who could devote their time totally for the cause of the Association and to risk their lives for the sake of their country, if necessary. No member of this Association was to join any other organisation without the consent of the district organiser.

Every member would try to avoid being suspected of revolutionary connections by the police or public. Members who betrayed were to be punished with expulsion or death and the authority of issuing such a verdict was to rest entirely with the Provincial Council.

Before enrolment as its member, the youngman was made to sign a pledge that he would hold the interests of his country above those of his community. It soon became clear, however, that the social objects of the Sabha were only a cloak for the dissemination of revolutionary ideas. As its political activities extended in the countryside, its workers and their activities became the centre of attention for the uneducated simple village-folk. They realised the unquestioned and unflinching sincerity of these youngmen for the cause of the country and the great and patriotic role they were destined to play in the near future.

The Sabha held the first provincial conference at Amritsar on 13 April 1928 and attracted a huge gathering. It declared its aim in explicit terms that it was to establish in India an Independent Socialist Republic of the workers and peasants by all possible means. The founders of the *Naujawan Bharat Sabha* had stern faith and belief in the philosophy of communism and the unavoidable class struggle of the peasants and workers against the Indian capitalists and also waging a revolutionary war against Britsh imperialism. Thus they had much sympathy and faith in the great and successful experiments being done in the Union of Soviet Socialist Republic of Russia.

They read with immense attention the speeches and literature of Lenin, Trotsky and other Russian leaders.

Promulgation of their Views

To flourish the ideology and the programme of the *Naujawan Bharat Sabha* in an effective way amongst the uneducated masses and simple village-folk, it was relevant to have literature which should be understood easily by everyone. It was, therefore, decided to form a Tract Society which was to publish the aims and objectives of the Sabha also containing popular poems and songs against the British *Raj*. The task was assigned to a dedicated, young and intelligent worker, Principal Chhabil Das, who had the scholarly bent of mind. To make it popular and mass-based medium of political propaganda in numerous regions, the policy of Naujawan Bharat Sabha was to sell it at a very cheap cost of two price which could be economically affordable for a common man. As these tracts contained articles on the economic and social status of an ordinary citizen under the British *Raj*, it gained a wide market for its circulation even in the remote areas of the Punjab, Haryana, Himachal, United Provinces, Delhi , Jammu and Kashmir and elsewhere. Its circulation touched a few thousands in a very short period. It is interesting to note that Principal Chhabil Das gave a dauntless and daring expression of his patriotic sentiments is one of the tracts :

Duniya se ghulami ka main nam mita dunga
Ik bar zamane ko main azad kara dunga
Jo log gharibon par karte hein sitam nahaq
Gar dam hai mere kayam gin gin ke saza dunga

Three momentous pamphlets were published by the Sabha. 'The Wealth of Nations' by Hardayal ; 'India and the Next War' by Agnes Smedley and 'Bharat Mata Ka Darshan' by Principal Chhabil Das.

All these writings were an inspiring appeal to the youngmen of India who were urged to follow the example set by the youths of Ireland, Turkey, Japan and China in their struggle for independence for their respective countries. These writings also enumerated the economic and social ills and the exploitation under the British *Raj* which had made the people of India impoverished, backward in every respect, and uneducated at a mass scale. They also criticised the prevailing system of justice prevailing for the people of India.

Thus it was a direct appeal to the people and the youths of the country to follow the principles, aims and objects of Communism which might gain ground by their dedication and sense of high degree of devotion and patriotism.

'The Naujawan Bharat Sabha did not confine its secularism to sloppy embraces. It struck at the very root of communalism and untouchability by organising joint dinners of Hindus, Muslims and untouchables. To make such dinners affordable and feasible, the menu was confined to items like *Khichri,*[4] *pulaos* of grams and curd. Sack cloth was spread on the ground to seat the guests. Earthen cups and earthen plates were used. The object was to embrace people of all communities together and have a dig at such superstitions that created a rift between man and man. Once a dinner was organised in which *jhatka* and *halal* meat were cooked together and Hindus, Muslims and Sikhs ate together.... Principal Chhabil Das cooperated with this type of work. Among Muslim comrades were to be found Fazal, Mansur, Ahsan Ilahi and others.'[5]

The *Naujawan Bharat Sabha* was reported to have revived at Amritsar and that a public meeting of the Society was held on 7 July 1930.

This revival of the Sabha led to the arrest of four leaders, *i.e.* Shaban Dutt, Ram Parshad Shastri, Ghulam Nabi and Dr. Sant Ram Arora under Section 17 (2) of the Criminal Law Amendment Act. Besides, action was taken against Babu Singh, Kuljit Sehgal, Bishen Dass and Sunder Dass—all active members of the Sabha at Lahore. They were, however, released on bail.[6] It was also reported that meetings of the *Naujawan Bharat Sabha* were arranged at Amritsar on 19th, 21st, 27th and 29th July 1930. On the 27th July, when a meeting of the Naujawan Bharat Sabha, Hissar, was held, it was announced that the Sabha had been re-organized. On this occasion, several persons who took part in the deliberate proceedings were taken into custody under Section 17 (2) of the Criminal Law Amendment Act.[7] The Sabha in Amritsar and its allied bodies had been in high gear during August 1930, when its members systematized a meeting which was dispersed by the police and five persons were arrested.

Their other meetings held on 15th and 17th of the same month, were interrupted by the police, and its members and presidents were arrested.

'The *Naujawan Bharat Sabha* at Amritsar has recently become openly defiant. On September 4, a meeting was held at which the President and the speakers after a few hurried speeches abandoned the stage and disappeared in the darkness, thus preventing the police from arresting them. Stones and brickbats were pelted at the police. After the mob became more and more agitated it was dispersed by the police. On the 5th September another meeting was held at which 4 arrests were made. The Amritsar Police raided the Jallianwala Bagh on the night between the 3rd and 4th September 1930. They demolished all the huts and took away all the property belonging to the Sabha and other lawful organisations.'[8]

Principal Chhabil Das reminisced, '...*Naujawan Bharat Sabha* encompassed two different trends of thought, because during those days,

India used to get revolutionary ideas either from Russia and Russian Revolution of Lenin or from Ireland—De Valera and Sinn Fein movement. So, naturally, *Naujawan Bharat Sabha* ideologically split into two fractions : One fraction emphasized on Irish revolution and the methods adopted by those people that was collecting arms, hurling bombs. The other section was like the Russians and wanted to create class consciousness amongst the masses, rural people, peasantry and factory workers.'[9]

From September 1930 onwards a number of prominent members of *Naujawan Bharat Sabha* visited various parts of the Punjab and delivered their open views against the misrule of the British *Raj*. These were mainly in connection with the first anniversary of Jatin Dass who breathed his last in the Lahore jail.[10] Master Laxmi Chand of Ambala City delivered such a speech at Shahabad in Karnal district on 16 September. 'The tyrannous Government has applied Section 124-A, Indian Penal Code and 144 Criminal Procedure Code, so that we may not be able to talk in a free manner. Besides, in other countries such as England, France, Germany etc. government cannot impose taxes without the consent of the public ; but in India the principles are quite different. Indians earn while *shaitan*[11] and mean Britishers enjoy luxuries in their bungalows. How much injustice is being done. Do you like to live such a disgraceful life? If not, then why don't you join this religious war and struggle for it? .... Look ! What plans these *saitans* have devised to ruin us. Don't you feel exercised upon your .... Mother ! If the men of Shahabad do not help their children and Mother India, you should join the warfare for the freedom of the country and for the safety of poor children. O ye men ! You should wear bangles and take their places .... Brethren ! It is not the time for sleeping. Make so many sacrifices so that these tyrants may give you freedom . ... Bread is placed before you, till it is not eaten it will not satisfy your hunger. Likewise nothing can be gained by merely uttering *Bande Matram, Hindustan Azad*, etc. unless something practical is done by making sacrifices—bodily, mentally and monetarily. . . . Gentlemen ! This *shaitan* Government came to India 325 years back as traders and have now become the owners of India. By the exercise of the principle of divide and conquer, they now claim to be our sovereign. This Government is so. You might remember the treaties which they (tyrants) made with Maharaja Ranjit Singh, Sher-i-Punjab and that after his death how through deception and fraud they ruined the Punjab and got possession of it having no regard for their agreement and treate. . . . Wake up and make sacrifices so that this tyrannous Government may be obliged to grant you freedom. You will get no other golden chance like the present one. If you do not come to the front now your coming progeny will abuse and hate you.'[12]

Pamphlets of Naujawan Bharat Sabha

The members of the Sabha who at no time exceeded about 30 in number, held several public meetings during the summer of 1926. In September 1926, Kidar Nath Sehgal and others printed a pamphlet on behalf of the *Naujawan Bharat Sabha* entitled 'An Appeal To The Young Punjab' attacking Lala Lajpat Rai as a traitor.[13] The pamphlet concluded with an appeal to young patriots to sacrifice everything including themselves, at the call of the Mother and exclaiming 'Victory to the Mother, 'Martyrdom to the Patriot'. The attack on Lala Lajpat Rai marked the beginning of the end of Sabha. Meetings continued to be held less frequently, and it was obvious that the attack on Lajpat Rai had divided the members.

In March 1927, Dr. Bhupendra Nath Datta, a renowned Bengali revolutionary, lectured on the youth movement in the west. This meeting indicates the close of the Sabha's activities for a year, and it was not until March 1928, that it was again heard of.[14]

On 28th March, S.A. Dange, and Philip Spratt of the British Communist Party spoke at a meeting organised by the *Naujawan Bharat Sabha* on the meaning of Indian Independence.[15] During the Punjab Political Conference at Amritsar in April 1928, a Young Men's Conference was also held and was presided over by Kidar Nath Sehgal, who gave the most culpable presidential address. A number of seditious and subversive resolutions were passed including *inter alia* resolutions prizing the sacrifices of certain convicts hanged in the Kakori Train Dacoity Case, advising youngmen to prevent the people from participating in a war of the future and appealing to the country to originate a regular agitation for the repeal of the Arms Act. At the same time great stress was laid on the necessity for the subjection of religion to politics in the cause of nationalism. A resolution proposing that no youngmen who wished for the complete independence of his country should become a member of any politico-communal organisation was, however, opposed by several Muslims and had to be aborted. During the Conference, it was agreed upon to organise the youths of the Punjab in a central body i.e., *Naujawan Bharat Sabha* with headquarters at Amritsar and branches in every district and to associate the Sabha with the Kirti group of Amritsar.

Thus it is evident that the proceedings of the Conference were generally directed towards the inclusion of a spirit of violence amongst the youths of the country.[16] This conference infused new life into the Sabha and encouraged it to take part in subsequent phases of anti-Government agitation. In conjunction with the group of agitators which at that time controlled the activities of the Congress and the *Kirti* parties, the Sabha was to aggrandize agrarian agitation over the failure of the wheat harvest. In this connection, a meeting was held on 23 May at village Jahman in the Lahore district to discuss the failure of the crops and was attended by prominent extremists such as Satyapal, Kidar Nath Sehgal and M.A. Majid.

While promulgated as a Congress meeting, there was logic to believe that it was in realilty inspired by the *Naujawan Bharat Sabha.* The attempt to augment agrarian agitation was, however, 'killed' by the large remissions of land revenue sanctioned by the government. The Sabha's next move was to begin a tract society for the discrimination of national literature. This society published three 'objectionable' pamphlets, strongly imbibed with Bolshevik and Communist doctrines, entitled '*The Wealth of Nations*' by Hardayal ; '*India and the Next War*' by Agnes Smedley and '*Bharat Mata Ka Darshan*' by Chhabil Das. In June, it grasped the occasion of students' week organized by the Lahore Students' Union, to publish and distribute another objectionable pamphlet *Naujawanon se do Baten*. (A Few Words to the Young Men). This pamphlet urged the young men of India to follow the steps of youngmen of—Ireland, Turkey, Japan and China in their struggle for independence, accused the British government for exploiting India and of keeping the inhabitants impoverished and uneducated, stated that the administration of justice in India was tainted by racial considerations, and that the state of slavery in which India was held had disastrous results on neighbouring countries, and exhorted the young men of India to study such movements as Communism and Bolshevism, the lives of political martyrs, the doctrines of freedom and equality, democracy and self-determination which could prove central to bringing self-government and economic freedom.

These pamphlets represented the Sabha's attempt to capture the Lahore Students' Union. It made an attempt actually to control the organization of the union, being content to allow the effect of its propaganda divert the activities of the students' union into channels which would run parallel to its own. In June the *Naujawan Bharat Sabha* supported the Congress in its campaign of agitation over the Bardoli reassessment, and held meetings to spread the belief that the *satyagraha* campaign in Bardoli was an economic protest against the highhanded policy of the Bombay government, and to hold up the movement as one worthy of imitation. In July 1928, Kidar Nath Sehgal, president of the provincial *Naujawan Bharat Sabha* issued a long statement to the press commenting on future programme of the Sabha in the course of which he wrote that in order to organize the youngmen throughout the Punjab, the Sabha had ruled upon having branches in all villages, towns and districts of the province.

He expressed the hope that the provincial workers would find it easy to reach the villages and towns if the branches of the Sabha were established at the headquarters of the districts of the province.

He supplemented by saying that prompt help would be much appreciated as the Sabha wanted to build up a strong organization before the Simon Commission came to India again. In July, the bond between the Kirti party and the Sabha was strengthened by the election of Sohan Singh Josh, the leader of the Kirti party, as president of the Amritsar branch of the Sabha.

The alliance of these two organizations culminated in their joint celebration, aided by Congress extremists, of the 'Friends of Russia Week', early in August when resolutions were passed stating that Indians would not assist the British Government in any future war, proclaiming that they had no enmity with Russia, and that they were in line with the anti-imperialistic policy of Russia.

The theme of the speeches was that England's engagement in war with Russia would be India's opportunity emancipate herself form foreign rule, while the argument was developed that the destruction of capitalism and the government of the country by labourers and peasants were the only road to freedom and prosperity.

Uniting Peasants

The *Naujawan Bharat Sabha* took prominent part in spreading propaganda for the workers and peasants' conference at Lyallpur at the end of September. In the absence of S.A. Dange, Chhabil Das was elected president and Ram Chandra as chairman of the reception committee. Ram Chandra delivered a discourse on Communism coupled with valuable references to revolutionaries and a denouncement of imperialism, capitalism and the present system of society.

He further recommended the nationalisation of wealth, a social revolution, the organization of workers and peasants to go against exploitation by capitalism and made specific demands to the assessment of the land revenue on the principles of the Income-tax Act, the unrestricted Indianization of the army and the withdrawal of the British army from

India. Another prominent worker and general secretary of the Punjab *Naujawan Bharat Sabha* expressed valiantly his patriotic feelings in the Jallianwala Bagh, Amritsar. The audience was advised thus : 'I learn with much regret that the police visited the camp of the Naujawan Bharat Sabha twice today[17] to arrest us, but I am sorry to say that both the President and I had gone out. When we arrived here, we learnt of the fact. Our hearts were greatly shocked at the fact that the police had to return unsuccessful. I request the police brethren that if they have got with them warrants for our arrest, they may inform us that fact in writing through a chit. We are prepared to come at the end of the meeting. They should not create disturbance at the meeting so that the public may not be put to trouble. I tell the policemen again that they should remember that if they create disturbance at the meeting, young men whose hearts feel rattled at the sentence of death passed on Bhagat Singh will get excited. They should not say afterwards that they were ignorant of this fact. O young men ! I have arrived at no decision regarding Bhagat Singh so far during these 24 hours, and have sent no reply to the *Naujawan Bharat Sabha.* Will our Bhagat Singh, Rajguru and Sukhdev break away from us in this way? O Young men ! if the existing savage Government made those three gems to the gallows, will you be able to show your face to the world?. . . . O Young men ! Make sacrifices in thousands and hand at the gallows in thousands, but save dear Bhagat Singh . . . He is a gem whose uncle Sardar Ajit Singh is at present wandering about in Persia like nomads. If there is any love for Bhagat Singh in your hearts, sacrifice yourselves like a moth over the lamp of freedom and tell the Government that it should release Bhagat Singh, in return for which we are prepared to give thousands of lives . . . . Today orders were passed that they would be executed on the 27th October.[18]

'O Young men ! Leave schools and colleges. Leave your parents. Come into the field of action like Bhagat Singh. . . (There were shouts of Bhagat Singh *zindabad*, Sukhdev *zindabad* and Ragjuru *zindabad*).

'The Naujawan Bharat Sabha still exists. This tyrannical Government has declared all the societies as unlawful but they must remember that the roots of the *Naujawan Bharat Sabha* have reached the northernmost regions and they cannot be destroyed. Its name will endure as long as the world lasts. . . If you want to see Bhagat Singh alive and if you want to see Rajguru alive you should plunge into the field of action. On that side, Bhagat Singh, Rajguru and Sukhdev have been sentenced to death and on this side you are sitting at your homes. Let us ask those in whose hearts abides the picture of Bhagat Singh. . . . Ask that old

Sardar Kishan Singh what were his feeling at the time when he heard of the sentence of death passed upon Bhagat Singh. Just enquire from the father and mother of Bhagat Singh what thoughts passed their hearts when they heard of the sentence of death passed against Bhagat Singh. O Young men ! Making yourself extinct at the tide of liberty you should tell the parents of this brother that Bhagat Singh is not dead and that we are at all times ready to die for Bhagat Singh.

'Without saying anything further, I request you to observe complete *hartal* in the city tomorrow. I make to those confectioners, green-grocers and fruit-sellers, the submission that tomorrow if they open any shop or expose any goods for sale, they must remember that the *Naujawan Bharat Sabha* will not be responsible if they suffer any loss. Tomorrow, at Amritsar, neither any hawker should sell his stuffs nor should any goods be sold at any shop. The *Mohalla* people will tell persons living in their *Mohalla* not to open their shops. If any one opens his shops he will have to suffer the consequences. Our volunteers will have their goods thrown into drains... I request my brethren—the *tongas*, but if they pity them no one should take a trip in them .... I request these students brethren not to attend schools and colleges tomorrow at all and observe a complete *hartal*.'[19]

Yet another prominent worker and president of the Punjab *Naujawan Bharat Sabha* delivered an emotional speech on this occasion.[20]

...'I now ask this Government. O Government people ! Just tell me where is your peace today? To what extent will young men remain sitting in your presence after keeping their strength under restraint? Listen ! Listen again ! The young men today make the announcement. On the execution of Bhagat Singh or on the execution of Sukhdev or Rajguru, it will become known to you that not one but thousands will become Bhagat Singh and I will be the first person to be executed on the gallows. ... Execute me on the gallows. I am prepared to be executed.

'We wish to arouse your independent views and feelings which have been suppressed owing to your living in slavery... If there is regard in your heart, take a vow here today that you will never live as slaves in this world. Those men are also like you who are to ascend the gallows.

'I know Sardar Kishan Singh whose beard has turned white. I know his mother and brethren who are yet of tender years. There is no one to earn a living for them, There was Bhagat Singh alone to earn a living for them... O young men ! You have organised the *Naujawan Bharat Sabha* in my absence. On the day of Bhagat Singh's execution, the British Government will, I hope, confine me within four walls and will put featers round my feet which I shall gladly accept you who will take my place! Keep in view my honour, God who knows of this fact will be with you'.[21]

The provincial government as well as the Government of India noted with much anxiety the objectionable and dangerous speeches by various leaders.

H.G. Haig, the Home Secretary, also expressed much concern over the whole episode at Amritsar.[22] 'I think we ought to address the Punjab Government with regard to the proceedings of this session of the *Naujawan Bharat Sabha* and ask what measures they have contemplated to deal with what appears to be highly seditious and inflammatory propaganda disseminated by this association.

We should refer to the correspondence on our file regarding the Secretary of State's suggestion that the *Naujawan Bharat Sabha* should be proclaimed an unlawful Association under part II of the Criminal Law Amendment Act. If the action under part II of the Criminal Amendment Act is either not feasible or not desirable, do they contemplate Prosecuting some of the more important speakers. J.C. Crerar stated, 'I agree. There are signs that this movement if unchecked may develop seriously'.[23]

The Punjab government felt that the Sabha meddled with the maintenance of law and order and constituted a danger to public peace, and, therefore, declared it to be an unlawful organisation.

On 23 June 1930 the office of the Sabha was searched and a list of members and other material were got hold of[24] by 1928, the activities of the Sabha had crossed the borders of the Punjab, and at this nick of time Bhagat Singh kept himself very busy in maintaining deep links with other contemporary revolutionaries working in the United Provinces. He and his associates like Sukhdev and Bhagwati Charan Vohra enrolled themselves as prominent members of a revolutionary organization of U.P., namely, Hindustan Republican Association.

It was formed in 1924 under the leadership of Sachindranath Sanyal, Jogesh Chandra Chatterjee and Ram Prasad Bismal. An important meeting of young revolutionaries was organised at Ferozeshah Kotla grounds in Delhi on 9-10 September 1928 when after rampant discussions and serious deliberations, the party was renamed as Hindustan Socialist Republican Association (HSRA). So Bhagat Singh, after 1928, was very active under the direction and mandate of the HSRA.[25] The Sabha, meanwhile, published the *Independent India Tract Series* and it highlighted the importance of peasants and workers. In another leaflet, 'Worst Sin in the World is Poverty', youngmen were incited to eradicate poverty, root and branch, to make an equitable distribution or wealth amongst one and all and also devise means for advancing opportunity for sharing power in perfect equality amongst the members of the society.[26] This kind of model had prominent impact on the thinking of the students, workers and peasants of north India. The Lahore Student's Union became almost part and parcel of the Sabha and its political activities had deep linkage with it. In various centres of the Punjab, youth leagues and students' union, with revolutionary fervour, were established. The D.A.V. College Lahore, one of the premier institutions in north India had become a prominent centre for the revolutionaries' activities and the Government showed its moderateness in recruiting young educated lot to government service.[27]

Even the Governor of the Punjab warned the school managements to the extent that their grants would be stopped if they failed to curb the revolutionary activities of their students. Besides, the teachers working in these institutions were threatened with dire consequences, if they extended any kind of political support to their students.[28] But this kind of approach on the part of the government did not help them in any way. The atmosphere everywhere was mingled with patriotic fervour and the youths were not at all hesitant to participate in any political activity which had anti-*Raj* stance.

References

1. Bipan Chandra, *Nationalism and Colonialism in Modern India,* New Delhi, 1979, pp. 224-25.
2. For details see Home Poll. File 492, 1930.
3. Transcript of interview with Jai Dev Gupta, *op. cit.*
4. Rice and lentil cooked together with salt and spices.
5. Manmathnath Gupta, *Bhagat Singh and His Times,* Delhi, 1977, p. 106.
6. Home Poll. File 173/VIII, 1930.
7. *Ibid.*
8. *Ibid.*
9. Transcript of Interview with Chhabil Das, NMML.
10. Home Poll. File 173/VIII, 1930.
11. Mischief-monger.
12. *Ibid.*
13. Home Poll. File 130, 1930.
14. *Ibid.*
15. *Ibid.*
16. *Ibid.*
17. *Ibid.*, File 173/VIII, 1930.
18. *Ibid.*
19. *Ibid.*

20. *Ibid.*
21. *Ibid.*
22. *Ibid.*, File 120, 1930.
23. *Ibid.*
24. *Ibid.*
25. See an analysis of the work of HSRA in the chapter on 'New Awakening'.
26. Sukhdeo Raj, *Jab Jyoti Jagi,* Mirzapore, 1971, pp. 26.
27. Home Poll. File 41/35/1931.
28. *Ibid.*

2

Revolution in Blood

As has already been stated that Bhagat Singh was born in a family with glorious revolutionary traditions. His uncle Ajit Singh was an important political leader and had great inclination for revolutionary activities. He finds a mention in the report of the Sedition Committee. This shows how influential he was among the leaders of the epoch.

The report enumerated that the Punjab (then united) was seething with discontent. To quote from the report :

"The Lieutenant Governor held that some of the leaders looked to driving the British out of the country or at any rate from power, either by force or by the passive resistance of the people as a whole and that the method by which they had set themselves to bring the government machinery to a standstill was by endeavouring a strong feeling of racial hatred. He considered the whole situation exceedingly dangerous and urgently demanding remedy. The remedy adopted was the arrest and deportation of Lajpat Rai and Ajit Singh, the Hindu and Sikh leaders of the movement."

United Punjab accounted for the bulk of the Indian army and the Sikhs were supposed to be very important in this respect. Says the report :

"The Punjab has for years been by far the most fruitful recruiting ground for the Indian Army and to-day enjoys the same. Of its total population 55 per cent is Muhammadan, 33 per cent is Hindu and 11 per cent is Sikh. But the most martial section is the Sikh, which during the present war with less than one hundredth of the population has supplied about one sixth of the fighting forces of the Indian empire."

Early Days

When Bhagat Singh was born in 1907, according to the above report "everywhere people were sensible of a change, of a 'new air' which was blowing through men's minds." The report further added that *Jugantar* was daily pouring forth poison in Bengal, "it is not surprising that simultaneously new ideas should be formenting elsewhere in India." Speaking in the House of Commons the Secretary of State Lord (then Mr.) Morley on June 6, 1907 said, "There were 28 meetings known to have been held by the leading agitators in the Punjab. Of these five only related, even ostensibly, to agricultural grievances, the remaining 23 were all purely political". Obviously Mr. Morley was of the view it was a crime for Indians to hold political meetings. The Viceroy also was not far behind the learned Mr. Morley. "On the first of the following November the Viceroy thus summed up the leading characteristics of the year when the new bill for preventing seditious meetings was before the Legislative Council. "We cannot afford to forget the events of the early spring, the riots at Lahore and gratuitous insults to Europeans, the Pindi riots, the serious view of the Lt. Governor on the state of his province, the consequent arrest of Lajpat Rai and Ajit Singh and the promulgation of the ordinance."

Ajit Singh

In this report it was further supplemented that Ajit Singh was only in custody for 6 months. For some time, after the arrests, there was peace in the province, but later seditious literature was published on a large scale. Lajpat Rai wrote in his memoirs that during the Calcutta Congress, Sufi Amba Prasad and Ajit Singh formed the Bharat Mata Society.

His Uncle: Ajit Singh

Ajit Singh wanted Lajpat Rai to help the society financially, but Rai imposed conditions that were not acceptable to Ajit Singh. Ajit Singh as an internee under Regulation 3 of 1818 was locked up in Mandalay Jail in Burma, then a part of India. As it could only be reached by sea, Mandalay was almost inaccessible to friends and relatives of political prisoners. Although Lajpat Rai was in the same jail, they could not meet. In reality the Lala had no inkling for a long time, that Ajit Singh was in the same jail. The Lala was more famous, but from the government point of view Ajit Singh was more formidable.

Ajit Singh was also more radical. Lajpat Rai too was a firebrand in the beginning, but very soon he began to give second thoughts all along the line. Such changes came about in a number of other important freedom fighters as well. In the Mandalay prison Ajit Singh was given Rs. 120/ per month as subsistence allowance and his wife outside was given Rs. 10/ per month. But Ajit Singh's spirited wife refused to accept the sum as it was too meagre. Ajit Singh utilised his stay in jail for studies. He also wrote a book, which was later published under the title *Mahibbane Waton* (Patriots) with an introduction by sufi Amba Prasad. Subsequently, he got it translated into Persian while he was staying in Iran. It is said that while Ajit Singh was in jail, his friend Kartar Singh appeared in a dream and told him that he would be released on the 11th of November, and actually he was released on the aforesaid date at 11 A.M. and reached Lahore on the 18th of November.

Along with his brother Kishan Singh, the father of Bhagat Singh, he went to Surat Congress, where he engaged himself with the extremists. He also participated in a meeting convened by Lokmanya Tilak, and when Tilak was arrested in 1908, he was very much anxious. Both friends, Sufi and Ajit Singh donned the garments of sadhus and took a vow to work for the freedom of the country until Tilak was released.

They also began to distribute revolutionary literature. They published a paper called *Peshwa*, of which 1500 copies were published on behalf of Bharat Mata Society. The British Government was visibly angry with these patriots. Kishan Singh received the news that they were to be arrested. He advised Ajit Singh to go abroad. Ajit Singh agreed. He stayed a few days at the family village house, then left India for good in the beginning of 1909.

Bharat Mata Society produced many patriots. 22 court cases were instituted against its members. Sirdar Kishan Singh was sentenced to 17 months R.I. and a fine of Rs. 200/, Ziaul Haq, the editor of *Peshwa* was sentenced to 5 years R.I., Nandgopal was sentenced to 5 years R.I., Munshiram was sentenced to 7 years R.I. From the above account it appears that Sirdar Ajit Singh was as valuable as Lala Lajpat Rai, and had he got indulged in the revolutionary movement, he would have been allowed to grow in stature as a public leader, and would have attained the eminence of Lajpat Rai. But as he did he had to flee and play hide and seek with Europe always serving the cause.

During the Second World War he broadcast speeches from Radio Rome. Although he served the cause every minute of his life, he remained an obscure figure like many other committed revolutionaries.

Bhagat Singh is Born

Bhagat Singh was born in the family on the 28th of December, 1907, at 9 A.M. in Banga village. Banga is now in Pakistan. It is said his grandmother named him Bhagat (Lucky) Singh , as on that date his uncle Subaran Singh was released, his father Kishan Singh returned from Nepal and also the news of the release of uncle Ajit Singh was announced.

Revolutionary Family

There is little doubt that their's was a revolutionary family. Bhagat Singh's grandfather Sardar Arjun Singh was the first to set the ball rolling by showing inclination towards *Arya Samaj* although he was a Jat Sikh, after meeting Swami Dayanand.

It is said that Swami Dayanand himself initiated him and made him put on the sacred thread. At that time the *Arya Samaj* was emerging as a radical sect. At present all the radical ideas preached by the *Arya Samaj* and other such non-conformist organisations have become part of the common man's legacy, and very banal, but at that time they were quite revolutionary. Arjun Singh became a loyalist to *Arya Samaj,* this does not necessarily mean that in the context of to-day or even in a historical sense the *Arya Samaj* is a more revolutionary organisation.

At that time there was no clear cut line between Hindus and Sikhs. Even now they freely intermarry. Arjun Singh's involvement with *Arya Samaj* only shows that he was ready to receive new ideas. He got Kishan Singh and Ajit Singh admitted to the Saindas Anglo Sanskrit School and he went through all the Arya Samajist literature that he had access to.

Sh. Arjun Singh and Sh. Kishan Singh

Arjun Singh was not a man to stop at half measures in any sphere. He was a *munshi* of Raizada Bhagatram and was quite happy. The government then decided to colonise the forest area and declared that every coloniser would be awarded 25 acres of free land. At this, Arjun Singh left his comfortable job, settled in Banga and adopted the hard life of a cultivator. In his leisure time he practised medicine as a *hakim.* The family had migrated to Banga about 1900. Arjun Singh died in 1932 surviving Bhagat Singh by some years.

Kishan Singh, the father of Bhagat Singh, as has alrady been mentioned, was involved in revolutionary activities. Arjun Singh was a hard task master and wanted Kishan Singh to be a successful man. Accordingly Kishan Singh had set up a small office in the city of Lahore at Lahori Gate for insurance work. Kishan Singh soon comprehended that insurance was not in his line, he could gain more by selling milk and other village products.

Bhagat Singh too had to give some time to this work to keep his family happy. When he gradually became more engrossed in revolutionary work, this office was turned into a sort of rendezvous of revolutionaries. Young men came and went. To maintain the dignity of the office, they did not lunch and dine there but visited cheap eating house nearby.

Influence of Yashpal

Yashpal was one of the young men who frequented this office. He was then a burgeoning writer and would write stories and articles sitting in this room. One day he was absorbed in writing and to concentrate he was playing with his foot with something which felt like an odd kind of footrest. He was so absorbed in his work, he writes, that he did not care to scrutinise the footrest. He was rather happy that it responded to pressure. Just then a penile Sikh gentleman who looked a hundred per cent villager walked up the creaking staircase. His flowing beard was snow white. He looked well to do and his cheeks were rosy. Yashpal did not take much notice of him nor did the old man think much of him. The old man dragged a chair near the hall and made himself comfortable. Yashpal continued to write, and abstracted inspiration from the rather fussy footrest. Occasionally their eyes met.

Suddenly Yashpal awakened from his reverie by yells from the old man, whose eyes were red with anger— 'You stupid unthinking ass I'll, break your neck. . .' he shouted.

The old man had raised his stick to hit him when Yashpal jumped away. With a choked voice the old man pointed towards the footrest and said, 'You fool. Is this a measure of your etiquette?' When Yashpal looked at the footrest closely, he was surprised to find that it was the holy portable *havan-kund* used by Arya Samajists. It was lying upside down. Yashpal had heard that Bhagat Singh's grandfather carried the portable *havan-kund* as a part of his travel kit. It is obvious that Arjun Singh himself was partly inclined towards the *Arya Samaj,* but he allowed his family complete independence, so that the family remained precariously poised between Sikhism and Arya Samaj. Added to this was the fact that at that time, Sikhs did not think it nonaggreable to stand out as a separate community. Arjun Singh's non-conformism took various forms, not easily identifiable as revolutionary. The land which he had bequeathed was very good for growing tobacco leaves, but tobacco is taboo in Sikhism. It is possible that the founding fathers of Sikhism seeing everybody succumb to the addiction of tobacco started a holy crusade against it.

Anyway, Sikh peasants are averse to growing tobacco. But Arjun

Singh decided to grow tobacco in his land because peasants in the neighbourhood had grown opulent by its cultivation. He turned a deaf ear to all the arguments of the Sikhs. Tobacco leaves were grown, harvested and marketed by him. After receiving the cash, he went to the orthodox Sikhs and said, 'Now all is over. I admit that I committed a mistake. Now that the dirty leaves are gone, you can tell me how to sanctify my house.'

This incident exemplifies that Arjun Singh was more erratic than revolutionary. He was by nature a man who did not like to toe the line. He was a Sikh at the same time an Arya Samajist. This kind of family atmosphere, in which everything was in a flux was, however, perfect for the burgeoning of a revolutionary.

I have already pointed out that the *Arya Samaj* at that time had a revolutionary image. Later, when the second generation of Arya Samajis became erudites and entered government service, the Samaj lost its revolutionary edge.

This degenerated people so much that Mahatma Hansraj derecognised his son because he had become a rebel. Had it been confined to one individual, it could be undermined as a case of aberration. Even an organisation like *Gurukul* passed a resolution thanking God for sparing the Viceroy in 1912 when Lord Hardinge had a hair-breadth escape from a bomb thrown by a revolutionary. God was futher requested to grant Lord Hardinge a long life. One need not give too much importance to such resolutions, as Yashpal suggests, because they were often forced down the throat of such institutions.

Swami Shraddhanand was seemingly a loyalist, but when the call for non-cooperation came, he broke free himself from the Gurukul nexus and joined the front rank of the non-cooperations. The Swami however was an exception. In the *Arya Samaj,* religious revivalism was executed to extremes. Yashpal was a student in the *Gurukul.* He testifies to it that students were taught that the Hindus possessed aeroplanes and other scientific means, and as they had monopolised science, they were victors of the universe.

The only excuse that can be forwarded in support of this type of myth making was that this gave boost to the morale of freedom fighters, but on the other hand it boosted religious chauvinism. It was a doubtful gain. Naturally infatuation for *Arya Samaj* even during its heyday was not beneficial to real revolutionary thinking in Arjun Singh. That is why many of the actions of Arjun Singh are not fully lucid.

Career of his Father

Bhagat Singh's father Kishan Singh was originally named Gobind Singh and as a child he was often called Gobinda. It was felt by some that this amounted to an insult to Guru Gobind Singh, the tenth and last *Guru*.

During these days the family collected at Anandpur to celebrate *Holi.* There Gobind Singh was given a drink of nectar or was baptised as Kishan Singh. In 1898 famine gripped Vidarbha, now a part of Maharashtra. Kishan Singh went there as a volunteer to help the people. At that time these were the only outlets open to a patriot. In fact people took their first came across patriotism in such social services. The famine was so severe that many children lost both their parents. Kishan Singh found some such children during his relief work. He did not know what to do with them, so he brought them back along.

An orphanage was opened in Ferozepur and the children were accommodated. In 1900 he visited Gujarat, on similar famine work. From there also he brought back some children. He also went for relief work to Kangra in 1904 to help people stricken by the tragedy of an earthquake, then he went to Jhelum which was in the grip of a devastating flood. Along with such work of benevolent nature, he associated with the extremists of the Congress in company with his brother Ajit Singh. When Ajit Singh was sent to Mandalay jail, Kishan Singh very wisely left for Nepal. About his life in Nepal, there are a number of unconfirmed legends. It is said that the Prime Minister of Nepal was so impressed by him that he employed him to teach his son. It is asserted that he had conversation with high-ups there about getting help for the revolution in India. This news leaked and the British demanded that he should be sent back.

The Government of Nepal could not resist this, so he was sent back, the legend goes, with due honour, on a palanquin, up to the border of India. The police tried to implicate him in a case of assault on a police officer named Philip. In the meantime, there was some change in policy and he was released on bail. One of the sources says that from 1910-11 he started meeting Shachindranath Sanyal. Once the latter often met him with a young man named Bibhuti. Kishan Singh looked at the new fellow and refused to recognise Sanyal. When Sanyal entered into conversation with him on revolutionary organisation, pat came his reaction, 'My dear you've come to the wrong place, I am just a social worker, I do not have any taste for politics. You had better gone to some other place.'

After this Bibhuti left the two alone for some time. Then Kishan Singh took Sanyal to task, 'Why did you bring this fellow to me? He appears to be a black sheep. Some day he will spill all the information and you'll be in a soup.'

Sanyal, it is said, had a long heated argument with him, but failed to convince Kishan Singh. Later, Bhibuti turned to be king's witness in the Benares conspiracy case. It is confirmed that Kishan Singh was all along known to Sanyal, but this conversation is not documented by any other source. Anyway it is a fact that Sanyal had much faith in Bibhuti, and in him he met his Waterloo.

Decades after this betrayal when we enquired about Bibhuti, he made a strange face as if remembering something that could have been avoided. It seemed that even then, he had not recovered from the shock which Bibhuti inflicted on him. Bhagat Singh's mother Vidyavati had a distinct personality, although at that time women in Indian villages, were not supposed to have any personality of their own. She survived snakebite 4 times. Although mother Vidyawati hailed from a Sikh family, and so did Kishan Singh, their marriage was organised according to *Arya Samaj* rites in 1898.

Contemporary Patriots

At that time marriage did not mean an immediate journey to the bridegroom's house. Marriages were held at a tender age, when the girl was not fully-ready to take up nuptial duties, neither was the boy. Mother Vidyawati came to settle in Kishan Singh's house when they got land in Banga village. She set her footsteps there with the normal aspirations of a bride, but she soon came to know that this was a strange sort of home. Maybe, for an instant, she felt alarmed. Apparently, shady characters, who visited this home occasionally, consisted of people like Sufi Amba Prasad and Sanyal. They did not augur well and it took her some time to get accustomed to their erratic ways. In the beginning it was difficult for her to understand them.

Once Sufi Amba Prasad happened to stay as Kishan Singh's guest when the latter was away from for two or three days. Whenever Vidyawati spied on him, she found him delving in his books-lost in his work—reading or writing. He did not care for food, not did any body ask him to eat. The Sufi continued with his ontoward routine without a morsel of food.

On his return, Kishan Singh soon discovered that during his absence his friend had not been fed. When asked Amba Prasad said, 'Nobody asked me to eat and I did not eat.' It is obvious that such people were difficult to deal with. Another distracting factor was the police, which was always round the corner.

Although they had got the land, father and son seemed to have other priorities in mind, rather than working on the land, with the result that there was never enough in the house. One day, the father rebuked the son for not concentrating properly on the fields. Kishan Singh resented this and since that day ate only once and always stayed away in the fields. Vidyawati, at particular that time, was at her father's house, Kishan Singh did not go to fetch her. When Vidyawati came during Diwali, she found Kishan Singh in the field, who instead of welcoming her said, 'Why did you come, when we are short of rations?' This was rather an odd reception for a newly married young girl. Fortunately Kishan Singh's mother came up and welcomed Vidyawati.

It is during these days of utter poverty in 1904-5 that Jagat Singh, the first son, was born. After this the situation improved as Kishan Singh became successful as an insurance man and so brought his family to Lahore. By this time Bhagat Singh and the girl Amar Kaur had been born. Soon there was another addition to the family. They could now afford to have some ornaments too. But a servant fled with them. The family remained well off, but the prosperity of ornaments never returned. Bhagat Singh then was born in a family, with some revolutionary background, but it would be unwise to assert that he became a revolutionary because of his family background. On the contrary, though Sardar Kishan Singh had been a firebrand as a young man, had sown his wild oats, and had had all the fun, excitement and suffering that go with trail-blazing, he put his foot down when he heard that Bhagat Singh was not just engaged with, but was seriously involved in revolutionary work. According to his close associate Yashpal, Kishan Singh was so unhappy over all this that he seriously disturbed Bhagat Singh and Bhagat Singh left his home to escape the pressure. However, he was coaxed to return. Now the police started visiting the house. This broke the precarious armistice between father and son and Kishan Singh again started pressurising him. He wanted Bhagat Singh again to marry and settle down in life, and accordingly, chose the bride. But Bhagat Singh was not interested. Finally, there was a confrontation. Kishan Singh asked, 'Tell me, what is your objection to marriage?'

Bhagat Singh parried the question, 'I want first of all to stand on my own legs, then I'll see.'

Kishan Singh like an antiquated patriarchal head of the family said,

'You marry and at the same time try to stand on your legs. I am not going to stand in your way.'

'—But I am too young for marriage,' objected Bhagat Singh.

At this the father quipped, 'In all other matters you pose as mature, but in this matter...'

The drift between father and son was complete. They passed each other silently in the house. Yashpal writes that the father expected a good dowry and he wanted to seal the deal. But Bhagat Singh was dogged and answered with an unequivocal no. This agonised the father and a bitter argument between father and son followed in the course of which Bhagat Singh said, 'If the girl is educated, I could think of it.' This further enraged the father and he lost his temper. Bhagat Singh said she should at least be a matriculate.

Sardar Kishan Singh now approached Bhagat Singh's friends and began to utter abuses at them. He said to Yashpal, 'Why don't you put the fellow on the right track? Now you fellows pose to be great revolutionaries and celibates, but you will cool off in a few days and then you'll be running through the lanes smelling panties.' When Yashpal repeated the argument about the bride being uneducated, Kishan Singh now fully aggreived said, 'Does education grow some new limb on the female? ... Do educated females beget educated children?' Continuing with new abuses he said, 'You and Jaichand are meaner than the meanest, on top of this you think that you are very clever. You are both well-employed having a damned good time, but you want others to remain unsettled...'

Bhagat Singh was distracted by the attitude of his father and felt that all his energies were being siphoned off in fighting over these small matters. As an outcome he led a more or less fugitive life where his home was concerned.

Personality of Bhagat Singh

Some admirers of Bhagat Singh have throught that he hailed from a rich family. It is such people, who started the rumour that the Nehrus got their linen washed in Paris. These people think that to augment the value of the sacrifice of the hero, it is necessary to put him on a jewelled pedestal. In reality Kishan Singh's was a struggling family dabbling in insurance, settling in a new village, cultivating tobacco, doing dairy work etc. to ameliorate their economic condition. Legends have a way of growing round the personality of all heroes, because the ordinary man cannot conceive his hero as one of them. When I was in Fategarh central prison along with Yashpal, one Shivram Pande (later an M.L.A.) told us in all graveness that when Bhagat Singh and B.K. Dutt were travelling in a ship, some Englishmen spoke against India. At this, Bhagat and Dutt picked them up by their ears and dumped them in the sea. It was just within 3 years of the hanging of Bhagat Singh that this type of legends had started doing the rounds.

In reality, Bhagat Singh and Dutt had never been out of India. Another legend which was relayed to us by Pande, a very sensible man and a graduate, was that during interrogation all the limbs of Bhagat Singh and Dutt were mangled and pulverised and *tutia i.e.*, copper sulphate was put on them. This was also refuted by us as exaggerated. At this Pande flared up and said that we were mean and jealous, therefore we refuted these stories of torture.

For an admirer and follower it may be just human frailty to regard his hero as a prodigy. Religious pedlars have developed much of this tendency. But while writing the history of a revolutionary, the writer must embody him as a man who rose from among the people and very much as one of them. He should not be painted as a superman.

3

Early Career

Bhagat Singh's mother Vidyawati lived in the village Banga in Lyallpur (now Pakistan). His father Kishan Singh was in the Lahore Central Jail that day to launch an agitation against legislation that modified Canal Colony tenures and raised canal rates in the Bari Doab. His uncle, Ajit Singh, who was in prison in Mandalay then, was, by all accounts, a figure.[1]

Influence of Parents

He established the Indian Patriots' Association, along with Syed Haidar Raza to deliberate the peasants against the Bill as well as a secret society, the Bharat Mata Society. Kishan Singh and another brother, Swaran Singh, were also its members.

When freed from prison, Ajit Singh opted for exile in Iran, Germany, Brazil and several other countries. He died in India on August 15, 1947, the very day the country became free.[2]

The mood of the people in the Punjab alarmed the Lieut-Governor, Denzil Ibbetson, who put it in a Report dated April 30, 1907 which became a mini-classic : "Everywhere people are sensible of a change of a 'new air' (*nayi hawa*), which is blowing through men's minds, and are waiting to see what will come of it . . . . In the towns of Rawalpindi, Sialkot and Lyallpur, an active anti-English propaganda is being openly and sedulously preached. In Lahore, the capital of the Province, the propaganda is virulent and has resulted in a more or less general state of serious unrest."[3]

Impact of First World War

The recent *nayi hawa* did not diminish. It acquired strength over a decade later, on December 10, 1917, the Governor General set up a Committee to investigate and report on "the nature and extent of the criminal conspiracies connected with the revolutionary movement in India" and to advise as to the legislation "necessary to enable Government to deal effectively with them". Its President was justice S.A.T. Rowlatt of the High Court of England. Its members were : Sir Basil Scott, Chief Justice of Bombay, Justice C.V. Kumaraswami Sastri of the Madras High Court, P.C. Mitter, a Calcutta lawyer and a British civil servant, Verney Lovett.

They quoted all along from Ibbetson's Report, not withholding his indignant reference to the fact that "on two recent occasions Europeans had been insulted as such". It was regarded as an injury deep enough for the Viceroy to denounce, in his Legislative Council, those "gratuitous insults to Europeans".[4] The Rowlatt Report recalled that nine batches of conspirators were tried by Special Tribunals set up under the Defence of India Act, enacted on the outbreak of the First World War.

The First Tribunal observed in its judgement that "a wave of sedition had been ebbing and flowing in the Punjab since 1907". Together these were popular as the Lahore Conspiracy cases.

Bhagat Singh's childhood witnessed the stories of exploits of his uncle and his father. The Ghadar movement left a deep impact on his mind. Kartar Singh Sarabha, got hanged when he was only too young at nineteen after conviction in the first Lahore Conspiracy case, became his idol.

The massacre at Jallianwalla Bagh on April 13, 1919 drove him to Amritsar where he kissed the earth sanctified by the martyrs' blood and came back home with a little of the soaked soil.[5] Lala Lajpat Rai, Bhai Parmanand and Sufi Amba Prashad formed the National College in Lahore in accordance with national schools and colleges and universities established in response to Gandhi's call to shun Government-aided institutions and establish, instead, national educational institutions.[6]

Bhagat Singh left the D.A.V. School in Lahore in 1921 and joined the National College where he met colleagues for future years like Sukh Dev, Bhagwati Charan Vohra and Yashpal. Prof. Jai Chandra Vidyalankar, who taught history was close to this pupil and introduce him to revolutionaries in the United Provinces, now Uttar Pradesh.

How self-consciously dedicated he had became is prominent in Bhagat Singh's famous correspondence with his father when he was forced again to marry.

Father and Son

"Respected Father,

This is not the time for marriage. The country is calling me. I have taken oath to serve the country physically, mentally and monetarily (*tan, man* and *dhan*). Moreover it is not a new thing for us. Our whole family is full of patriotism. After two or three years of my birth in 1910, uncle Swarn Singh died in jail. Uncle Ajit Singh is living a life of exile in foreign countries. You have also suffered a lot in jails. I am only following your footprints and thus dare to do this. You will kindly not tie me down in matrimony but give me your blessings so that I may succeed in my mission."

Kishan Singh's protest. "We have already settled your marriage . . . you should not create any difficulty" brought a firm refusal.

"Respected Father,

I am astonished to read the contents of your letter. When you, who are a staunch patriot and brave personality, can be influenced by such trifles, then what will happen to ordinary men?

You are caring for Dadi (my grandmother), but in how much trouble is our Mother of 33 crores, the *Bharat Mata.* We still have to sacrifice everything for her sake.

While leaving home he left this note :

"Revered Father,

Namaste. I dedicate my life to the lofty goal of service to the Motherland. Hence there is no attraction in me for home and fulfilment of worldly desires. I hope you remember that on the occasion of my sacred thread ceremony Bapuji had declared that I was being donated to the service of the country. I am just fulfilling that pledge. I hope you would forgive me."

This, when he was still in his teens and just a few years before that fateful act in Lahore on December 17, 1928 which was to cost him his life.

Bhagat Singh went to Kanpur where Ganesh Shankar Vidyarathi engaged him in a job at his press. Attempts to coax him to return proved unfruitful. Intercession by Maulana Hasrat Mohani, one of the great Urdu poets of the century and himself a revolutionary, succeeded. Kishan Singh's prodigal son returned home but with accentuated fervour for the causes to which he had devoted his life. For, in the six months he had spent in Kanpur, he had grown a lot wiser. Vidyarathi was a member of the AICC and knew Kishan Singh. His home was a rendezvous of political activists.

Bhagat Meets Comrade

It is here that he met Batukeshwar Dutt, who taught him Bengali, Chandrashekhar Azad, Jogesh Chandra Chatterjee and Bejoy Kumar Sinha. Bhagat Singh formally joined the Hindustan Republican Association formed by the UP revolutionaries. Its inspiration was Shachindra Nath Sanyal, who was involved in the Banaras Conspiracy Case along with M.N. Roy and Rash Behari Bose.

Formation of HRA

The HRA was formed in 1923. The object clause of its Rules and Regulations declared : "The object of the Association shall be to establish a Federated Republic of the United States of India by an organized and armed revolution."[7] Funds were raised by, among other things, committing dacoities. Three went unnoticed. The fourth was near the Kakori railway station near Lucknow on August 9, 1925. A train moving towards Lucknow was stopped and a safe laden with cash belonging to the Government was broken. The loot was not large, just Rs. 4,679, but the Kakori Conspiracy Case became a legend. Four of the accused were hanged, Ashfaqullah and Ram Prasad 'Bismil' to whom the famous poem "Sarfaroshi ki tamanna ab hamaare dil mein hai" is attributed ; wrongly, according to the scholar-poet Ali Sardar Jafri.[8] Five, including Jogesh Chandra Chatterji and Shachindra Nath Sanyal were sentenced to transportation for life while eleven were awarded sentences for various terms of imprisonment. These savage sentences languished the HRA but did not kill it.[9]

Bhagat Singh continued to remain in touch with his comrades in U.P. after his return to Lahore and established more contacts nearer home. In March 1926, he formed the *Naujawan Bharat Sabha* along with Sukh Dev, Bhagwati Charan Vohra and Ram Krishan. Kamlesh Mohan briefly sums up the function of this militant youth organization. It "took up the unachieved mission of the Hindustan Republican Association".

As well as the young, its members included men of eminence like Saifuddin Kitchlew, Satyapal, Mir Abdul Majid, Sardul Singh Caveeshar and the poet Lal Chand *Falak*.[10] Ram Krishan was its President ; Bhagat Singh, its Secretary. The Sabha's progress was impressive by all standards. Similar bodies also came up in other provinces. Branches proliferated in the Punjab. An All-India *Naujawan Bharat Sabha* was established in Delhi. Soon links were forged with the Hindustan Republican Association and the Kirti Kisan Party, founded by Sohan Singh Josh. Already, on his return to Lahore, Bhagat Singh had established contacts with the Kirti Kisan Party. This Party owed its existence to the united efforts of the emissaries of the Ghadar Party (Bhagat Singh 'Canadian') and of the Communist Party of Great Britain (Philip Spratt) and of Sohan Singh Josh, Mir Abdul Majid and Kedar Nath Sehgal with intension to be a Workers and Peasants Party, it was named the Punjab Kirti-Kisan Party.[11] Its organ *Kirti* was published in Punjabi and Urdu to make it available to the masses.

Manmathnath Gupta recalls : "In the Punjab, Punjabi was spoken and understood, but in schools only Urdu was taught . . . the sole reason why an Urdu edition of *Kirti* began to be published with additional pages." Bhagat Singh worked for some time, assisting Sohan Singh Josh, in the Urdu edition. This was the penultimate phase. The last phase is characterised as "the conspiracy" in the Judgment of the Tribunal which sent Bhagat Singh to gibbet. It presents a total contrast to later works by scholars. Their researches and insights provide the reader with good insights of the mainsprings of the actions by the participants in the drama, their motivations and their distinctive styles. The Judgement records conclusions from evidence adduced by the prosecution alone. The defence did not assidiously contest the case and produced no evidence. The Judgement, as in all such cases, seeks of tedious, albeit relevant, details of houses rented and abandoned and such. It is related essentially with culpability, individual and collective. Scholars and Bhagat Singh's colleagues have since shown light to some significant facts missing in the Judgement. Both are relevant. Where all agree is that the crucial moment was when the revolutionaries met at Feroze Shah Kotla in Delhi on September 8-9, 1928 and decided to launch a new body to bring about union of the provincial groups on one platform.

Revolutionary Groups Unite

There existed the Bihar group which included Phonindra Nath Ghosh, Man Mohan Bannerjee and Kanwal Nath Tewari, the U.P. group of Shiv Varma and Bejoy Kumar Sinha and the Lahore group comprising Bhagat Singh, Sukh Dev, Jai Gopal and Hans Raj Vohra. There was, of course, considerable interaction among them ; particularly between the

U.P. group and each of the other two. Phonindra Nath Ghosh, for instance, was well apprised of the U.P. group. So were Ajoy Ghosh, Gaya Prasad, Sachindra Nath Sanyal and, possibly, Lalit Kumar Mukerjee.

The Tribunal

The "conspiracy" was unravelled before the Tribunal by the participants who became approvers. They were none other than the leading figures like Phonindra Nath Ghosh and Man Mohan Bannerjee of the Bihar group, Jai Gopal and Hans Raj Vohra of the Punjab and Lalit Kumar Mukerjee of the UP group.

Of these, Phonindra Nath Ghosh's case was the most pathetic. He had joined the revolutionary Bengal Anushilan Party way back in 1916 and organized groups in Bihar in 1926. The prosecution case had, not September, but August 1928 as the commencement of the conspiracy by the renting of houses for use as rendezvous for the party to be formed in the next month. It was Bejoy Kumar Sinha who invited Phonindra Nath Ghosh to join the new party, towards the end of August, and proposed a secret meeting in Delhi on September 8 and 9. Phonindra checked Bejoy Kumar's credibility from Sachindra Nath Sanyal when they met in Allahabad *en route* to Delhi. The meeting was held on September 8, 1928.

Phonindra Nath Ghosh and Man Mohan Bannerjee sat under a tree in Feroze Shah Kotla Fort in Delhi where Kundan Lal also joined them on Sinha's introduction. Little away from them another meeting commenced on at which Bhagat Singh, Sukh Dev, Jai Dev, Shiv Varma, Bejoy Kumar Sinha and, another one who was to turn approver, Brahm Dutt.

Phonindra Nath Ghosh did not know Bhagat Singh but was introduced to him and to Sukh Dev the following day. On that day, September 9, the participants came together at 8 a.m. in the Fort and took important decisions. A Central Committee of the new party was appointed consisting of seven members, namely, Bhagat Singh, Sukh Dev, Bejoy Kumar Sinha, Phonindra Nath Ghosh, Kundan Lal and, most important of all, one who was absent—Chandra Shekhar Azad, already famous for evading the police dragnet in the Kakori Case. Of those present, Jai Dev and Man Mohan Bannerjee did not make it to the CC. There was another absentee, the Bengal revolutionary party. Various explanations are offered for that from its opposition to terrorism to the young revolutionaries' rejection of the leadership of the old.

HRA revived Beats were assigned to members—Sukh Dev, Shiv Varma and Phonindra Nath Ghosh were, respectively, assigned the Punjab, U.P. and Bihar. Chandra Shekhar Azad was appointed head of the Military Department. Kundan Lal was given the charge of the Central office at Jhansi. Bhagat Singh and Bejoy Kumar Sinha were appointed to maintain link between the various provinces.

The Hindustan Republican Association was revived with a new and highly significant name—the Hindustan Socialist Republican Association. The only change, "Socialist", was on Bhagat Singh's insistence. There was otherwise no change in the Rules and Regulations of the HRA. Other decisions arrived at the conference were : To take active part in the boycott of the Simon Commission and to throw a bomb on the train carrying it, open bomb factories at Calcutta, Saharanpur, Agra and Lahore ; arrange a good instructor for giving training to its members in making bombs ; murder the informers in the Kakori Dacoity Case and to flee Jogesh Chandra Chatterjee from jail ; and add punch to the commission of dacoities for raising funds but, as far as possible, to loot Government treasures rather than individuals.[12]

The most unfortunate thing was the watch man who interrupted. Bara Singh, Sukh Dev and Bhagat Singh assured him that they were students preparing for their examinations. They never suspected that he would, one day, testify against them along with some of their trusted colleagues. The Tribunal's Judgement said that the name of the new party was "Hindustan Socialist Republican *Army*"and the IB's Director J.M. Ewart repeated the assertion in the text of his compilation, *Terrorism in India*, 1917-1936 (p.73).

The texts of two Manifestoes he appended to it belie that. It was an "Association," and an "Army" only when it acted. It had a unique credo which one of the manifestoes proudly proclaimed : "The food on which the tender plant of liberty thrives is the blood of the martyr."

References

1. Vide Gurudev Singh Deol, *Shaheed Bhagat Singh,* Publications Bureau, Punjabi University, Patiala; 1985 and K.K. Khullar, *Shaheed Bhagat Singh,* Hem Publishers Pvt Ltd., New Delhi, 1981.
2. Bejoy Kumar Sinha, *Bhagat Singh and His Times in India's Freedom Struggle,* edited by J. Sarkar, A.B. Bardhan, and N.E. Balaram, People's Publishing House, New Delhi, 1986, pp. 51-52.
3. For the text see Khullar, pp. 98-110.
4. Superintendent Government Printing Press, Calcutta. Report of the Sedition Committee, 1918, pp. 127-28 and p. 157.

5. B.K. Sinha, p. 53.
6. Vide the writer's account of the formation of one such institution, the Jamia Millia Islamia in *President Zakir Hussain,* Popular Prakashan, Bombay, 1967.
7. Vide Ewart, pp. 195-99 for the text of the Rules and Regulations of the Association.
8. Interview with the author on September 17, 1995. The poem was written by a poet in Bihar. He was Bismil Azimabadi.
9. B.B. Mishra, *The Indian Political Parties,* Oxford University Press, p. 273.
10. Kamlesh Mohan, pp. 79-81.
11. *Ibid.,* p. 106.
12. Kamlesh Mohan, p. 324; and Deol, p. 30.

4

An Eventful Youth

In 1921, boycott of councils, courts, schools and colleges was a part of the non-cooperation movement. Leading people were aware of the need to the revolutionaries to be educated to cruise in the proper direction. National institutions came into being in various parts of the country for the benefit of those students who had abandoned their schools and colleges to participate in the National movement. The Kashi Vidyapeeth of Varanasi, Gujarat Vidyapeeth and the Bihar Vidyapeeth of Patna were among such institutions. A similar school was started at Lahore by Lala Lajpat Rai and other national leaders. Although it was called 'Tilak School of Politics', it was popularly known as the National College. Not to lag behind, Bhagat Singh also left the DAV school to get enrolled in the National College. He was then in the 9th class and over 14 years of age.

From his parents he had inherited a tall and well built body, broad shoulders, a fair and smiling face and a determined look which mesmerised everyone. Now, the problem was how to admit a ninth class student to the college. According to Bhagat Singh's class fellow Jai Dev Gupta, who had quit DAV school to join the National College, Bhai Parmanand, who was incharge of the college as a nominee of Lala Lajpat Rai, gave both of them two months time to clear the matriculation examination which they did with their dedication. Thus they were able to get admission in the National College. The head of the college was Acharya Jugal Kishore who had returned to India and had dedicated himself to the cause of the nation after completing his education abroad. He was a man of independent views with a good heart. He nurtured great love for the young men who had dedicated their lives to the national causes. He had by all mean made the atmosphere of the college very open and natural.

Influence of Teachers

One of the teachers at the college was Chhabildas. He was a studious and thoughtful young man who had a deep love for the country. Although, as a student he had been quite excellent and always won laurels he had left college when he was studying for his MA degree, had devoted his life to the service of the country and had joined the 'Lok Sewak Mandal' of Lala Lajpat Rai and had written a number of pamphlets, such as 'Chingariyan', 'Hum Swarjya Keyon Chahte Hain', 'socialism', 'Bhookha Bahisht', 'Rajneetik Kahaniyan', 'Inqlabi sharaare', 'Kyon Aur Kaise', to arouse national consciousness among the people. He published his autobiography in 1985 bearing the title 'Meri Inqlabi Yaatra'.

Let us see what he has to say about the National College. "My services were immediately placed at the disposal of the National College. There I started teaching English to the college classes. Next year, on the retirement of the principal, Acharya Jugal Kishore, I was made the Principal and I started teaching History in addition to English".

After gathering how the college functioned in the Bradlaw Hall and how about two hundred students had come to Lahore to get national education at this college, he recalls :

"In the beginning Lala Lajpat Rai used to come and himself teach the students. Education at the National College was quite different from that of other colleges. History, Economics and Politics were the subjects taught there. Although education was imparted through the medium of Hindi or Hindustani, students were also taught English because all the books were available only in English."

The teachers of the National College themselves wrote their lectures from books written in English. There was no entertainment such as sports or physical exercise for the students. However, with a view to equipping the students with practical knowledge, debates had been made a regular feature from the beginning. Although there was adequate arrangement at the National College for teaching in the various branches of humanities i.e. History, Economics and Political Science along with Science, it was History which gripped the atmosphere of the college and which was the main subject of discussion.

Ancient Indian history was taught by Pandit Jaichand Vidyalankar who was a graduate of Gurukul Kangri while European and Modern

History was taught by Bhai Parmanand. He was also teaching at the DAV college, Lahore concurrently. He had been deputed by the *Arya Samaj* to go to South Africa to spread Vedic religion. From there he had gone to England and, sitting in the main Research Library of London, he had written a history of India which became undigestible to the Government of India. When he returned to India, the government outlawed his book. The Governor of Punjab got him implicated in a political conspiracy and he was awarded the capital punishment. Pandit Madan Mohan Malviya and father C.F. Andrews appealed to the Viceroy saying that it was highly unjust and despotic to award some one capital punishment simply for writing one book.

The Viceroy converted Bhai Parmanand's punishment to life sentence and he was sent to the Andamans from where he was released after five years. The history of Europe that Bhai Parmanand used to teach was nothing but the history of wars, revolutions and bloodshed.

"All the students of the National Colleges were young men who had left their colleges with a smile on the appeal of Mahatma Gandhi. When these students learnt about the events of European history, as taught by Bhai Parmanand, they used to grow sceptical how Mahatma Gandhi could claim that he would secure India's independence through peaceful and nonviolent means when other countries of the world had to resort to arms and violence to shake off the bridle of slavery. The students often asked themselves the question, was not Mahatma Gandhi building castles in the air? Some of the teachers of the National College were also entertaining such doubts."[1]

Impact of Chhabildas

The word 'Principal' became a permanent prefix to the name of Chhabildas and he is still known as principal Chhabildas. He has further stated under the caption 'Bhagat Singh and National College' :

"While Bhagat Singh was a fervent revolutionary, he was also a good student. As his teacher, I can say with confidence that he enjoyed studying. He was greatly fond of reading. Whenever the name of some book was mentioned to him, he wanted to read it at once. Although Bhagat Singh had read numerous books of history, I *still remember that* the book he liked best was *Cry for Justice*. He had marked many portions of this book with red pencil. This shows how strong was his desire to fight against injustice."[2]

A prominent teacher at the National College was Jai Chand Vidyalankar who was a graduate of Gurukul Kangri. He used to teach ancient and modern history of India.

The curriculum included the Rowlatt Committee Report and the non-cooperation movement. The Rowlatt Committee Report contained a vast account of efforts for India's freedom. It was a report as long as a hundred and twenty-six pages. The main object of the report was to prove guilty the revolutionaries.

The Rowlatt Committee was also called sedition committee. The British Government considered all revolutionary efforts to be seditious. The report comprised a detailed account of revolutionary conspiracies, the difficulties that had been faced in suppressing such conspiracies and recommendations for the enactment of repressive laws for the future. These recommendations included the proposal for equipping the police with powers to arrest without cause, to carry out searches, to detain people and to refuse bail. These proposals made the blood of youth to boil and imbibed in them a feeling of hatred for the foreign rule.

Jai Chand Vidyalankar was affiliated to the revolutionaries of Bengal. As he would analyse the non-cooperation movement in the light of the repressive policy of the British, it used to become patently clear that the philosophy of peaceful *satyagraha* was anti-revolutionary which taught us not to hate and to bear repression by the enemy without retaliating. The story of Professor Jai Chand Vidyalankar coming into contact with the revolutionaries and of his being vital in bringing students like Bhagat Singh and Sukhdev hand in hand with the revolutionaries, is an interesting one. In the words of Shachindra Nath Sanyal :

"I had gone to Fategarh with Shri Chhedilal in connection with organisational work. We had to go to some parts of the city and also to the countrywide. Strategy of our organisation was to appoint brave, determined, self-sacrificing and devoted young men at as many places as possible who would, in course of time, become the nuclei of a big party. After our visit to the city and the countryside, we rested for a while at the banks of the Ganges. Thereafter, we walked along the bathing ghats and tried to find a place where an outsider could stay. We were closely looking all round to see if, in the crowd of children and old men and women, we could find an educated young man. Suddenly, I saw a young man sitting and reading a book in a room with open doors. I straightaway entered the room followed by one or two of my comrades. On finding us there, the young man lifted his gaze from the book and looked at us. From his looks I could guess that he had been reading that book with great concentration. When I looked at the book I found that it was in English. I apologised to him for the intrusion and explained to him that we had felt drawn when we saw a youngman reading with such concentration. He graciously asked us to be seated on the bed lying by his side. The poor man was all alone. I picked up the book that he was reading and found that it was the latest book by Mr. Jatir on Indian History. We learnt from him that his sister Shrimati Parwati Devi was serving a two year sentence in the Fategarh jail for making a seditious speech during the *Satyagraha* movement. We also learnt that he was a teacher in the prestigious National College of Lala Lajpat Rai at Lahore, that his name was Jai Chand Vidyalankar and he was a graduate of the Gurukul Kangri, and that he had written two books on Indian history based on his own research work. In the context of his sister, we started talking about politics and the *Satyagraha* movement. We also had a long discussion about violence and non-violence, about Mahatma Gandhi's policy and about the revolutionary movement. When Jaichandra came to know that I had been confined in the Andamans jail for four years, he felt very much attracted to me... In this way Jaichandraji joined our party. He invited us to Lahore where we stayed as guests in his house. In Lahore I became acquainted with some young men. Among the young men at Lahore, some were from Gujranwala, some from Gurdaspur and others from Hoshiarpur. All of them were students of the Tilak School of Politics of Lala Lajpat Rai. I had long talks with these young men separately. I particularly emphasised before them that India could not become independent except through armed struggle and that armed struggle was definitely possible and I also narrated to them the history of the bygone revolutionary era and, thereafter, I initiated them in the revolutionary path."[3]

Along with Bhagat Singh, some other youngmen also federated the revolutionary party. Among them were Sukhdev, Bhagawati Charan Vohra, Ram Kishan and Yashpal. In addition to the National College.

Lala Lajpat Rai had also founded the Dwarka Das Library which not only contained valuable books on History, Politics and Social Science but was also gathering revolutionary literature and magazines and journals from all over the country. These young men used to borrow books from this library very frequently, read them and debate many issues. Their teachers also created curiosity among them and infused in them the art to judge everything on the basis of logic rather than accepting it with blind faith. Bhagat Singh has written : 'During the non cooperation movement I got admitted to the National College. There I started to ponder freely about all the religious problems, even about God. I started discussing the ideological aspect of these issues. But I still had firm faith in God. I had grown my hair and my beard but I could never put my faith in Sikh mythology and ideology and in that of any other ideology and religion."

(*Main Nastik Kyon Hoon*).

National Dramatic Club

In order to propagate and popularize patriotic ideas among the people, this young man set up a 'National dramatic club.' The club used to stage plays like 'Bharat Durdasha' and 'Chandra Gupta' in which Bhagat Singh used to play the protfagonist. It has been recorded that Bhai Parmanand was so enchanted by Bhagat Singh's portrayal of the character of Emperor Chandragupta that he embraced Bhagat Singh on the stage itself and said "My Bhagat Singh would really prove to be Chandra Gupta one day."

Some plays has also been written on the theme of Hindu-Muslim unity and some which beleagured religious superstition. These plays were staged in Lahore, Lyalpur, Gujranwala, Rawalpindi and in every city or town where Congress Party held a conference. Three of the songs that used to be sung in the plays are as follow :

1

"Galiyaan de vich phiran nivane
desh di izzat de matwaale.
Hindu Kahain main sabton vadda, meraa
hindustan....
Muslim Kahe ek Kaarhoon saada,
Sanoo miliya hukim rabaaba."

2

'Saree duniyan main din hind main raat hai
Hind waalo batao yeh kya baat hai?
Baat baaton se hargiz banegi nahin,
Mar mito baat par baat ki baat hai.'

3

'Zara bhi lagan azadi di lag gayee
jinhan de man vich
Oh majnoon bane phirde her sahra her ban de vich
Din noo chain kadee naan lainde raat noon
oh naan sonde ve
Bad-bada de nind de vich, dath ke
kehnde ve....."

1

(The lovers of the country's honour
roam about in the streets and lanes
The Hindu says, I am superior to all
Hindustan belongs to me
The Muslim says, ours is the only cause
we have received God's command).

2

(All over the world there is day but in Hindustan it is still night
Speak, O Residents of Hindustan why is this so?
Nothing can come out of mere words
Sacrifice every thing for the word (that you give) honouring your word is all that matters).

3

(Even a little longing for freedom, makes them roam about the word like Majnu
(seeking freedom) from hill to date
They neither rest in the day nor sleep in the night.
Even in their sleep they mumble and say...)

The government condemned all these plays. While in Punjab the loyalist moderates had no influence whatsoever and the National Education was playing the role as described above, let us see what shape Gandhi conferred on National Education in Gujarat. Only a comparative study will help us to differentiate between truth and untruth, between patriotism and loyalty to the British. While urging the students to boycott schools and colleges, Gandhi had drawn up a programme of regular study of Asian civilisation, Western Science, religion, politics and history and a vocational training for the students. However, he suddenly aborted this programme and on 19th January 1921, he threw a bombshell by unilaterally announcing in the young India, quite a different programme for the National Institutions :

"We are struggling in a spiritual age. We are not living in an ordinary age. In an extraordinary age, normal work come to a stop. If we are firm in our determination to achieve freedom within one year then we should divert our attention from all other work and concentrate on this objective. Therefore I dare advise all the students of Hindustan (those who are studying in the National Institutions) to give up the usual type of education for one year and devote their time to spinning yarn by hand. This would be the greatest service to the motherland and will obviously be most helpful in achieving swarajya. During the last war, our rulers had converted every factory into an arsenal for manufacturing zinc bullets. In this war of ours, I advise each one of our national schools and colleges that they should convert themselves into factories producing tops of hand spun yarn for the sake of the nation."

Addressing the enthusiastic students of Bengal he had stated : "In lieu of your suspended education. I would emphasise on your taking up as far as and as quietly as possible, the study of the means of achieving *swarajya* within one year or sooner. I offer you the *charkha* as a gift and wish to tell you that our economic liberation depends on it. But, if you like, you may reject my suggestion and could join the college which Deshbandhu has promised you. The students of the National College of Gujarat have accepted the responsibility of spinning at the charkha for at least 4 hours every day."

Far from being of service to the motherland, this proposal seemed no less than a fraud on the motherland and the young generation. To set parallel yarn tops with zinc bullets and to claim to achieve *swarajya* within one year with their help, was nothing but tall talk by an anti-revolutionary loyalist ; his only aim was to main us by diverting all our thoughts and activity towards the charkha. Indu Lal Yajnik was one of the senate members of the National College that had been set up in Gujarat.

He has written on the basis of his personal experience that a Jain Muni was foisted on the head of Mr. Gidwani, who was the principal of that college and was a man of great political understanding with a scientific temper. Within the college campus, a unique institution was set up which was known as *Swarajya Ashram* and in which charkha was given the epitomic status. Soon the high schools and primary schools also were subjected to the same treatment. Very downtrodden type of schools were opened in hideous buildings where broken charkhas were set up. Some bundles of cotton yarn which often contain mill spin yarn, some tops to tangled yarn, which could not be mounted on the charkhas, were also kept there...... "Deep down in my heart I had begun to have misgivings even at that time whether it was not a sin against the interests of the education of our new generation to create such a spectacle in the name of a holy war."[4]

Service to Motherland

Young men had given everything in order to save the country's future ; their own future was hideous. Consequently, all these developments led to a reaction. Many committed suicide, many became Vinoba Bhaves (although Vinoba also committed suicide eventually) and many went back to the schools and colleges that they had left.

Was it the service of the motherland or of imperialism? Still, our brother Manmathnath Gupta writes in *Bhagat Singh our Unka yug*. "Here it would be worthwhile to draw attention to the fact that non-cooperation helped in taking the call of the *swarajya* to the remote villages. Other thoughts also percolated which proved very beneficial. Thus it can be said that the non-cooperation movement suddenly raised the intellectual level of the people. Their consciousness increased." He goes on to contradict himself by saying : "But this increase was limited. As we have seen, so far as the Muslims are concerned, this consciousness in, the case, proved to be regressive rather than progressive." How was it possible that the new consciousness helped the others to progress while it took the Muslims backward? Guptaji also says that despite differences with Gandhiji, it can be said that he was an honest man. But what kind of honesty was this? And honesty towards whom? Guptaji has himself doubted this honesty by saying : "The excited peasants of Gorakhpur district surrounded the Chauri Chaura police post on 12th Feb. 1922 and set fire to it. When 21-22 policemen died in the fire, Gandhiji called it violence and withdrew the movement." Guptaji writes on to say :

"It would be proper to pause and mention that in the history of the Congress it has not been revealed in the context of the Chauri Chaura incident that the policemen continued to fire till all their bullets were exhausted. It has also not been revealed that the bullets fired by the policemen killed some people and many were badly wounded. Whatever may be the fact, Gandhiji suspended the movement on this pretext. So the factual position was that Gandhiji did bring the people into the agitation—for which he deserves all praise—but he did not want that the people should move towards revolution which he should logically have helped them to do..... ."

The core of the matter was that war had thrust a revolutionary urge among the people. After starting the movement, Gandhi took the wind out of its sails and served the Indian and foreign vested interests by annuling the revolution half way. Principal Chhabildas has written :

"I very well remember that when some over enthusiastic Indian young men set fire to the police station in their zeal and out of anger resulting in 21-22 policemen being burnt to death, and when, moved by this incident, Mahatma Gandhi totally suspended the non-cooperation movement against the British Government Lala Lajpat Rai was in the Lahore central jail. In anger, Lalaji remarked that eventually Gandhi had turned out to be a Bania. I myself heard Lala Lajpat Rai making this remark in the outer quarters of Lahore central jail....."[5]

College Education

After passing the FA or the Intermediate Examination from the National College, Bhagat Singh got admitted to the BA class. He was then in his seventeenth year. This was the year 1924. In those days the language issue was being debated all over Punjab. The controversy was between Urdu and Hindi. The Punjab Hindi *Sarmya Sammelan* had invited articles on the problem of language and script in Punjab. A reward of Rs. fifty was declared for the best contribution. Bhagat Singh also participated in this contest. His article proved to be one of the best contributions. As such, the general secretary of the Sammelan, Bhimsen Vidyalankar preserved the article and it was later published in the *Hindi Sandesh* of 28th February 1933. This was the first article written by Bhagat Singh. The article gives ample evidence of the fact that after two years education in the National College, Bhagat Singh had grown wiser in his thoughts ; his thinking on the language issue was quite clear and appropriate. He began by saying:

"Knowledge of the literature of a country or society is a prerequisite for knowing that country or society. For achieving progress, a race needs to have literature of a high standard. This rise of a country is commensurate with the progress of its literature. All those who love their country, whether they are reformers or politicians, pay the greatest attention to their country's literature. If they are not able to create literature which reflects contemporary problems and situation, then all their efforts go waste and their work fails to acquire permanency."

Even today, language and script continue to be a problem. The Hindi-Urdu and the Hindi-Punjabi controversy has taken a religious and communal form. Bhagat Singh had given his own views on this issue :

"Here it would not be wrong for us to take up the question of language. We shall begin by placing the Muslim viewpoint. They are staunch supporters of Urdu. Presently, this language is also widely used in Punjab. The Muslim also claim that Urdu script can be used to convey more in less space. All this may be right ; but today the question before us is that we should have one language for the country. We may not be able to achieve this instantly ; we shall have to tread in that direction step by step and we should at least have a common script. The Urdu script cannot be said to be complete in toto. Above all it has its base in the Persian language. The Urdu poets, even if they be Indians, can only conceive of the saki (bar maid) and date trees. Kazi Nazrul Islam has repeatedly referred to Vishwamitra and Durwasa in his poetry but our Urdu, Punjabi and Hindi poets have not been able to do this. Is it not remorseful? The main reason for this is their ignorance of Indian literature and of whatever is Indian. They are not able to inculcate in themselves the Indian virtues. How can then we become Indians by virtue of the literature created by them? Students who only know Urdu cannot acquire knowledge of the ancient Indian literature. Not that the works of literature cannot be translated into a language like Urdu, but such a translation would be good enough only for an Irani who wants to get accustomed to Indian literature.

"In respect of the above statement, we would only mention that when ordinary words like *swarajya* and *arya* are so spelled in Urdu as to read 'Ariya' and 'Save rajya' then how can we talk of (translation of) subjects that are more profound. Only the other day, while translating the Urdu book entitled *Kaumen Kis Tarah Zinda Rahati Hai* written by Lala Hardyalji MA, the government translator read the name of Rishi 'Nachiketa' written in Urdu, as 'Neech Kutiya' and translated it as 'a bitch of low origin.' It was due to the imperfection of the Urdu script and the Urdu language and their distance from the Hindi language and literature.

"In the rest of India, it is the Indian languages and scripts that are prevalent. In such a situation, why must we isolate ourselves from the rest of India by propagating Urdu in Punjab? We must not do that. But what is more important is the fact that in the Urdu used by those Muslim writers who are staunch supporters of Urdu, there is a preponderance or Persian. So much so that in the Muslim newspapers like *Zamindar* and *Siyasat* there is a preponderence of Arabic which the common man cannot understand. Then how can it (Urdu) be propagated? We want that our Muslim brothers, while remaining steadfast in their religion, should become as mush Indian as Kamal Tarak is. We should look at the language question from a wider angle and should not make it an emotional issue....".

Mythology has always been a coherent part of the culture and tradition of a country. It is mythology which unites the common man and his culture and tradition. Without knowing the history and mythology of our country and without understanding the special features of our nation, it is impossible for any of us to become patriots and to lead the revolution. Bhagat Singh had comprehended and would stand it well even during his student life. That is why we find that his views about language, literature and mythology are so clear. In the present scientific age, the world will ultimately have one language. But this possibility falls at the very distant future. For achieving this, man will have to pass through a process of development for several centuries. In this regard, Bhagat Singh has aptly stated, "This cannot be done immediately. For that, we shall have to go step by step." For moving towards that eventuality intellectual development is required. Such a development in the initial stage is possible only with the help of the mother tongue and through the regional literature. He considered Nagari Script to be more suitable than the Gurumukhi script. Advising the former to be accepted as the script for Punjabi, he stated :

"We say to the gentlemen of the Hindi press that assuredly Hindi will ultimately become the sole language of the country. But in the initial stage, its propagation will prove very inconvenient. With the adoption of the Hindi script, Punjabi will become like Hindi. There will be no difference between the two, but this is what is required. Let us take for example, the following Punjabi couplet

"O reahiye raahe jandian
sunja meri gal
Sir te pag tere vilayat di
isnoo, phoonk moitada laa".

"Even the best of the Hindi couplets will not be able to create the same impact because they would still not have been imbibed by the common man. They appear to be so strange because of the fact that Hindi is based on Sanskrit. Punjab has moved quite far from it. Punjab has been more influenced by Persian. For example, the plural of the word *'Cheez'* is *'cheezan'* on the Persian style and not *'cheezain'*.

This principle seems to be operating all along. What is suggested is that by writing Punjabi in the Hindi script and trying to make it more literary, it would be possible to bring them shoulder to shoulder.

"After giving all these arguments, we would still like to say one thing. Many people feel that the Punjabi language is devoid of sweetness, beauty and fine sentiments. All this is baseless. Only the other day poet Ravindra was charmed by the beauty of the following song :

"Lachchiye jithe tain paani dholia
Uthe ug payo sandal de boote"

He immediately translated it into English thus :

"Lachchi, where thy split water
where thy split water etc. etc."

Several such examples can be given. The following couplet is no less beautiful than those of other languages :

"Peepal de pattiya ve, kehi khad khad laayee-e

Patjhare puraane hun rut naviyan di aayee..."

(O peepal leaf why do you grumble so?

When autumn arrives old leaves must wither away as it is time for the new leaves to sprout).

Untouchability was a burning problem in those days. The annual session of the Congress in 1923 was held in Cocanada under the presidentship of Maulana Mohammed Ali. In his presidential address he had made the suggestion that the untouchables may be equally absorbed by the Hindus and the Muslims. Lala Lajpat Rai opposed this suggestion. Consequently, the problem of untouchability led to controversy. The Muslims started a campaign of religious conversion which was known as Tableeg. The *Arya Samaj* also launched a similar movement which was known as *Shuddhi* movement. The leader of the *Shuddhi* movement was Swami Shraddhanand. Opulent Muslims and Hindus gave financial support to the two respective movements. As a result of all this communal and disintegrating forces got encouraged. Principal Chhabildas has written.

"I was greatly impressed by the fact that Lala Lajpat Rai paid special attention to eradication of untouchability in addition to the *Arya Samaj* and other reform movements. An Achchootodhar Mandal, (for the emancipation of untouchables) was set up under the auspices of the *Lok Sewa Mandal* and Lala Mohan Lal continued to be its secretary for several years. Seth Birla of Calcutta was contributing rupees five thousand per month for the work connected with the emancipation of untouchables. A similar assistance was also given to Swami Shraddhanand, the *Arya Samaj* leader."[6]

Lala Lajpat Rai has said in his autobiography that he was receiving money from Birla and Maulana Mohammed Ali was geting money from the Agha Khan. Bhagat Singh also penned an article on this problem which was published in, *Kirti* of June 1928 under the pseudonym 'Vidrohi'. He called untouchability a doom on India and went on to write :

"Today a lot of noise is being created on this problem. These poor people are receiving special attention. In the process of evolution of freedom in our country, the introduction of communal representation has been beneficial at least in one respect, if not in other respects, in so far as now every community is worried about increasing its own numbers so as to be able to claim more power. Muslims have exerted themselves a lot ; they have started converting the untouchables into Islam thereby converting them into human beings and giving them the rights enjoyed by other human beings. This has hurt the Hindus and there have been arguments, and even riots have taken place. Gradually Sikhs also started thinking in this direction. They also started converting people to their religion. There were quarrels between Hindus and Sikhs over incidents involving the discarding of the sacred thread and the cutting of the hair. Now each of the three communities is trying to pull them (untouchables) into their fold. There is a lot of furore. The Christians are also quietly raising their status. All this activity is bringing Hindustan into ridicule.

"On the other hand, when the untouchables saw that people were quarelling over them and trying to gobble them up, they felt it best to have a separate organisation of their own. The British government may or may not have had a hand in this idea being born, but the government officials certainly did a lot to publicise this idea. The setting up of the Adi Dharm Mandal is the result of this."

According to him these were the causes of the problem. He also suggested his own solution and said :

"Now the question is what is the proper solution of this problem. The answer is quite simple. First of all we must decide that all human beings are equal ; consequently, there is no difference based on birth or occupation. The idea that a person will have to carry the night soil all his life simply because he was born in a *Bhangi* home and that he has no right to progress, is an absurd one. These people were subjected to atrocities by our forefathers (the Aryans) who cast them aside by branding them as lowly ; they made these people do mean work and, fearing their rebellion, they propagated the theory of rebirth implying thereby that all this was the result of sins committed in the previous birth, that there was no remedy for their suffering and that they should quietly live the life that was destined for them. They (the Aryans) taught these people the lesson of forbearance and thus silenced them for perpetuity. This was the greatest sin committed by them. In this way they deprived human beings of the spirit of human dignity, self-confidence and self-reliance. This was a great tyranny and injustice that was committed. Now it is time to atone for this sin."

"This brought another evil. People developed a dislike for essential work. We even pushed the *julahas* (weavers) away from us and today the weavers are considered untouchables. In UP even the *kahars* are considered untouchables. This has done a lot of harm. This has obstructed our progress.

"We should move forward keeping all these things in mind. If the untouchables are not called by that name and are not considered untouchable, the problem will be easily solved. The method adopted by the *Naujawan Bharat Sabha* and the Naujawan conference is very good. If we apologise to these people, whom we have been calling untouchable, for our sins, if we treat them as humans like us, and if we accept them amongst us without converting them into Sikh, Muslim or Hindu religions, then it would be the right method. But to pull them to this or that side without giving them any rights in practice, will not be proper."

These two articles were written at an internal of four years. The first was written when he was a student of the National College and the second was written after he had engrossed himself in the revolutionary movement and had become one of its prominent leaders. These articles show that he was a versatile genius. He had both vision and direction. This indicates why his mental development was very rapid.

In addition to political and social problems, he had an in-depth understanding of literature and his thinking was very rational. The thinking of even the present day Congress and Communist leaders on the problem of language and untouchability is not as mature and logical as was that of Bhagat Singh. Apart from this, our Congress and Communist leaders, and also our intellectuals, did not possess the same scientific understanding of our history and culture as Bhagat Singh had.

Freedom did not merely mean banishing the British ; it also meant changing the centuries old caste system highlighting exploitation which had made not only the *Bhangis* and *Chamars* untouchable but also those who work with the sweat of their brow.

When Bhagat Singh was still studying at college, circumstance enforced him to abandon his home. He had dedicated himself to his service of the country and had decided not to marry. But his grandmother Jai Kaur wanted him to marry and bring home a bride.

His father Kishan Singh also wanted to oblige his mother, so marriage negotiations were started and a wealthy man belonging to the Mannwala village of Shakhupur district came to see Bhagat Singh with the proposal of his sister's match for him. Perhaps at that time Bhagat Singh's family was at village Khasana 6-7 miles from Lahore where also they possessed some land, because Virendra Sindhu has written : "All the day Bhagat Singh remained very happy. He was bubbling with joy and he himself harnessed the horse to the tonga and drove the tonga to escort the visitor back to his village. The bride's brother had liked him and before going he had fixed the date for the engagement ceremony."

It has been further recorded : "A few days before the date fixed for the engagement, Bhagat Singh went to Lahore and from there disappeared to some unknown place. His father found the following letter in the drawer of this table :

Final Step in Life

'Respected Pitaji,

Namaste.

I have pledged my life to the supreme objective, i.e., freedom of the nation. Therefore, in my life, comforts and wordly desires have no attraction for me.

You would remember that when I was young, Bapuji had announced at the time of my sacred thread ceremony that I had been pledged for the service of the nation. Therefore, I am only redeeming that pledge. I hope you would pardon me.

Yours obediently

Bhagat Singh

From Lahore, Bhagat Singh made for Kanpur. Some writers are of the view that he had with him a letter of introduction written by Vidyalankar addressed to Ganeshshankar Vidyarthi. In any case, he did not approach him straightaway. Shachindra Nath Sanyal has written :

"On talking to Bhagat Singh I came to learn that his father Kishan Singh was making all preparations for his marriage. Although I was myself married, I had been feeling distinctly that I had committed a great mistake by getting married. I explained to Bhagat Singh that if he got married he would not be able to do much work for the revolutionary movement. Bhagat Singh was not keen on getting married. I had made it a rule to put a member of our party to test to find out how much sacrifice he was capable of making. According to us, only that person was a true member of the party who was always ready to leave his home to join the struggle. Following this rule, I asked Bhagat Singh to be ready to leave his home and told him that if he got married there would be no hope of his doing any work in the future and that if he remained at home, he would have to get married. I told him that I did not want him to get married, and wanted that he should leave his home and stay at a place where I asked him to stay. Bhagat Singh agreed to leave his home. At one stage I had thought of meeting Sardar Kishan Singh because in the past we had some relations with him, but after Bhagat Singh had left his home, I decided not to meet Kishan Singh. At my insistence, Bhagat Singh left his home and went to Uttar Pradesh. In the beginning arrangement was made for his stay at the residence of Mannilal Awasthi of Kanpur."[7]

In those days, Suresh Chandra Bhattacharya was the leader of the revolutionaries in Kanpur. He has written, "Bhagat Singh came to me with a letter from Shachin Da. I arranged for his stay at my mess. As Bhagat Singh had to remain all alone in that house in the afternoon, I introduced him to Batukeshwar Dutt. He started learning Bengali from Batukeshwar and within a short time he learnt by heart the famous poem 'Vidrohi' written by poet Nazrul Islam. Although he rarely went out of the mess, yet I noticed that the constables of the CID had started moving around that house at number 221 in Ram Narain Bazar. I also came to know that Durga Prasad, the Deputy Superintendent of the CID and Yatin Bannerji had been making frequent trips to Kanpur looking for the revolutionaries.

"Somehow Ganeshji (Ganesh Shanker Vidyarthi) came to know about the arrival of Bhagat Singh. Bhagat Singh's father and Ganeshji knew each other, both being members of the All India Congress Committee. One day, Vidyarthiji asked me 'Suresh Babu' is Bhagat Singh staying with you?" Although it took me a few seconds to answer this straight question, I gave a clear reply and said 'Yes'.

'You bring him to the Pratap Press', Ganesh directed me. 'He is being closely watched by the police. Will it be proper to take him there'? I asked.

'You need not worry at all about it : And I would teach him journalism. You know, recently there have been serious riots at Daryaganj in Delhi. I have to send him there to bring correct news.'

Sardar Kishan Singh had started running about to learn the whereabouts of Bhagat Singh. He inserted an advertisement in the daily *Vandemataram* asking Bhagat Singh to return home. It is probable that Ganesh Shankar Vidyarthi had come across this advertisement and come to know from some other source about his presence at Kanpur. That is why he asked Suresh Bhattacharya to bring him to the Pratap Press. Anyway, this was how Bhagat Singh came into contact with Vidyarthi.

Bhagat Singh visited Delhi as a correspondent of *Pratap*. He collected facts about the communal riots and on his return to Kanpur he wrote a two column report. Thereafter, he got involved with the newspaper with the assumed name of Balwant Singh. Vidyarthi's press was the centre of revolutionary activities and it was also publishing privy revolutionary literature. When Gandhi started his non-cooperation movement he had talked of achieving *swarajya* within one year. But when he called off the movement on the pretext of Chauri Chaura incident, there was great frustration in the country. People were disenchanted with Gandhism ; Revolutionary young men again stood on their toes they set up a secret organisation called the Hindustan Republican Association and declared that the aim of this party was to establish united republic through an organised and armed revolution.

The constitution and the final form of this Republic was to be framed and announced by the representatives of the people at a time when they would suitably poised to translate their resolve into action. The republic would be organised on the basis of universal franchise. In this republic all such institutions would be abolished which allowed exploitation of man by man. The second item in the party's published programme was following :

"In order to organise peasants and workers, capable persons must be sent by this organisation to factories, railways and coal mines so that they can arouse the sentiments of the workers and make the workers well understand that the working class is not merely a tool of revolution but that revolution will take place only for the benefit of the workers. The peasants have also to be organised like the workers."

The fifth item of the party's secret programme was as follow :

"Suitable persons should be sent abroad for military training and education in science so as to make them capable of taking charge of arms factories and army operations at the time of revolution."

Deep Study

A study of this constitution can help us to comprehend the change that was brought about in the revolutionary movement as a result of the national and international situations. Shachindra Nath Sanyal has eked out the difference between this new secret organisation and the old organisation of Bengal :

"The intellectual development of the members of the Dhakha Anusheelan Samiti was quite incomplete. They were not able to understand that the revolutionary movement was only a branch of the National movement. At the base of the National movement was the urge to create a new nation and a new civilisation. They could neither understand all this nor had they anything to do with it. The revolutionary leaders of Bengal were not familiar with history, philosophy, literature etc. These leaders were undertaking some stocks of study during the periods of their detention. But this study of theirs was very unsystemetic ; for example, they would read a book about China by Bertrand Russel but would not think of reading the biography of Sun Yat Sen and articles written by him. They had no knowledge of the revolutions that had taken place in different states of the world.

Even during their detention, most of them did not show much inclination for study."[8]

With reference to the revolutions that took place in Italy, China and Russia and new ideas that gathered momentum and the new literature that was created during these revolutions, he goes on to say : "In India great leaders like Shri Aurobind, late Swami Vivekanand, Ramtirth, Dayanand and Lokmanya Tilak brought about a great awakening through a philosophical approach and started a strong and new philosophical movement".[9]

A philosophical movement is always an inseparable part of a political movement. There is a dialectical relationship between the two and it is this relation which shapes the goal of the political movement and demarcates the interest of the particular class which takes up the role, of leading the revolution.

Till 1921, the emerging capitalilst class was playing the role of leading our national movement, and the persons mentioned above by Shachindranath Sanyal were all the spokesmen of the emerging capitalist class which was ideologically against the feudal ideology and the surrenderist ideology of the loyalist moderates. This class extracted inspiration from history and mythology ; their political aim was to achieve *swarajya* and thereby to reestablish for India its pristine greatness. *Swarajya* was not defined in concrete terms by them. It was thought to be sufficient to proclaim that *Swarajya* is our birthright and patriotism of the people was evoked to achieve this objective and break the shackles of slavery which bound the motherland. The old revolutionary movement had the same shortcomings which the national movement of that period had. Revolutionary youths would go to the hanging ropes with a smile on their lips and with the Gita in their hands ; they used to take the pledge that they would be reborn in this country and would dedicate their lives to break the shackles of subordination of the motherland.

The only aim of the rebellion, sought to be achieved with the help of the army, which was planned by Sanyal himself in 1915 with the collaboration of the revolutionaries of the Ghadar Party, was to throw out the Britishers. Their ideological vision had the same limitations and they continued to have these limitations till the last which also were the limitations of the capitalist ideology based on the aforementioned political objective.

These limitations have been highlighted by Bhagat Singh in the following words in his article entitled *'Main naastik kyon hoon.'*

"Then I joined the Revolutionary Party. The first leader whom I met was one who could not deny the existence of God even though he had a fully developed consciousness. Whenever I wanted to know about God he used to tell me to meditate about God whenever I felt like doing so. He lacked the courage of an atheist. The other leader whom I met had firm faith in God. His name was—honourable comrade Shachindranath Sanyal.....on the first page of his book *Bandi Jeewan*, God has been glorified in superlative terms. The last page of the second part of this book contains the essence of the thinking which is nothing but spiritual glorification of God based on the Vendantic concept.... ."

Thus the new revolutionary organisation set up by the armed revolutionaries in the form of the Hindustan Republican Association, whose proclaimed aim was to put an end to the system that encouraged all kinds of exploitation of man by man, was only the old revolutionary movement in a new form.

The new consciousness imbibed by this movement was neither conceived by Sanyal nor was it a God's bounty. It was the product of the new phase which our national movement had entered after the failure of the non-cooperation movement. In order to understand this new form of the national movement, we shall have to analyse the political situation that prevailed in the country in 1924 when Bhagat Singh reached Kanpur. Only then we shall be able to understand the role of the revolutionary party and the nature of suppressive measures unleashed against it.

Three days before Gandhi called off the non-cooperation movement on 12th February, 1922 following the Chauri Chaura incident, i.e. on 9th February, the Viceroy sent the following telegram to the Secretary of State for India in London :

"The lower classes in the towns have been deeply affected by the non-cooperation movement. In some areas, especially in Assam, UP, Bihar, Orissa and Bengal, peasants are bent upon fighting. So far as Punjab is concerned, Akali movement has reached the rural Sikhs. Most of the Muslim population of the country is angry and defiant....Government of India is prepared for a fearful eventuality which it never had to face in the past and it also does not want to hide the fact that this situation has caused great worry."

Rajni Palme Dutt has written :

"The discipline of the mass movement and readiness for decisive struggle were shown by the example of Guntur, where in spite of Gandhi's orders, through a misunderstanding, the No-tax campaign was inaugurated. Not 5 per cent of the taxes were collected until Gandhi's countermanding order came. On a word of command from the Congress centre this process could have undoubtedly been unleashed throughout the country and would have turned into a universal refusal of land revenue and rent. But this process would have meant the sweeping away, not only of imperialism, but also of landlordism."[10]

This was the situation that was causing worry to the Viceroy and on account of which Gandhi himself was worried. Giving an account of this revolutionary upsurge and of the Bombay and Madras incidents, Gandhi wrote to Jawaharlal in a letter on 19th February, 1922 :

"All this news, and more such news from the south were with me when the Chauri Chaura incident worked as a spark which ignited the fire. I assure you that had this thing not been suspended then we would have been carrying on a truly violent movement instead of a non-violent movement."

This situation had not developed suddenly but was the continuation of a long historical process of development. This situation was the outcome of the war. Workers and peasants were the lynch pin of this revolutionary upsurge. During the war, imports had stopped and the needs of the Government had increased.

This brought about the growth of industry, particularly the textile industry and the industrialists grew wealthy. They wanted to invest their savings in new ventures so as to multiply these saving. This could be materialised only by weakening the stranglehold of imperialism. With the setting up of new industries, the number of workers had grown, but their economic condition was poor. Wealth had been concentrated only in handful of people belonging to the upper class of society. Workers, peasants and the middle class were very restless. The soldiers who had returned from the war front were no longer submissive, they were now more knowledgeable and more experienced.

Apart from this, the socialist revolution that shook Russia in November 1917 had helped in the creation of class consciousness and a new zeal among the workers. A new path of emancipation from exploiters and rulers through revolution had been opened up before them.

Labour Revolution

By the time the war ended, workers were on the verge of a struggle. Towards the end of 1918 there was a strike in the textile mills of Bombay which engulfed all the mills by 1919, involving 1,25,000 workers. The workers participated actively in the general strike organised in April against the Rowlatt Act and they played a militant role in the national movement. Strikes continued to be organised throughout the year 1919 and a peak was reached in 1920. Some of the figures relating to these strikes are as follow: From 4th November to 2nd December 1919, 12,000 workers of woollen mills of Kanpur remained on strike ; from 9th to 18th January 1920, 35 thousand workers of the jute mills of Calcutta were on strike ; from 20th to 31st January, 2,00,000 mill workers of Rangoon were on strike ; on 31st January 1,00,000 workers of the British India Navigation Company went on strike ; port and dock workers were on strike from 2nd to 16th February ; from 24th February to 28th March 4,00,000 workers of the Tata Iron and Steel Works were on strike ; on 8th March 60,000 workers of Bombay went on strike; from 20th to 26th March, 17,000 mill workers of Madras were on strike, and in May, 25,000 workers went on strike in Ahmedabad."[11]

In the first half of 1920 there were 200 strikes in which 15 lakhs workers participated. Workers organisations began to be formed during these strikes. They started as strike committees which were shown the way by intellectuals belonging to the middle class. Usually, they were either reformists or careerists. There was total absence of class consciousness. The Indian Trade Union Congress was set up in 1920. The inaugural session of the Congress was held in October in Bombay which was presided over by Lala Lajpat Rai. The fourth session was held in 1924 and was presided over by C.R. Das, the leader of the Swaraj Party.

While the emergence of this new force in our national movement drew the attention of the Congress leaders, the Government also could not afford to ignore it. The government appointed the Bangali Committee on labour unrest in 1921. In 1922, an Industrial Disputes Committee in Bombay and a Labour department in Madras were created. From 1921 onwards, figures about strikes and lockouts began to be maintained regularly.

With an upsurge in the labour movement, the growth of Marxism, the ideology of the working class was inevitable. The Communist Party brought forth the following Manifesto in the Congress session which was held in Ahmedabad in 1921 :

"If the Congress would lead the revolution, which is shaking India to the very foundation, let it not put faith in mere demonstrations and temporary wild enthusiasm. Let it make the immediate demands of the trade unions its own demands ; let it make the programme of the Kisan Sabhas (peasant unions) its own programme ; and the time will soon come when the Congress will not stop before any obstacle ; it will be backed by the irresistible strength of the entire population consciously fighting for their material interests."[12]

"In 1924, the publication of the journal *Socialist* from Bombay was started. The editor of the magazine was S.A. Dange. The propagation of revolutionary ideas was dangerous in the eyes of the Government even though, in London, the Labour Party was in power. The Government of India lost no time in unleashing repression. Four communist leaders—Dange, Shaukat Usman, Muzaffar Ahmed and Das Gupta were arrested ; they were prosecuted in the Kanpur Conspiracy Case and each of them was awarded 4 years punishment in jail. This was the first step that the Government took against Marxist ideology and the growing labour power and continued subsequently. The continued growth of this ideology became the greatest headache for the Government in the thirties.

Thus, in the stage into which our national movement entered after 1920, it was the workers and their organised party which was required to play the role of leadership and Marxism was to be the guiding ideology of this leadership. But this ideology was still in an incipient stage. It was slowly growing within the confines of the capitalist ideology of the national movement as a chick grows within the egg, and the time to break the shell and come out of it, had not yet come.

According to the law of history, every age produces its own exponent. The most powerful exponent of the preceding age was Vivekanand. Old revolutionaries used to eke inspiration from him, so much so that Vivekanand's works used to be recovered in searches that were conducted in their houses.

Exponent of New Age

The exponent of the new age was Bhagat Singh. The proposal of marriage gave him an alibi to run away from home and flee to Kanpur. Kanpur was the biggest industrial centre of north India. The revolutionary youths of Kanpur, Suresh Bhattacharya, Batukeshwar Dutt, Ajay Ghosh and Shiv Verma, etc., were all proponents of the Marxist ideology. After coming in contact with them, Bhagat Singh also became aligned to this ideology.

He started studying Marxism, and it was here that his training for becoming the exponent of the new age began. We shall find that the credit for developing Marxist consciousness and giving it a nationalist from goes neither to comrade Shachindra Nath Sanyal nor to the Communist Party, but to Bhagat Singh and his revolutionary comrades. It was natural that widespread anger against the foreign government explode during the movement and assume revolutionary dimensions. Gandhi was repeatedly requested to renounce the condition of the freedom struggle being non-violent. Such a request was particularly made by his Muslim colleagues. But instead of doing that, Gandhi called off the movement on the pretext of violence having been committed.

In this way he extinguished the fires of revolution. As a result, the widespread anger found expression in conuter-revolution which gave ample opportunity to the British Government to incite communal riots. The revolutionaries were now mainly engaged in trying to prevent these riots and redirect people's anger against imperialism. Ganesh Shanker Vidyarthy's Pratap Press was playing a significant role in this regard.

Therefore, the first task that was assigned to Bhagat Singh was to go to Delhi and give an apt report about the Daryaganj communal riots to make the people alert and vigilant. Apart from this, the revolutionary literature printed at the Pratap Press was also being distributed among the people in privy. The aim of this literature was to prepare the people for an armed struggle. Bhagat Singh wrote many papers and pamphlets which were distributed at fairs and other such occasions in the same way as was done by the Bharat Mata Society.

The Pratapgarh fair is one of the well-known fairs of Uttar Pradesh held at Dussehra and which is attended by thousands of people from villages and towns. Bhagat Singh and his comrades went there to distribute a Hindi pamphlet. This pamphlet had been printed at the Pratap Press and was entitled *'Jago mere desh ke loggo'* (Awake my countrymen). The constables of the intelligence department were also posted in the fair in plain clothes. As soon as the young men started distributing the pamphlets, the constables pounced upon them and arrested two of them.

Bhagat Singh brewed a plan to free his comrades from the clutches of the police. He quietly threw to one side all the pamphlets that he had with him. People ran to pick them up. Thereupon, Bhagat Singh approached the policemen and started shouting, 'Look, the Congressmen are distributing pamphlets there.' Leaving behind two of their companions, the policemen ran in that direction and were lost in the crowd. This was the opportunity that Bhagat Singh and his comrades were searching for. They overpowered the two policemen and freed their comrades. Thereafter, all five of them made a quick get-away from the fair. The police, and some from among the crowd chased them. Bhagat Singh fired three or four shots in the air from his pistol, whereupon, the pursuers gave up the chase.

Gopinath Saha Attains Martyrdom

The main event that occured at that time was the martyrdom of

Gopinath Saha, which once again rivetted the attention of the people towards the revolutionaries and the event became an issue of public debate.

Gopinath Saha was a revolutionary young man. He had fired at the notorious police inspector Charles Tangart but, by chance, another innocent Englishman was killed. After his arrest, Saha boldly stated in the Court that he had intended to annihilate the oppressive Charles Tangart, that he had committed a great mistake due to which an innocent Englishmen had been killed. Saha was badly tortured in the jail ; he was made to sit on ice slabs to make him reveal the secrets of his party and his colleagues. But Gopinath Saha did not budge, he quietly tolerated all the oppression and did not speak a single word. On being sentenced to death, he went to the gallows with a smile on his face. In the cell in which Saha was kept before being hanged, people found the following words written on the wall "non-violence has no place in Indian politics".

The revolutionaries were, on the one hand, fighting against the British, and on the other, they were struggling against Gandhism. Gopinath Saha initiated this struggle after the non-cooperation movement by shedding his own blood. At this point of time a provincial political conference of Bengal Congress was held at Dinajpur. In the conference the heroism of Saha was eulogised by a resolution and a tribute was paid to him. This took place under the presidentship of the veteran Congress leader Chittaranjan Das who was the President of the Swaraj Party and the Trade Union Congress at that time.

Gandhi was arrested in March 1922 for committed the 'crime' of withdrawing the movement and was sentenced to six years imprisonment. But he was released in January 1924 after only 20 months because the British Government felt that he would be more useful outside the jail. He had been locked in the jail only to protect him from the wrath of the people.

Chittaranjan Das was being appreciated all over the country for the resolution eulogising Saha. Gandhi criticised this action and pleaded that such resolutions should not be brought in the conferences of the Congress party. This led to a controversy which continued for quite a long time in the form of letters to the newspapers. Youths, not only of Bengal but of the whole country, gave credence to action of Chittaranjan Das and opposed Gandhi's plea. In the AICC meeting held at Ahmedabad on 27th, 28th and 29th June, a motion against Gandhi was moved.

Congress historian Pattabhi Sitaramayya writes :

"The resolution of the meeting that excited much feeling was the one relating to the condemnation of the murder of Mr. Earnest Day by

Gopinath Saha which the Committee regretted. It offered its condolences to the family of the deceased, and, though deeply sensible of the love, however misguided, of the country prompting the murder, the AICC strongly condemned this and all such political murders and was emphatically of the opinion that all such acts were inconsistent with the non-violent policy of the Congress, and was of the opinion that such acts retard the progress towards *swaraj* and interfere with the preparations for civil disobedience." There was a battle-royal over this resolution. There was no concealing the fact that it was not to the Deshbandhu's taste ; not that he did not swear by non-violence, but that he would change the emphasis on the different clauses considerably. Gandhi was disappointed to find some of his dearest and closest followers voting against the resolution and that was one of the few occasions on which he wept in public.[13]

He goes on to write :

"But the bane of the year was the outbreak of communal violence in various places especially at Delhi, Gulbarga, Nagpur, Lucknow, Shahjahanpur, Allahabad, Jabalpur and worst of all at Kohat. The Kohat riots really broke the backbone of India. A committee was appointed to investigate the causes and conditions of the riot. It consisted of Gandhi and Mohammad Ali. The two produced a report, but unfortunately they differed in respect of the parties on which they fixed the blame for the disturbances. But a perusal of the reports on the Kohat outrages, printed and published for the Kohat Refugees Working Committee, by Lala Nandlal. Head Master, Bharati School, Kohat immediately after the riots, sends a thrill of horror through the reader. We cannot review the events beyound saying that after the shootings and carnage of 9th and 10th September a special train had to remove, 4,000 Hindus, of whom 2,600 were taken to Rawalpindi where they had to live for two months on charity and the remaining 1,400 to other places."

"It is no wonder that Gandhi decided to go on a twenty-one days' fast. He held himself responsible for all this fury and murderousness and felt called upon to expiate his own guilt. The fast was a critical test... the fast was commenced in Maulana Mohammad Ali's house, Delhi, but later he was removed to a house outside the city. Advantage was taken of the fast to gather the leading Indians of all communities at a Unity conference, which was attended by the Metropolitan of Calcutta. The committee had prolonged sittings from September 26th to October 2nd, 1924. The members of the Conference pledged themselves to use their utmost endeavours to enforce the principles of freedom of conscience and religion and condemn any deviation from them even under provocation. A central National Panchayat was appointed, Gandhi, as chairman and convenor, and Hakim Ajmal Khan, Lalaji, S.K. Nariman, Dr S.K. Datta and Master Sunder Singh of Lyalpur were its members. The conference laid down certain fundamental rights relating to the liberty of holding and expressing religious beliefs and following religious practices, the sacredness of places of worship, cow-slaughter and music before mosques, with a statement of the limitations they must be subject to. The press was warned to be careful in its writings, and the people were requested to offer prayers during the last week of Gandhi's fast. The 8th of October was marked out for mass meetings for thanksgiving."[14]

Gandhi rightly blamed himself for the riots. But this fast was not to reparate for the grave sin he committed by reducing the revolution to a counter-revolution. A close analysis of the incident leads us to the followng conclusions :

1. The fast was observed by Gandhi to stage a come-back in politics and to salvage his lost reputation.

2. Analysing the Russian Revolution of 1905. Lenin has written that the failure of the revolution sounded the death knell of Tolstoyism, because the masses, like an army, learn a lot from their defeat. Our masses had learnt a great lesson from the failure of the non-cooperation movement and Gandhism was dying. The fast was observed only to inject life into it.

3. Just as an unprincipled and opportunistic alliance with Khilafat movement had only encouraged religious obscurantism and blind faith, the Unity Conference also did the same on this occasion.

4. The only aim of holding prayers all over the country during the last week of the fast and to observe as thanksgiving day on the 8th October was to enhance the importance of Gandhi and to blunt the class consciousness resulting from the prevailing situation by making the people consume the opium of religion.

5. Gandhi said that the revolutionary act of violence by Gopinath Saha was an obstacle in the path of swaraj while the fact was that it was *satyagraha,* non-violence and fasts that were weakening the forces of revolution, and the native and foreign vested interests were using Gandhi for the purpose.

It is further written by Sitaramayya :

"The (all parties) conference... put down the unrest in Bengal to the withholding of swaraj, and appointed a committee of representatives of all political parties to prepare a scheme of swaraj and a communal settlement to report not later than 31st March, 1925. There was no doubt that the conference was not expected to achieve much. But very likely, Deshbandhu's arrest was obviated by it."

The committee, as was expected, did not achieve any thing. It was only a drama although it was appropriate to say that withholding of *swaraj* was the reason for unrest in Bengal. Lord Reading issued ordinance No. 1 in 1924 to suppress the revolutionary forces that were emerging as a result of this unrest. By the contents of this ordinance, any one, who was suspected by the local government of being affiliated to the revolutionary party, could be put under arrest and such persons could be summarily tried in the court of a special commissioner. The committee did condemn this ordinance, but it did not consider it necessary to make any reference to the revolutionaries. It meant for them little if they were subjected to repression. The next session of the Congress was held in 1924 in Belgaon. In his presidential address, Gandhi said only this much that all that repression was against the Swarajists. However, the action against the Swarajists was only play acting. Here is an example of the same. The Nagpur police had stopped a procession with the National Flag to pass through the Civil Lines on 1st March 1923. This was done under Section 144. The volunteers were insisting on their right to carry the flag wherever they pleased. This gave way to arrests and punishments and the issue led to a movement.

The Congress Working Committee gave its backing to this movement and it was decided that the coming Gandhi Day falling on the 18th would be observed as a flag day. Volunteers started coming from all nook and corners of the country and within no time it became an all-India movement. The contention of the Congress was that the road was meant for public use and they had the right to go wherever they pleased. Vallabhbhai Patel laid down the route of the procession and put an end to people's misunderstandings. In spite of Section 144, the procession was taken out and it was allowed to pass-through.

The pro-British papers said that it was Government's victory because the Congress Party had sought permission to take out the procession. However, the Congress Party denied having asked any permission. The Delhi Congress congratulated to the organisers of the Flag satyagraha movement at Nagpur and the volunteers for having, by their audacious endeavour upheld the honour of the country by carrying the fight to a successful finish.[15] Doesn't this satyagraha appear to be one which derailed people's mind from the real problems and the struggle that was being carried on to solve them? Does it not appear that words like 'honour of the country' and 'fight to a finish' used by Pattabhi Sitaramayya, are nothing but verbose? Yet, Sitaramayya has described this Flag Satyagraha in detail and with great pride.

Jawaharlal Nehru has, in his autobiography, referred to a similar *Satyagraha,* which was undertaken for protecting the honour of religion. The Kumbh fair was being held in January 1924. Lakhs of pilgrims had come for a holy dip on this occasion. But that year the flow of the Ganges had become somewhat overwhelming and the Government had imposed certain restrictions on bathing at the Sangam. Now, the importance of bathing was only in donig it at the *Sangam.* Therefore, Pandit Madan Mohan Malaviya objected to these restrictions and threatened to offer Satyagraha if the restrictions were not lifted.

Early on the Kumbh day, Jawahar Lal Nehru visited there just to see the Kumbh fair. According to him, he had absolutely no intention of bathing because he did not believe in sanctification by bathing in the Ganges. But when he saw Malaviyaji proceeding towards the *Sangam* with a band of two hundred people despite the prohibition imposed by the magistrate, he also joined the band of Satyagrahis in the zeal. The satyagrahis were beleagured by the mounted and the unmounted police. There was a mild lathi charge but Malaviyaji and the other satyagrahis remained unabetted. After some time, Malaviyaji suddenly got up and shot through the police cordon and had a quick dip. Nehru and other satyagrahis also followed him and all of them jumped into the water. After that the police contingent was removed from there.

After discussions with Gandhi, Chittaranjan Das and Motilal Nehru issued a statement regarding the future programme in which it was stated :

'In the second place, we must supplement the work of the Congress by helping the labour and peasant organisations throughout the country. The problem of labour is always a difficult problem to solve in every country but in India the difficulties are greater. On the one hand, we must find out a way of organisation by which we can prevent exploitation of labour by capitalists or by landlords, but on the other hand, we must be on our guard to see that these very organisations may not themselves be the source of oppression by nursing extravagant and unreasonable demands. Labour, undoubtedly, requires protection, but so do industrial enterprises. Our organisation must protect both from exploitation and the Trade Union Congress must be so organised as to be able to serve this useful purpose. We hold that in the long-term the real interests of both and of the country at large are identical.'[16]

The statement is self explanatory and needs no comment. The fear of the growing strength of workers and peasants is quite obvious in this statement. The Congress leadership was interested in protecting the interests of industrialists and workers by keeping the trade unions under check. The British Government was equally intimidated of this revolutionary force and it was enacting repressive laws, inciting riots and was using Gandhi's *Ahimsa* and *Satyagraha* as an ideological shield.

The All Party Committee to define swaraj had been appointed only under the pressure of this revolutionary force of workers and peasants. The committee did nothing as was kept expected. But it remained the most important issue of the day and could not have been aside. Dr. Sitaramayya has given a brief summary of Gandhi's speech delivered at the Belgaon Congress in the following words.

'I would strive for swaraj within the Empire, but would not hesitate to sever all connection, if severance became a necessity through Britain's own fault'.[17]

Not defining *swaraj* as complete independence and keeping the definition ambiguous amounted to checking the growth of class consciousness. The struggle between the Marxist class ideology and Gandhi's ideology of Trusteeship was the special feature of this era which asks for closer study.

Revolutionary Activities

Most of the writers who have written about Bhagat Singh opine that since Bhagat Singh had come to the notice of the police because of his revolutionary activities, Ganesh Shankar Vidyarthi got him appointed as head master of National School at village Saadipur in district Aligarh and it was from there that he returned to Punjab at the end of 1924. But his nephew Prof. Jagmohan, who has conducted valuable research on Bhagat Singh, holds a contrary view. According to him, Bhagat Singh became head master later, when he came to Kanpur the next time. We consider Jagmohan Singh's view to be authentic which is supplemented by other events. In any case, following is the story of his returning home.

Grandmother Jai Kaur was seriously ill and she was wishing badly to see Bhagat Singh, but there was no trace of him. By chance, at that very time, Bhagat Singh wrote a letter to his friend Ramchand who belonged to Jinar village of Rawalpindi district. He instructed Ramchand not to tell anyone about his whereabouts. But Ramchand mentioned the fact of his receiving this letter to another close friend of Bhagat Singh, Jaidev Gupta. This is how Kishan Singh got to know about it. Kishan

Singh sent Ramchand and Jaidev to Kanpur to apprise Bhagat Singh about the illness of his grandmother and to bring him back.

Both of them, however, returned without finding Bhagat Singh. Thereafter, Kishan Singh penned to his friend Maulana Hasrat Mohani to persuade Bhagat Singh to return home.

Maulana Tafazzul Hussain Hasrat Mohani was a noteworthy character in the political world of our country. Like Kishan Singh he was a follower of Tilak. Besides being a poet, he was a firm follower of his religion. In fact, he had an inseparable blend of politics, religion and poetry in his personality. He was equally devoted to all the three. While his political devotion gave him the inclination of a revolutionary, his religious convictions made him a firm follower of the Prophet and the holy Qoran, and his fascination for both found outlet in poetry. He was first sent to jail in 1906 for publishing anti-government articles in his Urdu journal Urdu-e-Mualla and consigned to the grinding stone.

For the first time, a resolution demanding complete independence was moved by him at the Ahmedabad Congress in 1921; but Gandhi got it rejected calling it 'irresponsible'. When the non-cooperation movement started, he commented in the context of boycott of foreign goods that since our fight was against British Imperialism, only the British goods should be boycotted. Gandhi did not nod to this too. He was also among those who had demanded that there should be no insistence on non-violence in the non-cooperation movement. He had been greatly moved by the Russian Revolution. In one of his couplets he had said :

'Kyon Gandhi ki tarah baith ke kaatenge charkha
Lenin Ki tarah denge na duniyan ko hila hum'

(we shall not sit quietly spinning on the charkha, like Gandhi, We shall, rather, rock the world as Lenin did).

When the inaugural session of the Communist Party was held at Kanpur in 1925, Maulana Hasrat Mohani chaired the Reception Committee. But he could not go nicely along with the communists because of his religious inclinations. Since he could not see eye to eye with Gandhi in the Congress Party, he joined the Muslim League. There too, he tried to get a resolution passed favouring socialism and fell out with Jinnah.

After the formation of Pakistan, he continued to stay in India and was elected to the Constituent Assembly. He, however, refused to sign the final draft of the Constitution asserting that what we needed was a Russian type of constitution.

To come back to our story, he advised Bhagat Singh to go back and to work in Punjab which was his field of work. Bhagat Singh liked the advice of the Maulana and he returned home on 15th January 1925 after an absence of 6-7 months. On seeing her grandson, grandma Jai Kaur recovered from her illness—so much was her love for Bhagat Singh. For some time, Bhagat Singh devoted himself to looking after his grandmother. After she had recovered a little, he started visiting Banga, Lahore and other cities to develop acquiantance with young men and bring them into the fold of the revolutionary organisation.

At this time, his father also entrusted him with some work and he displayed his wisdom and organisational capacity in accomplishing that task. The Akali movement against the corrupt Mahants was being executed with great vigour despite government repression. However, since March, 1924 the Jathas (contingents) were being sent to Jaiton town in Nabha state instead of Nankana Saheb. The reason behind this was as follows. A day of mourning had been observed to pay homage to the martyrs who had been brutally killed in the gruesome firing that had taken place at Nankana Saheb. On that particular day, people participated in the function displaying black armbands. Among these mourners the Raja of Nabha, Ripudaman Singh was also present with a black armband. This was something surprising because the five Sikhs states of Punjab, Patiala, Nabha, Kapurthala, Jind and Faridkote, had lent support to the British in the 1857 war of independence and soiled the fair name of Punjab. For this reason, the rulers of these states were called toadies by the people, who hated them. The Rajas were against every progressive measure as also to the Akali movement.

So it came as a great surprise when the ruler of Nabha joined the mourning with a black armband. In the eyes of the Government, this was sedition. The Viceroy was very angry. Ripudaman Singh was deposed and detained at Dehradun. Now the issue of reinstatement of Ripudaman Singh also became important along with that of the Gurudwaras, and the Jathas started coming to Jaiton instead of going to Nankana Saheb. The demonstrations that took place at Jaiton became memorable in the history of martyrdom. When the Jathas passed through, they used to be welcomed in every village. Government used to make all efforts to ensure that the jathas were not welcomed in any village because this would boost their morale. Pro-government jagirdars also gave their best to ensure that the jathas did not receive any welcome.

The thirteenth jatha of martyrs had to wade through Kishan Singh's village Banga. Jathadar Kartar Singh and Jwala Singh had come to Kishan Singh at Lahore and requested him to arrange a welcome to the *jatha.* Although Kishan Singh was not an Akali himself, he had sympathy for the Akali movement and he also had influence in his village. But he had to visit Bombay for insurance work. So he entrusted the work of welcoming the jatha to Bhagat Singh. The Jagirdar of that area, Dilbagh Singh was pro-government. In addition to holding the title of Sardar Bahadur, he was also a first class honorary magistrate. He decreed by drum beat that no one should welcome the *jatha,* nor should any one offer anything to the jatha. He ordered the removal of buckets from the wells in order to prevent the members of the *jatha* from drawing water from the wells to drink.

Sardar Bahadur Dilbagh Singh was a close relative of Bhagat Singh. He was the son of Surjan Singh, the elder brother of his grandfather Arjun Singh.

Surjan Singh and Arjun Singh had both participated as delegates in the Congress session that had been held in Lahore in 1893 under the presidentship of Dadabhai Nauroji. Subsequently, Surjan Singh had become pro-government and his son was decorated with the title of Sardar Bahadur and was made a first class magistrate as a reward. The police was at his disposal. As such, the entire village was in fear of him. It was a very crucial confrontation. People did not know Bhagat Singh much as he had been out of the village most of the time. Yet he was determined to discharge the responsibility that he was entrusted.

He reached the village with some of his friends. He had the experience of carrying out revolutionary work. Gradually, he dispelled the fear of the people and made arrangements for the supply of milk, bread, vegetables etc. to the *jatha.* Sardar Bahadur was relaxing in the belief that he had set the police to do his job. He and the police did not come to know of all the arrangements made by Bhagat Singh. On the appointed day, the *jatha* arrived and halted at a place outside the village—close to a sugarcane field. Bhagat Singh and his comrades, were hiding in the sugarcane fields. Milk, vegetables and bread had already been transported to the sugarcane field at night. These were served to the members of the *jatha.* The peasants of Roda village had also given a helping hand in this operation.

Subsequently, Bhagat Singh and his comrades set up fireworks to mark the welcome given to the *jatha.* The fireworks attracted the people who gathered there in good numbers Bhagat Singh delivered a speech before them.

New Phase of Life

As Gopinath Saha was in the news those days, Bhagat Singh related the story of his martyrdom to the audience which moved them greatly. One of the Mirasis of the village later related how he had wept after listening to the speech of Bhagat Singh. The *jatha* was given a memorable farewell and those in the *jatha* went away singing, 'Laaj rakh lee, laaj rake lee ; Bhagat Singh pyare ne laaj rake lee ; (our darling Bhagat Singh has saved our honour).

This was a great humiliation for Sardar Bahadur Dilbagh Singh. He had lost his respect. All he could do was to get a warrant of arrest issued against Bhagat Singh.

Kishan Singh had his own sources of information in the intelligence department. The information about the issuance of the warrant was leaked out. So Kishan Singh himself, sent Bhagat Singh to Kanpur to stay there untill limit of the warrant expired after six months. In this way, Bhagat Singh got a providential opportunity to renew his contacts with his revolutionary comrades and to learn from their experience.

Bhagat Singh spent some days in Delhi and worked in the editorial department of *Arjun* under the assumed name of Balwant Singh. Later on, Ganesh Shankar Vidyarthi got him appointed as headmaster of the National School at village Saadipur in Aligarh district. This gave him an opportunity to prophess the new generation the revolutionary teachings of patriotism. The teachers and the students of the school were pleased with Bhagat Singh's ability, way of teaching and his behaviour. During those days there was a heavy downpour of rain from 16th to 19th September which resulted inundated the Ganga, Yamuna and Ram Ganga. Many villages of Uttar Pradesh, which was then called the United Provinces, were flooded. Emulating his forefathers, Bhagat Singh took to the task of providing relief to the flood affected people. This dedication and sense of service were appreciated all round. The government did not provide any help which, naturally, must have led the people to draw their own conclusions. In addition to all this, Bhagat Singh, according to B.K. Dutt, continued with his engrossed study of the revolutionary experiences of the world.

When the Belgaon Congress was held in 1924 under the presidentship of Gandhi, Kishan Singh took along Bhagat Singh with him as a delegate. This gave him an opportunity to see and assess the national leaders at close quarters. A notable incident that took place there was that Kishan Singh introduced Bhagat Singh to the old revolutionary Niralamb Swamy. The two talked for a long time, many questions were put and answered. At the end of the meeting, the Swamy said to Kishan Singh, "Sardar Kishan Singhji, Bhagat Singh is growing into a great revolutionary. Let him go on."

It has been written : "In the beginning of 1925, Bhagat Singh was regularly coming to Kanpur from Lahore. At that time he was, in his own words, only a romantic fanciful revolutionary. Although the socialist and revolutionary communist thinking had reached India and among the Kakori martyrs, Rajender Nath Lahiri had make a lot of study in this regard, yet there was still much difference between precept and practice. Although it was due to Lahiri's influence that Bhagat Singh had named his younger brother Rajendra, he well understood Lahiri's shortcomings. On 9th August 1925 the government treasury near the Kakori railway station was looted to give a boost to the party. Following this dacoity, the martyr Ram Prasad Bismil and his comrades were arrested. Only Chandrashekhar who was absconding, was at large. In such a situation, Bhagat Singh took upon himself the task of reorganising and reactivating the party. The Party was called Hindustan Prajatantra Dal (Hindustan Republican Party). The party had to face conditions which have been described by Bhagat Singh in his own words, "till then I was only a romantic fanciful revolutionary. So far, we were only followers. Now the time had come to shoulder the entire responsibility. For some time, the very existence of the party had been in danger due to unremitting opposition ; not only excited comrades but even leaders started making fun of us. For some time, I was apprehending that I myself would start believing the failure of the party's programme. This was a turning point in my revolutionary career. I was feeling a great urge to study. My inner voice was urging me to study so as to equip myself to counter the arguments of opponents. So I started studying. The evidence given by common people during the Kakori Conspiracy Case thoroughly exposed the fact that the leaders of the party, who were otherwise dedicated, self-sacrificing and selfless, had failed to identify themselves with the masses".[18]

In November, a plan was sketched to help the comrades involved in the Kakori Conspriacy Case to flee from the jail. Bhagat Singh went to Kanpur to participate in this plan. However, the plan could not materialise as it was leaked out. Another plan was prepared in January-February which also failed. Out of the ten people who had been arrested, four were sentenced to be hanged and six were awarded long terms of imprisonment.

Now we have to see how the transformation of Bhagat Singh from a romatic fanciful revolutionary to a pragmatic socialist revolutionary occured and how he discharged the responsibility that had fallen on his shoulders. In fact, this turning point in the career of Bhagat Singh was also a turning point in the history of our national movement, and its aims and objectives which knowingly or unknowingly, lost sight of, had been resulting in the failure of the revolution and the present ills of the nation.

References

1. *Meri Inqilabi Yaatra,* pp. 24,26.
2. *Ibid.,* p. 33.
3. *Bandi Jivan,* pp. 268-70.
4. Quoted in 'Gandhi Benakab' from *'Gandhiji'* by Yajnik, pp. 194-95.
5. *Meri Inqlabi Yatra,* p. 32.
6. *Meri Inqilabi Yatra,* p. 30.
7. *Bandi Jeewan,* p. 277-8.
8. *Bandi Jeevan,* p. 258.
9. *Ibid.*
10. Rajni Palme Dutt, *India Today,* p. 327.
11. R. Palme Dutt, *India Today,* p. 377.
12. *Ibid.,* pp. 346-47.
13. Dr. Pattabhi Sitaramayya, *History of the Indian National Congress,* Madras, 1935, pp. 464.
14. *Ibid.,*.pp. 464-65.
15. *Ibid.,* pp. 433-34.
16. *Ibid.,* p. 462.
17. *Ibid.,* p. 470.
18. Introduction to '*Shaheed Bhagat Singh aur uske Saathiyon ke dastaavez'* (Documents of Shaheed Bhagat Singh and his Associaties).

5

The Bomb Incident

When the rulers turn deaf to the appeals of the people the only way to awaken them is to hurl a bomb in their ears. The Saunders murder shook the whole British empire. It was another deadly blow to imperialism. That the chief of police was murdered in front of the police headquarters, while policemen witnessed and the assailants escaped, was a humiliation on the whole system. It was a great embrassment for the Government to face. The police deduced that Bhagat Singh must be involved in this affair, but Bhagat Singh had completely vanished from the scene. He had shaved off his beard and moustache and was not recognisable. Fortunately Sohan Singh Josh has an account of that night which followed the historical day. At first he quotes what Ajoy Ghosh wrote ;

"Our party decided to strike a blow. In November (actually it was December) 1928 Saunders, the assistant superintendent of police, the man who had led the lathi-charge on the procession, was shot dead in front of the police headquarters in Lahore. Well-timed and daringly executed, it was an action that was acclaimed with joy. The first of the blows by means of which we expected to stir the country had been struck. On the same night (17 December) a little after 11 p.m. somebody knocked at my door in Bara Ghara, Islamabad, I was alone in the house, my family having gone to my village Chetanpura (Amritsar). I opened my door and to my utter surprise I found Bhagat Singh and Sukhdev standing outside. I welcomed them, but told them that it was rather risky to have come to my house because the police might raid it any time. But Bhagat Singh said, 'Don't worry, we have made all arrangements.' They came in and said, 'We are hungry, give us something to eat.' I could offer only two *chapatis*, some vegetable and a glass of milk. I told them we could cook fresh food. But they said, 'Nothing doing, we shall talk and sleep.'

Bhagat Singh was wearing a felt hat and an English style suit. He was quite unrecognisable in those clothes. Sukhdev was wearing an English hat and suit. Bhagat Singh took off his hat and placed it on a table nearby. He hung his pistol on a peg above the cot. Then after finishing the meagre meal, the first question he shot at me was—'What is the reaction in general to Saunder's murder?'

'The youths are happy,' I replied. 'But they would have been much happier if Scott had been killed.'

'We had gone there only for him (Scott), but the other devil came out,' he said. 'And we could not go empty-handed after all the pains taken for the preparation.' And then he added, 'Anyway, some beginning has been made.'

'There is another opinion also about this murder,' I put in, 'that of Gandhi's followers.'

'We knew it beforehand', he said, 'We discussed this before deciding upon the action.' Then he contemptuously added, 'Gandhi stabbed the nation in the back by withdrawing the non-cooperation movement (1921-22) after the Chauri-chaura incident. The people are still under the cloud of frustration and demoralisation which he brought to this country.'

'But leave that aside,' he continued, 'Do you know what has been the effect to Saunder's murder on the British rulers?'

'I do not know, it is too early to know that.'

'There is a great panic amongst them,' he said. 'Some of them have already booked their wives' and children's passages for England. They are terribly frightened.'

'But this panic is temporary,' I gave my opinion. 'It will wear off soon.'

'What do you think of this action?'

Sohan Singh repeated what he had been saying. To this Bhagat Singh said—'I don't agree. This action will rouse the masses and strengthen the movement.'

During this whole talk Sukhdev did not speak a single word. There were only two cots in the house. Sukhdev slept on one and Bhagat Singh and I shared the bigger one. They woke up a little before four in the morning to be ready to go. While going Bhagat Singh borrowed the book *Liberty and the Great Libertarians* by T. Sprading. Sohan Singh did not want to part with the book, but Bhagat Singh had his way. He promised to restore it after reading it.

Sohan Singh records that within a week he came across Bhagat Singh again in a shaving saloon in Calcutta. He writes—"After walking about a furlong , my guide and I entered a shaving saloon. To my utter surprise I encountered Bhagat Singh seated on a chair, waiting for me. I was taken aback. Just think, Josh entering a shaving saloon in Calcutta with a flowing beard and all the Sikh paraphernalia about him and CID shadowing him and hunting everywhere for Bhagat Singh. That was not only creating suspicious circumstances, but inviting the enemy to come and arrest us. I rebuked him for doing this foolish thing. He laughed and replied nonchalantly, 'Don't worry, nothing is going to happen. We have made all arrangements.' What arrangements he had made, I do not know till to-day."

Then after some talk on the conference he said, 'You do the organising of the workers and peasants and we shall do the disorganising of the British rulers. Let us have this division of work.' That was the last time Josh met Bhagat Singh. Indeed the plan of action, and the escape thereafter were prepared with great care. It was comparatively easy to kill a police chief, but the crux of the problem was to escape not only from the venue of action, but from the city as well. It was not possible to have a common plan of escape covering everybody. Every face had its limitations and disguises had to be adjusted and adopted within these limitations.

Accordingly, Bhagat Singh disguised as an Indian Sahib and travelied by first class, then a very great distinction for an Indian. To lend him additional credibility Durga, the young wife of Bhagavaticharan, along with her infant son Shachi, accompanied him as his wife. Rajguru with his rough exterior aptly assumed the role of the servant of the young Sahib. Taking advantage of winter, Bhagat Singh put on an overcoat and also a hat, thus further hiding his person. He clasped the infant in such a manner as to expose very little of his face. Both Bhagat Singh and Rajguru carried loaded pistols at that moment.

Chandrashekhar Azad, being a unique personality could not fit into this bourgeois set up. The contours of his person were so sedulously imprinted on the minds of the policemen that he would have been immediatley recognised. So he invented his own disguise. He joined a group of holy beggars and sang and danced out of the city, which had now become too hot for revolutionaries. All this was made possible because of the timely monetary assistance given by Dr. Gopichand Bhargava, an important Congressman. It was apprised to him that the murder was committed by revolutionaries. The names of the participants were not however confided to him. After 3 hours he conceded the emissary Yashpal Rs. 200, at that time a big sum, but from then he avoided Yashpal. This was natural, because Congress leaders, from the biggest to the ordinary ones, wanted that the revolutionaries should always be on the prowl, because this increased their bargaining power, but they did not want to jeopardise their ownselves. Dr. Gopichand Bhargava gave Rs. 200 but Durga gave with Rs. 500 willingly, at the request of Sukhdev. Thus Bhagavaticharan who had been almost underground since his house was searched in connection with the Meerut conspiracy, fully contributed to this affair, through Durga. Bhagavaticharan was in Calcutta in connection with the Congress session there.

When Bhagat Singh reached Calcutta with his Durga and son, Bhagavaticharan was there on the platform along with Sushila, an important revolutionary, to them welcome. On the journey, at Lucknow Durga had telegrammed to her husband that she was coming with her brother, but as she had written under the name Durgavati in the telegram, Bhagavaticharan was not clear about Durgavati and her brother until he saw them on the platfrom. This was the eve of the Calcutta session of the Congress and there was inflow of travellers from all the states. Policemen from all the states had come too. During his stay in Calcutta Bhagat Singh napped during the day. At night, dressed like a Bengali in *dhoti* and *chadar* he met Bengali revolutionaries like Trailokya Chakrabarti, Pratul Ganguli, Prof. Jyotish Ghosh. He also met Jatin Das. At first Bhagat Singh and Durga put up at a hotel, but later on they shifted to the house of Sir Seth Chhajjuram, who along with his wife, were of great service to them. It appears that Bhagat Singh had started planning to throw bombs in the Central Assembly just to make the deaf hear. Jogesh Chatterjee revealed later, that the revolver found on Bhagat Singh after the incident, had been given to him by Pratul Ganguli. Also his photograph with the felt hat that reached every betel seller's shop was clicked in Calcutta.

It spite of this, the Bengal revolutionaries did not make any substantial contribution to his plans. Bhagat Singh left Calcutta very soon and travelled to and fro in northern India in connection with organisational work. It is during these days that he met Ajoy Gosh, later the secretary of the CPI While taking a stroll in Calcutta, Bhagat Singh noticed that a cinema house was showing 'Uncle Tom's Cabin'. Bhagat Singh, who always kept his mind open, was eager to see the picture. But where to get the money? The party allowed only four *annas* for meal. Two *annas* bought bread and six pice was spent on *ghee* and two on tea.

And the lowest ticket was available four *annas*. Bhagat Singh and party decided to miss a meal, but when they reached the hall, the four *anna* tickets were already sold out. So they had to procure eight *anna* tickets. Later on, they appealed to Azad that as it was a revolutionary film, they had to see it. At this Azad graciously agreed to reimburse the sum, otherwise they would have had no alternative but to remain hungry for a whole day.

Once Azad was eating *chapatis* with *gur* (solidified molasses). The whole meal cost him only an *anna*. Bhagat Singh did not like the idea that he should eat a shabby meal for the sake of money. He said, 'You are overdoing it.' But Azad said, 'Let me go my own way, don't bother.' Bhagat Singh snatched a piece of *gur*, at this Azad got angry and threw the whole *gur* away. Comrades present there realised that Azad should not be disturbed. But the pieces of *gur* thrown away had fallen near the sewage. These were picked, washed and shared by all the comrades. Such was the poverty in which the revolutionaries chose to live. They really lived in dedicated poverty. This was in tune with the traditions of the party. After the Saunders affair, people began to contribute more liberally to the funds of the party and revolutionary work became stead fast. But the standard of living of the comrades was not allowed to go too high, as the contributions were all public money.

Like a hawk, Bhagat Singh carefully watched over the Indian scene. He noticed that the labour movement was also taking big strides. Bhagat Singh, Bejoy Kumar Sinha and the party intellectuals thought that all the different agitations should be brought to a confluence. They were aware of the fact that the Government, unhappy at the phenomenal growth of the labour movement, was poised to strike at it with all its strength. The Trade Dispute Bill, now in the Central Assembly, had been sponsored to deliver a fatal blow at the movement. There was tremendous opposition to the bill throughout the country. But the government as usual ignored it. The revolutionaries studied the bill thoroughly. When searched, a copy of the bill was found in the Agra hide-out of the revolutionaries. The party had struck at a very psychological moment, and had gained tantamount popularity as even Nehru concedes. Now, another opportunity was in the offing. The new stance of the party weged that it should identify itself with the labour movement. Before we proceed to recollect the events, it would be appropriate to see what the revolutionaries were thinking of during this interregnum between the Saunders murder and the Central Assembly Bomb affair, because posterity is going to judge them according to these ideas—especially their ideas on life in general, outside of politics, are very important.

Yashpal writes : "Up to that time, Azad laboured under a very antediluvian idea of *brahmacharya* (celibacy). Once or twice comrades had shown dereliction of duty because of women. Azad smelled a rat and looked askance whenever the topic touched the fair sex, love and beauty. Comrades enjoyed bringing good books for Azad, but he was upset when he saw nudes and books on sex,"

In the light of future events, Azad's thinking on these points stands defended and emerges as sound and healthy. The revolutionary has to operate in the battle field not in a bed of roses. It is a job that demands absolute loyalty leaving scarcely any room for luxuries. This stark fact governed Azad's judgements. At the same time, he never objected to such couples as Bhagavaticharan and Durga or Mohan and Sushila. But he certainly felt that those comrades, who were not married, should not further complicate and encumber their lives.

Somebody calculated, that in Russia the average active life of a revolutionary was 6 months, but according to the calculations of Shachindranath Sanyal, the duration of the active life of an Indian revolutionary was on an average two years. Seen from this viewpoint. Azad's active life lasted seven years, an all time record. I think Azad was quite right in not wanting comrades to increase their susceptibility during these years. As a born leader, he very well knew human weaknesses. He was cautious, but not dehumanised. In Jhansi he stayed in the family of Master Rudranarayan as a normal brother of his wife. He never said to Rudranarayan that as he was a married man, he did not befit from revolutionary work. Azad was very cautious in handling the money of the party. Parting even with a pice was torture to him.

From all accounts it is proved, that had Azad not kept a tight grip on the coffers of the party, comrades would not have been so economic. This was so, not because others were less aware, but because Azad coming from a poorer than the poorest class had a lower standard of necessities.

The Jolly Event

Dr. Mahore has recorded an anecdote, which brings forth this aspect of the life of the comrades. Mahore was suffering from bronchial troubles. Somebody suggested that an ounce or two of brandy would give relief. So money was obtained from Azad to 'buy the medicine.' At that time a bottle of brandy cost only Rs. 4. Mahore who was ignorant that this was alcohol, carried his bottle bravely wherever be went. He arrived with his bottle in the Agra hide-out where important revolutionaries were putting up. The bottle was recognised, but Mahore, innocently explained it was a tonic and the supremo had paid for it. The comrades took it as great fun and suddenly everybody developed bronchial trouble and consequently helped himself with a dose of the medicine. Gayaprasad, Sadashiv and Rajguru had already taken a dose, and now came the turn of B.K. Dutt, who was rather hesitant. In the meantime, Bejoy Kumar came in and threatened to relate the whole thing to Panditji (Azad). But Mahore refused to be threated, because he said Panditji had himself paid for the medicine. Bejoy kumar brought the whole affair to Azad's notice. Bhagat Singh himself did not like all this, but now the joke had gone so far, he too wanted to eke some fun out of it by nailing Azad down to a wrong type of partiality. Sadashiv, Vishwanath Bhaishampayan and Mahore were considered Azad's young men as they belonged to the Jhansi period of Azad's absconding life.

Bejoykumar, now that he had been aroused fully, said to Azad, 'Under the influence of wine Mahore with hardly a stitch on his back, performed a solo throughout the night. He would neither sleep nor let others sleep.'

Bhagat Singh further aggravated the lapse by delivering an extended lecture on the undesirability of comrades taking alcoholic drinks. Azad reacted very sharply. Said he—'Such men have no business to be in a revolutionary party. Then Bhagat Singh stoking the fire said, 'Panditji, it is you who paid for the bottle and now that the cat is out of the bag, why fret about it?'

Then Azad told the comrades that he had paid because he thought that it was medicine, he had no knowledge about this being some kind of wine. Somehow the matter was wound up and Mahore was ordered to break the bottle. Azad was insisted upon not to get the bottle broken as some situation might arise in the bomb factory when a comrade might need a drink. Azad modified his orders, but put the bottle among the bottles of chemicals. These slices of life help us to form a fair idea of the day to day lives of the revolutionaries and the philosophy which governed their actions. Bhagat Singh and Chandrashekhar Azad, combined together, harboured a balanced philosophy of life.

Bhagat Singh's natural makings were those of a bon viveur, Azad was every inch a saint, but both of them adjusted themselves to the goal which they had set for themselves—the goal of ultimate martyrdom.

Bhagat Singh was a lover of books and had worked as a journalist in the *Pratap* at Kanpur, *Arjun* at Delhi and in the *Kirti*. Some of the subjects of Bhagat Singh's reading were mentioned by approver Phanindra Ghosh—

(1) The History of the Revolutionary Struggle in British India—Open and Secret, (2) The Ideal of Republic, (3) 1914-15 Rising, (4) Ideal of Equality, Liberty, Fraternity, (5) Indian Princes and Revolutionaries (Sarkar's pamphlet), (6) Turkish Message to India's Muslim Rulers, (7) Berlin Committee and the German Plot, (8) Non-co-operation, (9) Swaraj—Clear Definition, (10) Failure of the Non-cooperation Movement and the Revolutionary Parties, (11) Communist Thought, (12) Spiritual Report, (13) Advanced Socialist Thought, (14) Communist School of Thought, (15) Nehru Report, (16) Terrorists and Mass Revolutionaries, (17) Anarchism versus Socialism, (18) Communism, (19) Syndicalism and Collectivism, (20) Revolution and World Revolution, (21) Modern Breach Loaders, (22) Use of Explosives, (23) Monopoly or How Labour is robbed.

Apart from these subjects, psycho-analysis, novels and road maps were gone through by Bhagat Singh. Bhagat Singh was fully aware of the fact that if he was arrested, he was sure to be hanged. He and Azad both were advised to flee the country, but they did not listen. They had the example of so many, who had given their lives. Rashbehari had settled down in Japan, married a Jap lady and was writing books in Japanese on Indian affairs. He had not abjured politics. This was proved later when he organised the INA. When Subhas Bose went, he willingly handed over the organisation to him because he felt that this was in the best interests of the cause. M.N. Roy, Birendranath Chattopadhyay, Shyamji Krishnavarma, Barkatulla and other prominent revolutionaries were working from abroad. Bhagat Singh refused to go abroad. Instead he started thinking on more and more dangerous lines. His argument was that if he were to die, he must do something more before the end approached. It is said that even when he was a student at the National College, the incident of a French anarchist Vaillant dropping a bomb in the French Assembly had appealed to him.

As Sohan Singh Josh points out Bhagat Singh had written an article in the Punjabi *Kirti* on Vaillant. He wrote :

"In Europe repression, suppression and oppression had gone beyond limits. Anarchists began to confront the governments and their police. One day, the bomb-throwing hand of Vaillant, while in action aiming at the French Assembly (government benches) was deflected by a woman in the attempt to restrain it, could injure only some deputies and could not impress very much, yet he gave a thundering statement saying, 'It takes a loud voice to make the deaf hear' and further added that he was not afraid of any punishment they would give. He resorted to that action because they oppressed the poor and sucked their blood.... Vaillant was hanged."

The zero hour seemed to be approching. Some oppressive bills were before the Assembly and the Government was adamantly backing them through into the statue book. Azad shared the thoughts of Bhagat Singh. The problem was how to communicate this to the masses. Unfortunately, they were lost in deep slumber and could be roused only by something like an explosion. All the comrades said that the party should not take this onslaught against the rights of labour lying down. It should lodge a loud protest that would echo through the corridors of time and send a clear message that the party stood for the toiling masses. This being an urgent matter, it was put before the Central Committee. It was resolved that the apt moment to drop the bombs would be after the house had voted the bill down, for the Viceroy, using his special powers, would smuggle it into the statue book.

After this decision, started the reconnaissance of the terrain and the plans on the *modus operandi*. Jaydev Kapur was asked to stay in Delhi and arrange for passes, needed for entry into the Assembly. He introduced himself as a student of economics in Hindu College, and some Congressmen agreed to help him to procure the requisite passes. After Jaydev had done the reconnaissance, Bhagat Singh himself went to familiarise himself with the building. By chance he stumbled on Dr. Kitchlu, who immediately recognised him though he had shaved off his beard and moustache. Dr. Kitchlu agreed to help him in his endeavours.

Chandrashekhar Azad went to the Central Assembly and took notice of the proceedings. His purpose was to make an on-the-spot study, whether it would be possible to drop the bombs and manifesto, raise slogans (Long Live Revolution) and escape. Azad was of the opinion that escape would be possible, if something like a car was available. The first blueprint prepared by Azad was that, as in the Saunders affairs, he would escort the comrades to the automobile and drive away.

Everyone gave consent that Bhagat Singh should spearhead this action. He himself was eager to lead the party. He argued that hanging was certain in his case, so he should deliver as much as possible of himself. He did not concede to the view that after dropping the bombs and the manifesto he should escape. He thought that he should get himself arrested on the spot and then bring forth the party point of view in the courtroom. Bejoykumar Sinha, a party theoretician preferred the Bhagat Singh blueprint.

When all this was still on the discussion stage, news was got that the Vicerory would attend a party on the occasion of Holi, thrown by a loyalist Indian. The group decided to attack the Viceroy, but it so happened that at the eleventh hour the route of the Viceregal was changed and this programme had to be given up.

Revival of Central Assembly Plans

The Central Assembly plan was revived. Dr. Mahore writes : "Sukhdev was not present in the meeting of the Central Committee in which the Central Assembly scheme was approved. Bhagat Singh insisted that he should form one of the party, but other members did not see eye to eye with him because it was well-known that the Punjab police was after him, and arrest in his case meant nothing short of hanging. The Central Committee supported the opinion of the party that not Bhagat Singh, but two other young men should lead. When Sukhdev returned and was told about the scheme, he opposed it. His stand was that after arrest only Bhagat Singh could successfully pilot the scheme of advocating the new ideology of the party in the courtroom. He hand talked to Bhagat Singh on this aspect long before the Central Committee decision. When Sukhdev failed to convince the other members of the Central Committee, he took Bhagat Singh aside for a *tete a tete*.

He was in a frenzy. He spoke in short bursts to Bhagat Singh, 'You have become an egoist, you think that you are indispensable to the party. You have started fearing death, you are a coward.'

The burden of his culminations was : 'When you knew that you were the only person, who could do justice to the party's new stand, why did you suffer the Central Committee to take the decision that somebody else might by sent to drop the bomb?' He recalled the justice of the words of Lahore High Court on Bhai Parmanand —'Although the brain and the spirit behind the party, he was a coward at heart, he sent others to the stake, himself managing to remain in the background.' Staring at Bhagat Singh he said, 'Someday a judge would write the same about you.'

Bhagat Singh refuted these charges. But Bhagat Singh's arguments added fuel to the flame of his fury. At last Bhagat Singh said, 'You are just insulting me.'

To this Sukhdev, stoically said, 'I am just doing my duty towards my friend? At last Bhagat Singh left him saying, 'In future please never talk to me.' At the instance of Bhagat Singh a meeting of the Central Committee was convened and the question was reopened. Sukhdev did not speak a word. The Committee had to bow before Bhagat Singh's will and had to change its decision. Sukhdev, without informing anybody, went away to Lahore, reaching there the next day with his eyes heavy and red. It appears that he had been weeping bitterly. But on that day he neither wept nor showed any sign of weakness, though he was very much disturbed internally. He had sacrificed the dearest thing for the cause."

Mahore has not revealed the whole truth. Here is Sukhdeoraj —

"Bhagat Singh had heard that his stay at Calcutta with Durga had been misconstrued, and this got on his nerves. Another event that really unbalanced him and Bhagavaticharan was that Diwan Chamanlal in whose favour they had worked in an election against Lala Lajpat Rai, and had distributed that leaflet *Lost Leader*, had publicly branded the killer of Saunders as an assassin. Diwan Chamanlal had said, 'That an assassin killed Saunders, makes me bow my head with shame.' Naturally the papers had given this utterance good publicity.

Diwan Chamanlal did not of course know that Bhagat Singh and Rajguru were involved, but he certainly was aware that it was the work of revolutionaries. Under the circumstances, the statement was inappropriate, unexpected and almost a stab in the back. It had to be refuted, but how? Only one method was open to the revolutionaries. To get oneself arrested and then give a bold statement in the courtroom.

On the one hand, Bhagat Singh was very much hurt that Sukhdev was at the campaigner of character assassination, on the other, he was very much pained at the mindless statement of Diwan Chamanlal. When all this debate was going on, the Public Safety Bill and Trade Dispute Bill were turned down by a majority vote in the Central Assembly. The only course that was open for the Viceroy was to make us of his special powers and sanction the bills. At last Bhagat Singh and Bhagavaticharan returned to Lahore with a heavy heart. All this pinched the former on to the desperate remedy of getting himself arrested and then issuing a bold statement exposing mindless intellectuals like Chamanlal.

In the meantime he received a letter from Sukhdev—'You are now in the grip of a woman, you can now do nothing worthwhile.' This letter completely unsettled him. It was like Brutus aiming a dagger at Julius Caesar. He took the letter and went straight to Bhagavaticharan's house. At the time Bhagavaticharan was sleeping, so Bhagat Singh was able to catch Durga alone. Later on sister Durga related this most crucial interview—'When Bhagat Singh came, he was ready to burst into tears.' When I asked him, 'What is wrong?' He could not answer immediately. He handed over Sukhdev's letter to me and said in his broken voice—'Just see, sister, what nonsense they are saying about our relationship.'

Bhagat Singh sat near Bhagavaticharan's feet and continued, 'On the one hand we have these people (Sukhdev etc.), who are flinging mud at my character for nothing, on the other here is divine Bhagavaticharan who turns a deaf ear to all this idle gossip. It is better to die than to lead such a life'.

Sukhdev Instigates Bhagat Singh

According to Sukhdeoraj (not to be confused with Sukhdev) whose book throws a lot of light on the subject, Bhagat Singh had gone to talk over this matter with Bhagavaticharan, but he abruptly left the place weeping. After this he decided to go himself to the Central Assembly, drop the bombs and manifesto and court arrest. He wanted to vindicate his own character, at the same time, he wanted to make the stand of the party clear. Thus it was a political decision muddled very badly with a personal situation. The mechanics of history does not over rule such intermixture of motives. Out of this complicated web of psychic jumble the pure honesty of Bhagat Singh emerges and emanates with irrefutable clarity. He was an honest and dedicated revolutionary. May be he was spurred on to action by the calumny circulated by Sukhdev, may be he was not.

It would not be honest to pin down Sukhdev as an unmitigated villain, until it is proved that he had some sordid motive. His only motive was to pin on Bhagat Singh in such a manner as to make it impossible for him to evade the work which he wanted to do. Was Sukhdev jealous because he had no charisma and had no success with women, although he was almost a top intellectual of the Party?

We have no evidence on these matters. On the other hand we have evidence that after that initial burst of weakness, he behaved as one of the most audacious throughout, and went to the gallows as bravely as any other comrade in a similar situation. Bhagat Singh chose Batukeshwar Dutt as his second. This also was, as I have already mentioned, not accepted by everybody. But again we must keep in mind that this was not out of any foul motive, this difference of opinion had its origin in the desire to be the first on the sacrificial altar. When the blueprint of the Central Assembly bomb affair had gone through all the stages except the ultimate, all revolutionaries who had not been assigned any role in the affair, left, Delhi. Chandrashekhar Azad went away to Jhansi, where he had a few hide-outs. It is strange that nobody has left any account as to how he allowed Sukhdev's allegations about Bhagat Singh's character as a weapon to instigate the latter on. It is of course inconceivable that he was not aware of the unhappy episode. May be that in spite of being fully in the know, like the head of a family, he decided to keep out of it as long as things moved on the right track.

Chandrashekhar Azad knew that he was going to lose Bhagat Singh for ever, because he was certain that Bhagat Singh would also be tried for the murder of Saunders as soon as he was arrested. Theirs was not a casual companionship, but was a deeply emotional involvement. The imminent separation cast a spell of gloom over Azad's mind. For years they had nourished their dreams together. They had needed each other, they had supplemented each other. And now the day had come to part, part for ever. Duty had called them together and now duty was forcing them to part. They talked and talked through the night till the cock's shrill clarion woke them up. When Azad had said the last good-bye he confided to Shiv Verma, 'In a few days, history will claim them (Bhagat Singh and Dutt) and only a legend would survive through the corridors of time.' Thus Azad bowed out, but he would have been happier to execute the first plan, in which he was to rescue Bhagat Singh and Dutt from the clutches of the police.

Bomb Dropped

The plan had been hatched in great detail. To make it most effective it had been decided to drop the bombs at the psychological moment, when the announcement of Viceregal approval would be given.

There were some other revolutionaries inside the Central Assembly when on the 8th of April 1928 Sir George Schuster, made the pleasure of the Viceroy known to the members. As he was ready to make the anti-democratic announcement, the comrades who had no role to play left the hall. They took away with them the passes issued to Bhagat Singh and Dutt, so that there remained not a small evidence against those people on whose recommendation the passes had been issued. The zero hour at last approached. When George Schuster had told the house that H.E. the Viceroy by virtue of his special powers had O.Kayed the bills turned down by the house, Bhagat Singh and Dutt stood up.

Bhagat Singh took a step forward and dropped a bomb behind Schuster, which resulted in an earshattering explosion. Then Dutt moved a step and dropped the second bomb. This caused a great commotion, followed by a stampede. George Schuster took shelter under his desk.

Balshastri Haridas writes in his book : "Sir Schuster was on his legs when the bombs were thrown. Bhagat Singh fired two bullets at the desk opposite to Sir John to frighten him, at the sight of which he was so terrified that he took cover under another desk nearby."

On the contrary, on his death bed, B.K. Dutt told Chamanlal, "We carried the bombs wrapped in newspapers. They were ready with fuse and all. The pistol had been taken only so that we could not be overpowered before the action. The bombs were in such a sensitive state that they could explode if somebody collided with us. To prevent this we were walking together so close that nobody could come between us. Bhagat Singh carried his bomb in his right pocket and I carried mine in the left pocket."

All sources are agreed that Vithal Bhai Patel, Motilal Nehru, Jinnah and Madan Mohan Malaviya remained glued to their seats even when there was confused running in the visitor's gallery. Through this confusion came the slogan *Long Live Revolution* in English, which in its Hindustani translation *Inquilab Zindabad* has become the battle-cry of all Indian leftists. When B.K. Dutt was almost in his death bed in 1965, in the Medical Institute, I asked him to clarify whether it was true, as Bhagat Singh's niece had claimed, both the bombs were dropped by Bhagat Singh. He specifically mentioned that one bomb was dropped by Bhagat Singh, the other by him, as the police had alleged. I also asked him in what language they had raised the slogans, to which he replied, 'In English.' These were the slogans :

Long Live Revolution !
Down with Imperialism !
Workers of the World Unite !

A red leaflet was also thrown at the same time. It bore the heading *The Hindustan Socialist Republican Army.* According to Batuknath Agarwal (as per his letter dated 3-1-1976), it was an inspiring appeal typewritten on red letterhead, the same as was used on the occasion of the 'Saunders' murder.' It began with the statement—

"*Explosion Necessary to Make the Deaf Hear*"

Then it proceeded—'A French martyr and anarchist Vaillant (not Balley as Balshastri writes in his book, p. 339) said a loud explosion was necessary to make the deaf hear.' Then it dwelt on the fact that on the one hand some people were expecting crumbs from the labours of the Simon Commission, on the other the Government had come out with two oppressive bills—the Public Safety and the Trade Dispute bill and a third bill—The Press Sedition Act was on the anvil. Under these circumstances the HSRA had taken upon itself the duty of tearing off the mask. We consider human life sacred. We believe in a glorious future in which every individual shall be assured of full freedom and peace.

Long Live Revolution

—Balaraj "

Had they taken advantage of the stampede due to explosion, Bhagat Singh and Dutt could have escaped. But they decided to stand where they were and got themselves quietly arrested. Yashpal says that had George Schuster not concealed himself under the desk, Bhagat Singh would have shot him. Anyway they got themselves arrested peacefully. When they were being escorted to the police van, Bhagavaticharan, sister Durga, sister Sushila and Sukhdev were very near. Shachi, the young son of Bhagavaticharan in his mother's lap saw Bhagat Singh, raised his hand and screamed *Lambe Chachaji* (Tall uncle) but his voice was gently muffled by his mother.

Thus occurred the great event, which gave a shriek to British imperialism and gladdened the hearts of freedom fighters throughout the world. The stand of the revolutionary party was made public for the first time, in such a way, that it reached the ear of every Indian. The deaf and dumb masses had been told through a detonation that the fight for their liberation was going on. Bhagat Singh again and again threw light this statement in court. In one stroke Bhagat Singh had done more for popularising the cult of socialism than all his illustrious Indian predecessors brought together. Nehru introduced this slogan inside the Congress (this was the third bomb) a few months later and created a mild stir.

To continue, when the confusion gave way and the smoke cleared Bhagat Singh and Dutt as mentioned earlier were peacefully standing to court arrest. All the gates of the Assembly had been closed in the meantime, and Sergeant Terry with a posse of armed constables approached him, but he dared not go near them. For a little while there was hesitation. Bhagat Singh then assured the sergeant, "We offer ourselves for arrest. We have no arms.' This is what Dutt told Chamanlal.

After the arrest the police took a lot of long time to make their minds about the two prisoners while they were made to wait in the veranda. Ultimately, Dutt was sent to the Kotwali, Old Delhi and Bhagat Singh to what is now known as the Parliament Street Thana. At Kotwali a man came and told Dutt, 'Young man, you have made history to-day.' He introduced himself as a press photographer and urged Dutt to be photographed. He was in reality a police photographer and this photograph, as Dutt told Chamanlal, was misused and shown to witnesses for his identification.

Bhagat Singh and B.K. Dutt were kept in separate cells. That old rascal Tasadduq Hussein had been sent to lure B.K. Dutt. He had failed to induct Ashfaqulla some five years ago. He got B.K. Dutt's clothes, which had become dirty by then, changed. He showed that he was doing this on humanitarian grounds, but in reality they were being sent for chemical examination. He also asked Dutt if he had watched 'Passing Show', a film that had recently been shown it Delhi in which there was a bomb-throwing scene in it. His purpose was to know from where they got their ideas.

An official room in the jail was converted into a court and a bench was put for the two accused to sit. When they were brought to court, they raised their slogans *Long Live Revolution* and *Down With Imperialism*. The magistrate Mr. Pool was offended and asked the police to handcuff them, but Mr. Asaf Ali, their counsel, succeeded in pacifying him. It is awkward that Asaf Ali failed to see the political implications of the case and like a short-sighted lawyer, advised the accused to deny that they had not thrown the bomb at all. This the accused refused to do and they gave the already prepared statement. In this statement the objective of the party had been described as the installation of the dictatorship of the proletariat, but at the urge of Asaf Ali the word dictatorship was changed to sovereignty. This was un exercise in futility of which only a lawyer is capable. This was unexpected from Asaf Ali, who as a member of the Congress Working Committee should have known better. However the original statement as prepared by Bhagat Singh was published in a special supplement of the newspapers, which they had already acquired. As soon as the correspondents saw that the statement was submitted to the court they made it available to every newspaper reader within two hours. This created a shock in Government circles. Obviously a copy had been smuggled out. I wonder why Asaf Ali insisted on changing the word dictatorship. Even legally, it hardly made any difference. The accused were given the highest sentence in spite of the change. As for his promise to get them released if they denied that they had nothing to do with the bombs was sheer nonsense, as any legal hack would know.

The court refused to admit the statement in full. It only admitted the following sentence, 'We admit that we entered the Central Assembly and had thrown the bombs.' Mr. Pool transferred the case to the court of Mr. Middleton. When the accused were asked if they wanted to produce any witness in their defence, they named two people—Madan Mohan Malaviya and Dr. Moonje. When Pt. Malaviya arrived, he was asked only one question—

"In the atmosphere created by the arbitrary certification of the Trade Dispute bill and the Public Safety bill by the Viceroy in utter disregard of the duly elected members of the Assembly, do you think that a young man may have been forced to take extreme measures?"

The court disallowed the question on grounds that it was motivated by propaganda. After it was disallowed the old leader went first to Bhagat Singh, then to Dutt. He put his hand on their shoulder and said, 'Don't worry. I shall get you out of jail within 2 years.' He had tears in his eyes.

Bhagat Singh wrote a letter to his father from Delhi jail (the present Maulana Azad Medical College stands on the site) :

Delhi jail.
26-4-29.

"Revered father,

Vande Mataram,

We were moved to Delhi jail (from police custody) and now we are here. The hearing of the case will start on the 7th of May, inside the jail. It appears that the whole drama will be over in a month's time. Don't worry too much. I came to know that you had come here, had met some lawyers and had tried to see me. But at that time things were not ready. I received the clothes the day before yesterday. You can now come any day and see me. There is no great need for a lawyer. I want to have consultations on one or two points, but they are not that important. Don't strain yourself too much. Do come alone, if you come at all. Don't bring mother. She would burst into tears for nothing, and this would pain me very much. When you come, you could tell me all the news about home.

If possible bring 'Gita Rahasya' (by Tilak), Napoleon's long biography from among my books, and a few good novels in English. May be you could get the novels from Dwarakadas Library. Well, find out. Don't worry. I do not know your present address, so I am sending this letter C/o the Congress office.

Your tabedar
(servant),
Bhagat Singh."

Even in this short letter, Bhagat Singh comes out as a passionate lover of books.

6

Trials of Bombing Case Hunger Strike

Although conceivable, people awaited wondering the fate of the revolutionaries, Bhagat Singh and others. In the year 1929, 7th May, started the hearing of the case of Central Assembly bomb dropping in the court of Mr. Pool, inside Delhi prison. Afterward this case, as we are already aware of, was transferred to the court of Mr. Middleton, special magistrate. The Indian press and the world press gave importance to this case as a *cause celebre*. In the past Khudiram (hanged on 11 August 1908) and Kanhailal (hanged on 20 November 1908) and been given great importance. Mandanlal Dhingra's hanging in England on 16 August 1909, was naturally international news. Poets, most of them unknown, sang songs on them.

But Bhagat Singh transcended them all, because of one great factor—the statement which they issued on the 6th of June 1929 in which the party's commitment to socialism was explained. In that statement they discussed the fact of the case first :

"We stand charged with serious offences and at this stage we venture to explain our conduct.

The following questions arise—

(1) Were bombs thrown into the chamber, if so, why?

(2) Is the charge as framed by the lower court correct or otherwise?

To the first half of the first question our reply is in the affirmative, but some of the so-called eye-witnesses have committed perjury. By way of illustration we may point out that the evidence of Sergeant Terry regarding the seizure of pistol from one of us is a deliberate falsehood for neither of us had a pistol at the time we gave ourselves up.

In our reply to the next half of the first question, we are constrained to go into some detail to offer full and frank explanations of our motive and the circumstances leading to what has now become a historical event. When we were told by some of the police officers, who visited us in the jail that Lord Irwin in his address to the joint session of the two houses after the event in question, described it as an attack directed against not individual, but against the constitution itself, we readily recognised that the true significance of the incident had been correctly appreciated.

We are next to none in our love for humanity and so, far from having malice against any individual, and holding human life sacred beyond words, we are neither perpetrators of dastardly outrages and therefore a disgrace to our country as the pseudo-socialist Diwan Chamanlal is reported to have described us, nor are we lunatics as the *Tribune* of Lahore and some others would have the people believe.

We claim to be no more than serious students of history and the conditions of our country and human aspirations, and we despise hypocrisy.

Our practical protest was against the institution, which since its birth has eminently displayed not only its worthlessness, but also its far-reaching power for mischief. The more we have pondered, the more deeply we have become convinced that it only exists to demonstrate to the world India's humiliation and helplessness, and it symbolises the overriding domination of an irresponsible and autocratic rule.

Time and again the national demand has been pressed by the representatives of the people, only to find the wastepaper basket as its final destination. Solemn resolutions passed by the House has been contemptuously trampled underfoot on the floor of the so-called Indian Parliament. Resolutions regarding the repeal of repressive and arbitrary measures have been treated with sublime contempt and Government measures and proposals, rejected as unacceptable to the elected members have been restored by just a stroke of the Viceregal pen.

In brief, in spite of earnest endeavour we have utterly failed to find any justification for the existence of an institution, which despite all pomp and splendour organised with the hard earned money of sweating millions of India, is only a hollow show and a mischievous make-believe.

In the same manner we failed to comprehend the mentality of public leaders, who help to squander public time and money on so manifestly a stagemanaged exhibition of India's helpless subjection. We have been ruminating upon all this, as also on the wholesale arrests of the leaders of labour movement. The introduction of the Trade Dispute Bill brought us into the Assembly to watch its progress. The course of the debate only served to confirm our conviction that the toiling millions of India had nothing to expect from an institution that stood as a menacing monument to the strangling of the exploited and the serfdom of the helpless labourers.

Finally an insult, which we considered inhuman and barbarous, was hurled on the devoted heads of the representatives of the entire country and the starving and struggling millions were deprived of their primary rights and the sole means of their economic welfare.

None who has felt like us for the dumb driven labourers could possibly witness this spectacle with equanimity, none whose heart bleeds for those, who have given their lifeblood in silence to the building up of the economic structure of the exploiters, of whom the Government happen to be the biggest in the country, could repress the soul-agonising anguish, which is so ruthlessly wrung out of our hearts. Consequently, bearing in mind the words of the late Mr. S.R. Das, once the law member of the Viceroy's council executive, which appeared in the famous letter he addressed to his son, to the effect that the bomb was necessary to awaken England from her dreams, we dropped the bombs on the floor of the Assembly Chamber to register our protest on behalf of those, who had no other means left to give expression to their heartrending agony. Our sole purpose was to make the deaf hear and to give the needed timely warning.

Others have as keenly felt as we have done and from under the sea of the Indian humanity a veritable storm is about to break out. We have hoisted a danger signal to warn those who are speeding along without heeding grave danger ahead. We have only marked the end of an era of utopian non-violence of whose futility the rising generation is convinced beyond a shadow of doubt. Out of sincere goodwill and love for humanity we have adopted this method of warning to prevent untold suffering, which we like millions of others clearly foresee.

Utopian Non-Violence

We have used the expression utopian non-violence in the foregoing para, which requires more explanation. Force when aggressively applied is 'violence' and is therefore unjustifiable. But when it is used in the furtherance of a legitimate cause, it has its own moral justification. Elimination of force at all costs is utopian and the new movement which has arisen in the country and of which we have given a warning is inspired by the ideals which guided Guru Gobind Singh, Shivaji, Kamal Pasha, Reza Khan, Washington, Garibaldi, Lafayette and Lenin. As both the Indian Government and the Indian public leaders appeared to have shut their eyes and closed their ears against the existence and voice of this motive, we have felt it our duty to sound the warning, where it could not go unheard.

Our Intentions

So far we have dealt with the motive behind the incident in question and now we must define the intention. It cannot be said that we have no personal grudge or motive against anyone of those, who received slight injuries or against any other person in the Assembly. On the contrary we hold human life sacred beyond words and would sooner lay down our own lives in the service of humanity than injure any one else. Unlike mercenary soldiers of imperialist armies, who are inclined to kill without compassion, we respect and in so far as it lies in our power, we attempt to save human life. And still we admit to have deliberately thrown bombs into the Assembly Chamber. Facts however speak for themselves and intention should be judged from the result of action without drawing upon hypothetical circumstances and presumptions. Despite the evidence of government experts, the bombs thrown in the Assembly Chamber resulted in slight damage to an empty bench and slight abraisons in less than half a dozen cases. While the government scientist ascribed this to a miracle, we see nothing but a precise scientific process. The two bombs exploded in vacant spaces within the wooden barriers of desks and benches. Secondly even those who were within two feet of the explosion, for instance Mr. Rau, Mr. Sanker Rao and George Schuster were either not hurt or received slight scratches. Loaded with an effective charge of Potassium Chlorate and sensitive, Picrate, the bombs would have smashed the barriers and laid many low within some yards of the explosion. Again had they been loaded with some other high explosive with a charge of destructive pellets or darts, they would have sufficed to wipe out a majority of the members of the Assembly. Still again we could have flung them on the official benches chockful with people of note. And finally we could have ambushed Sir John Simon, whose luckless commission was hated by all reasonable people and who was at that time sitting in the Presidential gallery. All this was however beyond our intention and the bombs did not do more than what they were designed to do and the miracle consisted of no more than a deliberate aim which landed them in safe places.

We then deliberately offered ourselves to bear the penalty for what we had done and to let the imperialist exploiters know that they can crush individuals but, they cannot kill ideas. By crushing the insignificant units the nation cannot be crushed. We wanted to emphasise the historical lesson that *lettres de cachet* and Bastilles could not crush the revolutionary movement in France. Gallows and the Siberian mines could not crush the Russian revolution. Can ordinances and safety bills snuff out the flames of freedom in India? Conspiracy of young men who cherish the vision of the greater ideal could not check the march of revolution. But timely warning, if not unheeded, can help to prevent loss of life and general suffering.

What is Revolution?

Bhagat Singh was asked in the lower court as to what he meant by revolution. In answer to that question, we would say that revolution does not necessarily mean sanguinary strikes, nor is there any place in it for individual vendetta. It is not the cult of the bomb or the pistol. By 'Revolution' we mean that the present order of things, which is based on manifest injustice must change. Producers or labourers in spite of being the most necessary elements of society, are robbed by their exploiters of the fruits of their labour and are deprived of their elementary rights. On the one hand the peasants who grow corn for all, starve with their families. The weaver who supplies the world markets with textile fabrics cannot find enough to cover his own and his children's bodies. Masons, smiths and carpenters, who build magnificent palaces live and perish in slums. On the other hand, capitalists, exploiters, parasites of society squander millions on mere whims. These terrible inequalities and forced disparity of chances are heading towards chaos. This state of affairs, cannot last and it is obvious that the present order of society is merrymaking on the brink of a volcano and the innocent children of exploiters, no less than millions of the exploited, are walking on the edge of a dangerous precipice. The whole edifice of this civilisation, if not saved in time, shall crumble. Radical change is therefore necessary, and it is the duty of those who realise this to reorganise society on a socialist basis. Unless this is done, and the exploitation of man by man and nation by nation, which goes masquerading as a civilising force, but in reality is imperialism, is brought to an end, the suffering and carnage with which humanity is threatened today cannot be prevented and all talk of ending wars and ushering in an era of universal peace, is undisguised hypocrisy. But revolution we mean the ultimate establishment of an order of society, which the sovereignty of the proletariat should be recognised and as a result of which the world federation should redeem humanity from the bondage of capitalism and the misery and the peril of wars.

Fair and loud enough warning. This is our ideal. With this ideology for our inspiration we have given a fair and loud enough warning. If however it goes unheeded and the present system of government continues to be an impediment in the way of the national forces that are swelling up, a grim struggle must ensure involving the overthrow of all obstacles and the establishment of the dictatorship of the proletariat to pave the way for the consumination of the ideal of revolution. Revolution is the inalienable right of all men. Freedom is the imprescriptible birthright of all. The toiler is the real sustainer of society. The sovereignty of the people is the ultimate destiny of the workers. For these ideals and for this faith we shall welcome any suffering to which we may be condemned. To the altar of this revolution we have brought our youth as incense, for no sacrifice is too great for so magnificent a cause. We are content to await the advent of the revolution.

Long Live Revolution!"

Bhagat Singh and Dutt from the very first day of their trial used the courtroom as a launching pad for their ideological missiles. They utilised every small occasion to issue a statement. After some time they angled their attack on a different plane. They were being treated as ordinary criminals. During British rule the European or pseudo-European criminals were, as a rule, treated better than Indian criminals. This was totally a racist policy. The Kakori prisoners had fought against it and had won a limited, and as it proved later on, a temporary victory some 3 years ago. They were extended European treatment on medical grounds, but as soon as they were convicted and their bargaining power was diminished, they were deprived of this privilege. To protest against this they went on hunger strike, which they broke at the insistence of Ganesh Shanker Vidyarthi, who had been duly assured by the Government that special treatment would be offered to them. But the Government did not stand on this promise. Thus the position in Indian jails had gone back to square one as in 1925.

Bhagat Singh and Dutt picked up the fight from where it had been left by their predecessors, specially the Kakori prisoners, who at least, had secured a temporary victory. As has been repeated time and again the revolutionaries did not think like Gandhi that an imprisoned freedom fighter should give up all fight. Revolutionaries believed that prison only changes the *modus operandi* of the struggle. Therefore they smuggled out articles, even whole books from jail and they made the best use of the courts.

On the 12th of June Bhagat Singh and Dutt were sentenced to transportation for life. Immediately Bhagat Singh was transferred to Lahore jail and Dutt was sent to the jail at Mianwali.

They were separated, but Bhagat Singh impressed the English sergeant so greatly that he allowed him to meet Dutt during the journey to their respective jails. Bhagat Singh knew what was going to happen. He knew that he had only a few days to live and he decided to make the best use of those days. He instructed Dutt to go on hunger-strike as soon as he reached Mianwali jail. Accordingly, they both went on hunger-strike from the 14th of June, 1929 in their respective jails.

In the meantime, the police had decided to reopen the Lahore conspiracy case. Though some arrests had been made, they were still in the process of nabbing others. From Delhi jail, Bhagat Singh and Dutt had been sent to stand their trial in this case. Later on, the Government decided to exclude Dutt in this trial, in his case transportation for life was supposed to be enough because there was no evidence to implicate him in the Saunders murders case, so there was not much chance to hang him.

The hunger-strike started by Bhagat Singh and B.K. Dutt developed into an all-India affair. 30th June was celebrated throughout India as Bhagat Singh Day. But the Government did not give in. On the 10th of July the revolutionaries arrested to try in this case alone, were brought together in jail for the first time. All the comrades were excited and wanted to jump into the fray. But Jatin Das of Calcutta opposed this emotional approach and advised caution. He said, 'It is a long struggle different from and more difficult than gunfights.' He further said, 'Inching to death in a hunger-strike is far more difficult than death in a gunfight or on the gallows. It would be against revolutionary traditions to withdraw from the strike without attaining the objective. It is better not join the strike than to suffer a premature withdrawal.'

Before we proceed to describe the full story of this epic hunger-strike, let us recall the story of the martyrdom of Bhagavaticharan as described by Vishwanath Baishampayan.

Thus Jatin Das advanced towards, meeting his end. The whole country was woked up. Subhas Bose despairing of compromise, sent Rs. 600 for his body to be sent to Calcutta. Bombay and the Punjab came forward to bear the expenses. The whole of India prepared for his glorious martyrdom. The Government immemely tense that his body might be taken out in a procession. A discordant note was aired by certain sticklers for non-violence that Das was not a believer in violence, that is why he was dying so gloriously. Indeed it was Gandhi, who said this after his death, trying thus to glorify non-violence. Anyway, Jatin Das died at 1-5 P.M. on the 13th of September. The doctors for some reason could not force-feed him even for a day. This was an achievement in fasting. Terence Macswiney, the Irish mayor of Cork, lasted 74 days and our Jatin died on the 63rd day.

His body was escorted by train from Lahore to Calcutta. Large crowds turned out to pay tribute at all stations. When it reached Calcutta, a procession of 6 lakh mourners accompanied the body to the cremation ground. Only Tagore at a later date was given such a homage. Gandhi kept mum over the whole affair, and when he did speak after a few days, he most inadvertently spoke of violence and non-violence. He prophesed that Jatin Das did not belong to the 'School of violence.' The revolutionaries had a good laugh at Gandhi, because they knew that Jatin was an ardent revolutionary.

The Plot at Lahore

The explosion on the 23rd of October, during the *Dashera* holidays, in 1928, elucidated certain facts that created the suspicion that Bhagat Singh was connected with some grave conspiracy. But as yet the police were just in the dark. On the 15th of April 1928 the police raided a house and arrested Sukhdev, Jaigopal and Kishorilal. Jaigopal opened up within 8 days of his arrest, though in Bhagat Singh's estimation, he was a jewel. On 27th May a house was searched in Saharanpur resulting in the arrest of Shiv Verma and Jaydev. Hansraj Vohra became a witness.

On the 7th of June a dacoity was reported in a village named Maulania in Bihar. Regarding this Phanindranath Ghosh was arrested and though he belonged to the old guard, deposed as king's witness. Thus the case started with 16 accused—(1) Sukhdev, (2) Kishorilal, (3) Shiv Verma, (4) Gayaprasad, (5) Jatin Das, (6) Jaidev Kapur, (7) Bhagat Singh, (8) B.K. Dutt, (9) Kamal Nath Tiwari, (10) Jitendranath Sanyal, (11) Asharam, (12) Deshraj, (13) Premdutt, (14) Mahavir Singh, (15) Surendra, (16) Ajoy Ghosh. The absconders—Bejoykumar Sinha, Rajguru and Kundanlal were arrested in Bareilly, Pune, and UP respectively. B.K. Dutt, in the end exclued in the conspiracy.

When the trial started, the revolutionaries involved were crystal clear in their views as to how to make the best use of the courtroom.

Bhagat Singh constituted a 3-member committee for this purpose, which comprised of himself, Bejoykumar Sinha and Sukhdev. Thus Bhagat Singh and his colleagues proved to be unbearable annoyance to the judges and police officers threatening them at every step, with the prisoners always managing to publicize revolutionary propaganda in court. In prison, visitors were discouraged and correspondents were harassed. Bhagat Singh was against all this. The trial began with slogans of *Long Live Revolution, Down with Imperialism* and *Workers of The World Unite* and the singing of *Vande Mataram*. During these performances the judge and the officials looked like guilty and helpless by-standers. But the court had to do something to demonstrate its authority, so it ordered all the accused to be handcuffed. More slogans. When an approver made some stray remarks, the accused shouted 'Shame', but the youngest of them Premdutt, disgruntled with this hurled his slippers at him. The proceedings were stopped and it was ordered that henceforth the accused must remain handcuffed in court. Bhagat Singh's immediate reaction was—"Under these circumstances we won't attend the court."

Despite all efforts the accused could not be forced to attend court. Only five accused were somehow commuted to the gate of the jail, where the court was sitting, in a vehicle, but they could not be made to get down from it. So the court had to compromise. It was agreed that the accused would be handcuffed before reaching the court, but once inside the courtroom, their handcuffs would be taken off. The accused kept to their part of the agreement. They came to court in handcuffs. But the proceedings started without taking off their handcuffs. The accused kept quiet at this breach of trust. At noon their handcuffs were taken off to enable them to take lunch. After lunch they started handcuffing them again, but they refused. This gave way in a scuffle and the Pathan police was called to deal with them, tilting the struggle a communal. These simple Pathans of the frontier viewed they were dealing with dangerous criminals. They swooped down on the prisoners, specially on Bhagat Singh, on whom 8 Pathans fell and began to beat him with sticks and shoes. All this happened in broad daylight in the presence of visitors and correspondents. The judge just sat still, looking on. While this continued for some time, the visitors and correspondents were asked to quit. The government hoodlums got tired, but the accused did not surrender. Ultimately the police authorities disposed the court that the accused would rather be killed, but could not be 'disciplined.' The story of this gruesome assault was printed in the papers with big captions and was condemned by everybody. Gandhi kept mum again, although what the accused were going through was nothing but non-violent passive resistence. The Government realised that it could not overpower. The judge had to eat his own words and annul his orders. Jitendra Sanyal, one of the accused, has written that the news of this judicial vandalism reached the world press and a Polish lady sent some money. Also money poured in from Japan, Canada and far away South America. The whole country in protest celebrated Bhagat Singh day. Top leaders came to see the accused—Subhas Chandra Bose, Jawaharlal Nehru, Baba Gurdit Singh, Nariman, the Raja of Kalakankar (a patron of litterateurs and patriots), Rafi Ahmed Kidwai, Mohanlal Saksena (a lawyer for the Kakori prisoners and later member of Nehru's cabinet), Ganesh Shanker Vidyarthi, the idealist editor of Hindi *Pratap*, and the dean of Congress leaders Motilal Nehru.

Although Gandhi ostentaciously talked of non-violence all the time, many of his archbishops admired the revolutionaries. Motilal Nehru saw Chandrashekhar Azad many times and encouraged him to keep up. In reality, the Nehru family was close to the revolutionaries. Jawaharlal Nehru writes about an interview with Azad in his Autobiography, in which he unfortunately says, "Many of them, it seems to me, have definitely the Fascist mentality." This was a complete mis-statement, because he knew that they were not at all Fascists, on the other hand, they were pioneers of the socialist ideology.

A few names in this socialist heritage were Madame Cama (who attended the International Socialist Congress at Stuttgart in 1907), M.N. Roy, Birendra Chattopadhyay and of course Bhagat Singh. It seems that Bhagat Singh went to the Nehrus for some money after the Saunders murder, but came back empty handed, because they did not know him. Later on, when they got to know him, he was helped. No detail of this incident is available.

The publicity gained by the Lahore case prisoners caused unrest in the dovecote of British bureaucracy. A solution was suggested that the presence of undertrials in the court should be dispensed with by an ordinance, and that the presence of their lawyers should be deemed sufficient. Finally, the Government passed the decision and in violation of all legal norms the necessary ordinance was made public. The accused attended court, but they insisted on singing the National Anthem before the proceedings started. The court now asked the police and jail authorities to control this, it was reiterated by them that they could kill the accused, but could not stop their singing. Ultimately the accused decided not to attend court.

Sardar Kishen Singh was deadsure that Bhagat Singh would

certainly be sentenced to death. Somebody, convinced him that he should forward a petition to the Government that on the fateful day, Bhagat Singh was far away from the place of occurrence. Even a letter bearing a postal stamp was produced to substantiate this alibi. Sardar Kishen Singh writes in detail and argues the cause of his son being not guilty.

This was published in all the papers. In view of the statements of the approvers this plea appeared ridiculous and childish. Bhagat Singh was very much embarrassed as he thought that some people might get the notion that all this was being done with his consent. He wrote a strongly worded letter to his father in which he said :

"I was very much surprised to note that you have written a petition to the special tribunal in my defence. This distressed me very much and I cannot take it lying down. As a son I have the greatest respect for your paternal sentiments, at the same time I think you had no business to send such a petition without my consent. From the very beginning you have tried to impress upon me that I should give the highest priority to my legal defence, I have always thought that political workers should ignore the court and should accept and bear the heaviest punishment with a smile on their faces.

I assure you that my life is not as precious as you think. As least I do not hold life so important as to imperil the priceless ideals to save it. Had somebody else done what you have done, I would have straightaway branded him a traitor, but your case is different. I must however accuse you of a low type of sloppy sentiment. This is an occasion when you, I, everybody is on trial. I must say that you have failed in this trial. I know that you have been a tried battle-scarred patriot. I fail to understand why you could not rise to the occasion in the case."

Under Bhagat Singh's instructions this letter to his father was printed in all the papers, as the mischief wrought by Sardar Kishen Singh's 'petition' could only be negated by this method.

When attending court, Bhagat Singh made good use of the occasions. Everyday he gave some message to the youths. Lenin day, Kakori day and other revolutionary days were celebrated after informing the court. His object was to inspire the youths to read the works of Lenin. Lenin was not an arm-chair politician. Bhagat Singh maintained that clarity of thinking should not be kept apart from struggle. Thus, Bhagat Singh, within the course of a few months, emerged as the greatest factor contributing to the understanding and study of Marxism-Leninism. I have already shown that Madame Cama lit the flame of socialism in 1907, M.N. Roy, Birendranath Chattopadhyay and others made the word meaningful to some intellectuals, but Bhagat Singh burst like a bomb to make its fame encircle, enrich and fill every aspect of the freedom struggle and even Jawahar Lal Nehru was forced to declare himself a socialist and a republican in the Lahore Congress. This aspect has not been conceded the importance it deserves.

When approver Phanindra Ghosh came to depose in court that he had learnt how to make explosives, Shiv Verma, at the urge of Bhagat Singh subjected him to a rigorous and detailed cross-examination. The object aimed at teaching young men how to make explosives, because detailed report of the court proceedings reached the press. During the hunger-strike, Bhagat Singh had sent telegrams to jails where political prisoners had gone on hunger-strike sympathizing with the Lahore prisoners. These telegrams were sent through the court. He asked his father to send similar telegrams too. When he learnt on the 5th of April 1930 about the passing away of the veteran revolutionary Shyamji Krishna Verma in Europe, he sent a telegram C/o Hindustan Association of Europe, Berlin, which read —

"We condole the death of Shyamji, pioneer and veteran freedom fighter. His life-long struggle for independence is a national heritage, that will inspire generations of freedom fighters."

In the same manner Bhagat Singh mourned some Hungarian freedom fighters who had passed away in jail. These telegrams were sent on behalf of the Lahore prisoners.

His lawyers put their foot down against celebrations of Lenin day, Kakori day, May day and other such days, because in their legalist eyes this constituted an indirect corroboration of the charges levelled against them, but the revolutionaries ignored such warnings.

As time passed Bhagat Singh began to realise about the fact that the hunger-strike in which Jatin Das conceded his life had not as yet yielded any results although a jail commission had been set up. There was no doubt that the Government was using the jail commission only to hoodwink the Lahore prisoners and the masses. Bhagat Singh foresaw that it was his duty to make sure that the supreme sacrifice of Jatin Das be made meaningful before he himself was hanged. The Government was waiting for the case to finish and Bhagat Singh etc. to be hanged. Then the jail commission could escape by producing a futile report full of banalities signifying nothing.

Bhagat Singh and his young men saw through the making and retook to the hunger-strike with the same old demands. Public leaders had promised them that they would fight, declaring that it was now their fight.

But they had failed to show results. Bhagat Singh was certain that even if only a single Lahore prisoner were sentenced to death, it would be he, so the fight for special treatment for freedom fighters hardly personally concerned him . It was a fight, which concerned the future of all except the condemned prisoners.

His attitude towards life and death was like a born fighter. He didn't mind hanging, but not like a fatalist. And, in the meantime, he wished to use every minute of his life for the fight, which was the salt of his life. After being sentenced to death, he wrote to B.K. Dutt from the condemned cell :

"I am sentenced to death and you are sentenced to transportation for life. You shall live and show to the world that revolutionaries can die as well as live for their ideals in the face of heavy odds. It would be wrong to welcome death as a means of escaping from worldly pinpricks. Revolutionaries, who are spared hanging by chance, should demonstrate to the world that they defy the life of torture in dark cells."

What Bhagat Singh said was in line with ideas of revolutionaries. In the same manner Rajendranath Lahiri (hanged on 17 December 1927) had told of me on the day he was sentenced to death, 'I don't care. In my case the agony would be over within a few days, but you have to trudge for years and years.'

The hunger-strike started on the 4th of February 1930. The Lahore Congress had been convened in the meantime and Jawaharlal Nehru created quite a stir by declaring 'I am a socialist and a republican'. This was, in fact, a success for Bhagat Singh, Chandrashekhar Azad and his youths that after Bhagat Singh had named his party a socialist republican party, Jawaharlal endorsed his words inside the Congress. No doubt it was clever on the part of Nehru. Very few can recapitulate what Nehru actually said in the Congress. He said :

"I must frankly confess that I am a socialist and a republican and am no believer in kings and princes or in the order which produces the modern kings of industry, who have greater power over the lives and fortunes of men than even the kings of old, and whose methods are as predatory as those of the feudal aristocracy. I recognise, however, that it may not be possible for a body constituted as is the national congress and in the present situation of the country to adopt a full socialistic programme. But we must realise that the philosophy of socialism has gradually permeated the entire structure of society the world over and almost the only points in dispute are the pace and the methods of advance to its full realisation. India will have to go that way, if she may evolve her own methods and may adopt the ideal to the genius of her race."

After nearly 50 years of its existence, the Congress had, finally declared complete independence as its objective and was poised for a Gandhian type of fight. It was against this background that Bhagat Singh and his brave colleagues engaged on hunger-strike. This electrified the atmosphere and freedom fighters, lingering in jails all over India, took part the strike. Kakori prisoners—Rajkumar Sinha, S.N. Bakshi, Mukundilal and Manmathnath Gupta—who had already spent more than four years in jail, joined the strike on the 7th of February 1930, i.e., 4 days after the Lahore comrades. Other prisoners also jumped in. The Government had before hand knowledge of this hunger-strike and the blueprint of an 'Operation Hunger-strike,' technically perfect, was all set to tackle with the strike. It was found out that although Bhagat Singh, Dutt and others had been on hunger-strike for a longer period than Jatin Das, they did not die because they were force-fed everyday. Jatin Das could not be force-fed, although a few attempts were made to do so. The Government deduced that force-feeding hunger-strikers gave them more days for propaganda and thus psychologically helped them. It was therefore decided to lessen force-feeding to the minimum, to be taken up only when the prisoners were about to pass away and to be abandoned as soon as they revived a little. This new policy was meant to keep the growing pangs of hunger always alive and thus increase chances of surrender. Medical science and psychology were requisitioned to derail the freedom fighters.

But this new policy did not bear any fruit. Political leaders, editors and philanthropists visited the Lahore and the Kakori prisoners. Bhagat Singh and others told their interviewers that their object was to ascertain that the supreme sacrifice of Jatin Das was not meaningless. Thus a movement was created through the length and breadth of the country. This movement naturally helped to increase the strength of the bigger movement that was being launched by the Congress. The new policy of force-feeding only to keep the lamp of life burning called for a quick solution, because the Government had realised that one Jatin Das was enough, they could not afford to let another freedom fighter starve to death at this very crucial moment. Quick consultations were held and on the 19th of February 1930 the Government came out with a communique, creating A, B and C classes of prisoners. This classification saw the end to the racist discrimination prevalent in Indian jails till now. Europen convicts were now rechristened B class prisoners and Indians with higher standard of living, with higher cutural and educational backgrounds were now entitled to this class. Class A was reserved for people of status convicted in crimes not involving 'moral turpitude'.

Thus the demands for which Jatin Das had given his life were not fully attained, but it had at least removed racial discrimination. It was no doubt a victory, but at the same time it was not a full victory. Bhagat Singh and his colleagues thought that thcy should considcr this enough for the time being, and called off the hunger-strike. But Kakori prisoners at Bareilly jail, refused to call it off, as they had been cheated once. Mukandilal, however, broke the strike. The remaining trio continued. Granted that now there existed a B class, they argued, what was the guarantee that they would be kept in this class? In spite of telegrams from Bhagat Singh, Sardar Kishen Singh and other public leaders they did not give in. The new policy of force-feeding reduced them very soon to skeletons, each striker having lost much weight. Many leaders came to see them, but they remained dogged. To make the story shorter on the 53rd day of their hunger-strike when they were assured, that on breaking the strike, they would be given B class, they callcd off the strike. By this time each of them had lost 50 to 60 lbs of weight. Thus they became the first three to benefit from this new classification. There is a sequel to this story showing how the bureaucracy took its revenge. Bhagat Singh, Rajguru, Sukhdev were of course hanged, but others of the Lahore case were not given B class.

In parenthesis, we must note one thing that is very important. Although in 1921, 1930 and 1942 large numbers of Congress prisoners, were put in jail, it was the revolutionaries who fought for and created this classification, which is still prevalent in Indian prisons. In the 1930 and the 1942 movements, hundreds of Congress prisoners enjoyed the awards of this classification. But neither Gandhi nor any Congress leader ever gave any credit for this to Jatin Das or Bhagat Singh because this naturally would open the uncomfortable question—'Who won independence for India?' The battle begun by Ramrakha in the Andaman jail (although fought on a lower key) was thus brought to a meaningful end by Bhagat Singh. The supreme sacrifice of Jatin now yielded some tangible result.

7

Pronouncement of Verdict

Views of Jury

Finally arrived the day of judgement, judgement, that was already anticipated. The Lahore prisoners had their last supper. In many respects, it showed semblance to the last lunch of the Kakori prisoners on their judgement day (6th April 1927), but was different as some jail officials also joined it. According to the revolutionary traditions everybody was in his Sunday best. They knew what the morning was to bring for them. The accused did not attend court in its final stages. But the trial had continued.

The judgement was pronounced by an emissary of the tribunal. The Government was aware of the fact that judgement would be followed by a tremendous demonstration which would shake the whole nation. It appears that the day of judgement was not disclosed and not even to the accused. That is why the last supper was held 2 or 3 days earlier.

The judgement was delivered on the 7th of Oct., 1930, and Bhagat Singh, Sukhdev and Rajguru were sentenced to death. Bejoykumar Sinha, Kamalnath Tiwari, Jaydev Kapur, Shiv Verma, Gaya Prasad, Kishorilal and Mahabir Singh were sentenced to transportation for life. Kundanlal was given 7 years R.I., Premdutt, 3 years R.I. The rest were freed.

The judgement could not be kept under cover and people came to know of it immediately. It was a fifty page document. Wherever the news reached, it resulted in a spontaneous *hartal* and a wave of anger and disobedience gripped the country. On the 8th of October not only Lahore, but all cities in northern India witnessed strikes. Some institutions closed automatically, other were forced to close. Naturally Lahore was the most agitated. Many students and 17 women were arrested. A crowd that had gathered round the Government College was attacked. The sky blazed with the cry of "Bhagat Singh, Rajguru, Sukhdev Zindabad." The police entered D.A.V. College and beat up 80 students and one professor practically to death. The Government was ready with its oppressive bulldozers.

The *Naujawan Bharat Sabha* convened a meeting of students and youths at Bradlaugh hall, once the centre of activities of Bhagat Singh and Bhagavaticharan. In this meeting, the revolutionary leader were eulogised and very exciting speeches were made. On the field outside Mori Gate, 12 thousand men collected in a meeting presided over by the veteran freedom fighter Parvati Devi.

Eminent personalities like Jinnah took upon themselves to deliver the message to the British *Raj* by way of presenting the case of Bhagat Singh and others. He amply supported the unhappiness of youth with the suppression by British. A legel battle was begun to save the heroes. An appeal was made in the Privy Council. The public agitation gathered momentum every day. Many people were arrested, others were lathi-charged. People were aware that the appeal to the Privy Council was an exercise in futility, in spite of this it was made, to allow time for the public agitation to consolidate.

Seen from a purely legal point of view, so the legal pundits said, the appeals had a number of good points and any just appellate court could crush the judgement to shreds because the case had been conducted without the participation of the accused.

Bhagat Singh, Rajguru and Sukhdev were now lying in condemned cells. Now that the courtroom was no longer available to propagate revolutionary propaganda, they sent an appeal to the Privy Council, to highlight the high-handedness of the tribunal and trumpet the fact that the revolutionary party in India stood for socialism. The agitation to get Bhagat Singh released very soon, got on its feet. Had Gandhi wanted to, he could have utilised it to give fire to the movement that was in the offing. But he did not do this, as it would have meant boosting up the revolutionaries.

Basically, Gandhi stayed away from all this, because he was mortally afraid of revolution. All the time, he brandished the big stick of revolution, but in the pit of his stomach he always wanted a compromise, because he was aware of the shortcoming of this weapon— *Satyagraha*. Bhagat Singh's thoughts on the subject were recorded in a letter, which though written at this time could only be published on 2nd February 1931, in the *Punjab Kesari*. The letter addressed to his comrades said —

The Punjab Kesari

"Dear friends,

Our fight for freedom is passing through a critical period. After a year of hard struggle the Round Table Conference has pinpointed on certain positive reforms and the Congress leaders have been asked to assist in shaping them. Under the circumstances, the leaders of the Congress seem to be heading toward switching off the movement. It does not matter much to us, if they stop the movement or continue it. Their present agitation can only end in a compromise, just now or after some time.

In reality, compromise is not as detestable as people make out, on the contrary judicious compromises are sometimes necessary to advance the struggle. A nation struggling against a despotic system meets with initial defeat, but in its long struggle it becomes stronger and stronger through reforms acquired and through compromises. Thus gradually, it becomes so powerful that its final assault breaks the backbone of the system. Even at the final stage a compromise may give it a breathing space. This is illustrated in the Russian struggle against the Tsar.

In 1905 waves of revolution started in Russia. The revolutionary leaders were very hopeful. Lenin returned from abroad and took the reins in his own hands. People slew a handful of capitalists and burnt a few houses, the revolution however did not come off. But the Government as a result was forced to concede some reforms and the 'duma' was established. At that time Lenin said that the 'duma' should be accepted. But in 1906 he started opposing it. Again he said in 1907 that one should go in the 'duma', although the powers of the 'duma' had been curtailed in the meantime. He wanted to convert the 'duma' into a platform for his agitation.

In the same manner when the question of peace arose after 1917, everybody, except Lenin was against the compromise. But Lenin said, 'Peace at all cost. Peace even if we have to cede some districts to the German militarists.' When some Bolshevik leaders opposed this, he said, "At present the Bolshevik government is weak, just now our first duty is to consolidate our government."

What I want to impress upon you is that compromise is a weapon that has to be used during a political struggle to give respite to a tired nation for some time, so that it can pick up the thread of the struggle with renewed vigour at a later date. But during all these compromises we should not lose sight of the ideal, which should remain as a target before our eyes all the time. We should be very clear and determined about the goal of our struggle. If you are fighting for 16 annas and you get only one *anna*, pocket that one *anna* and continue the fight for the rest. What I despise about the Indian 'moderates' is that, they lack a goal. They agitate to get one *anna* with the result that they get nothing.

The Congress aim is to liberate the country, but after liberation it does not seek to liberate the *mazdurs* and *kisans* from the clutches of the capitalists and landlords. The liberation struggle is manned by middle class people, naturally its goal is very limited. The Congress wants to pressurize Great Britain through the capitalists and shopkeepers and thus secure certain rights, but this would not set the teeming millions, the *mazdurs* and *kisans,* free. The real fight for freedom can only be fought by mobilising the *mazdurs, kisans* and the common people. Along with liberation from the foreign yoke, they have to get rid of the capitalists and landlords.

I maintain that the Congress does not stand for total revolution. They want to pressurise and secure certain rights. They want to secure certain privileges for the bourgeoisie, that is why I think that the Congress agitation can only end in the smoke of some kind of compromise or failure.

Under the circumstances youths should remember that bad times are ahead. They should fight against frustration and confusion of ideas. Having experienced two agitations sponsored by Mahatma Gandhi, it has become necessary to formulate precise aims and programme. Having said this let me spell out what I want. *Long Live Revolution* has become your battle cry. But it is very sacred and we should use it with good care. I take it that you stand by the slogan you raise. During the Assembly Bomb Case I thus defined revolution—'By revolution I mean that the present set-up and system must be uprooted. For this purpose we have to grab the state machine, which is now in the hands of the capitalists. For the good of the common people and for giving a practical shape to our ideals, we must wrest the state machine according to the principles of Marx. This is the object of our fight. Keeping in view this objective, we must educate the masses.'

What should be the yardstick for measuring and evaluating the reforms for those who are engaged in the fight for revolution. All reforms must stand these 3 tests —

(1) To what extent the administration is passed on to Indians.

(2) What is the character of the government that is called upon to

take over and to what extent the people are called upon to participate in it.

(3) What are the future prospects and to what degree its progress is blocked.

Universal suffrage must be advocated.

The type of provincial autonomy proposed by the Round Table Conference, is, according to my opinion, not provincial autonomy, but provincial *Zulam* (tyranny) because of the class on which it confers power. Having considered all this, I have come to the conclusion that we must have a clear-cut picture before us. Compromise may not mean always a surrender, it may add up to only one step forward, and then there may be a pause. At the same time we must all the time be very clear that this is not our ultimate destination and not a point for final pause.

I would like to say something on the object and the means of our party. It is named 'socialist republican', its object is to establish a socialist society. The difference between the Congress and our party is that the Congress after the power has passed from the hands of the British to the hands of Indians, will rest on its oars, but our object is to bring power to one and all, who are committed to socialism. For this the toiling masses have to be mobilised, because for them it won't matter much if Lord Reading is replaced by Sir Tejbahadur Sapru or Purushottamdas Thakurdas.

Our party means all this by complete independence. Even during the Lahore Congress (where the Congress ceremonially passed the resolution of complete independence) the Mahatma said, 'We have not banged and bolted the door to compromise it is still open'. This means that he was aware of the fact that his type of struggle could only end in some sort of compromise. His aim was a half-hearted advocacy of complete independence. It is this half-heartedness that we abhor.

To youths I say, they should enlist as workers in this cause, as for leaders we have them galore. Our party does not need leaders. If you are a worldly man, a family man, don't come to us. However, if you are sympathetic to our cause, help us in other ways. Only strictly disciplined people can take a movement forward. It is not necessary for the party to work in secret for these objectives. We may propagate our ideas everywhere through leaflets, pamphlets, booklets, small libraries, lectures, private conversations.

Our party should have a military wing. Let me make myself clear. It is said that I am a terrorist, but in reality, I have been all along a revolutionary with definite ideals and ideology. I may be blamed as they blame Ramprasad Bismil that the condemned cell wrought a change in his ideology, but this is not true. I am the same man as I used to be, and have the same ideas. It is my considered opinion that bombs cannot serve our purpose. This is proved by the history of the Hindustan Socialist Republican Association. Throwing bombs is not only useless, but is often harmful as well. They are to be used on certain occasions only. Our chief aim should be to mobilise the toiling masses. The military wing should collect material for war for use on special occasions.

Finally, I would appeal to the youths to work fervently for the establishment of a socialist republic. If they carry on the struggle relentlessly, then they can attain the objective, 'not within a year' but after heavy sacrifices and passing through very gruelling trials."

While Bhagat Singh was in the condemned cell, he was allowed an interview with Bejoykumar Sinha, who was awarded transportation for life. It is a historical fact, whether one believes it or not, though there was a countrywide agitation to get Bhagat Singh released, and all sorts of attempts, legal and illegal, were in the offing to rescue him from the clutches of the hangman, while he himself wished to be hanged. This was not out of despondency or frustration or a will to die. But a manifestation of a simple mathematical calculation as to how far under the circumstances he was useful, alive or otherwise when hanged for the country.

Views of Sinha

Bejoykumar Sinha writes about the interview : "Even after such a long time, I remember vividly the interview which I had with Sirdar Bhagat Singh in Lahore Central Prison. From almost his deathbed Motilal Nehru had entreated through a special emissary, that we should not stand in the way of legal appeal. He wanted to gain some time. He thought that the compromise talks were on the way, and he hoped that the Sirdar could be saved."

In parenthesis, let us note that Motilal Nehru in all probability (he was never dogmatic) wished try everything possible to save the Sirdar, but Gandhi, as we shall later on see, was reluetant.

Bejoykumar Sinha further says : "But he viewed this problem from a different angle. He confided to me in great anguish. 'It would be a calamity, would it not, if I am spared the rope.' I told Bhagat Singh very plainly, that the government had to two-edged policy, namely, on the one hand it was trying to befriend the Congress and on the other, was crushing all the revolutionary elements and so, there was no chance of the rope eluding him. I told Bhagat Singh that if the hangings are delayed or the sentence commuted, there would be more time for revolutionary propaganda. At long last he agreed to put his signature to the appeal, but this he did most unwillingly. Thus the appeal was forwarded, but we did not say in it that our sentences should be reduced. We demanded that the whole case should be quashed and declared *ultra-vires* as we had been tried under an ordinance. The whole country was clamouring to save the Sirdar, but he himself wanted to be sacrificed on the altar. He maintained that he could serve the revolution better this way. The moments that I spent with him are unforgettable. People cling to life so badly, but here was a man just a little above 20 years, who wanted to ring down the curtain of life, to have a rendezvous with death, for the good of the country."

All this brings into bold relief the fact that Sirdar Bhagat Singh was not only a believer in socialism, but at the same time he believed, like Mazzini, that it is the martyr's blood that ripens ideas. This is where a real revolutionary vary from the brand of socialists and communists that the world has been seen mushrooming in all countries, specially since the Second World War. They adore soft life, they address meetings, they lead any type of strikes and they think that they can incorporate socialism without a revolution.

Sardar Bhagat Singh embodied in himself true socialism. He wrote in a letter just before being hanged :

Koi dam ka mehman hun ai ahle mahfil
Cherage sahar hun bujna chahta hun,
Meri hawa men rahegi khyal ki bijli
Yah mushte khaq hai fani, rahe na rahe.

'O friends of the tavern, I am just a fleeting guest, being the morning lamp about to burn out. The atmosphere bequeathed by me its surcharged with the electricity of ideas. This my body is only a lump of dust, it may be there or may not be.'

One of the men who had a glimse Bhagat Singh when he was confined in the condemned cell was Shri Prannath, whom I met later on and did a programme along with him on Bhagat Singh for television. He writes :

"On that day I was privileged to stay near Sirdar Bhagat Singh's condemned cell for nearly an hour. I had met him many times at the same place. I had witnessed him as a hunger-striker, and had seen him in action in the courts, but I had never felt that he was that courageous and so great. He and I both knew that he was walking through the valley of the shadow of death, the hands of the clock were moving fast towards the zero hour of hanging, but I found him cheerful. His face glistened as always. When I approached his cell he was pacing it like a tiger in a cage. As soon as I stepped inside the cell he asked : 'Did you bring the book?' I handed over the book quietly, *Krantikari Lenin* (Revolutionary Lenin) to him. He was very pleased at the sight of the book. I told him : 'Would you give some message to the country?' He said, 'Down with Imperialism, Long Live Revolution.' I asked him. 'How do you feel today?' He said briefly, 'I am feeling fine.' I persisted and asked, 'Have you any last wish?' He answered, 'May I be reborn and serve the motherland again.' He conveyed his thanks to the leaders, who had taken interest in the case and expressed his good wishes to his friends, specially the absconding ones. In that atmosphere of death I felt shaken, but he seemed to be entrenched firmly in the faith that looks through death. He seemed to be so much at peace with himself, he was so much free from fear and unattached that he appeared to be divine."

During these last days Bhagat Singh wrote to a friend :

"It is but natural that I should desire to live. I do not want to conceal this, but it is conditional in the sense that I do not want to live with my freedom curbed. My name has become a symbol of revolution and the ideals and sacrifices of revolutionary parties have placed me on a high pedestal. It is such a high pedestal that I may not be able to do justice to it as a living being. My weaknesses are not known to the public. If I am saved from the gallows, they would become known to everybody. Thus, the symbol of revolution would fade and even dissolve, but if I die wreathed with smiles, Indian mothers would wish their children to emulate Bhagat Singh, and thus the number of formidable freedom fighters would increase so much that it would be impossible for the satanic forces of imperialism to stop and stem the march of revolution. Of course, there lingers a hidden hankering in my heart that I have not accomplished even a thousandth part of what I proposed to do. Could I live, may be I could get the opportunity to fulfil the tasks and thus be happy.

Apart from this there was never any temptation to be saved from hanging. Otherwise I am the luckiest man. Nowadays, I think too much of myself. I have no lurking desire. Now I am impatiently waiting for the last test. I wish it could be nearer.

Yours comradely,
Bhagat Singh".

Politics is but a part of life. It would be interesting to know what

Bhagat Singh ruminated sitting on the dividing line between life and death. I had seen Rajendra Nath Lahiri (hanged on the 17th of December 1927) under the influence of Shachindranath Sanyal, a theist revolutionary, turning from agnosticism back to the border of theism. Sanyal was responsible no doubt, but death sentence, which was round the corner, may have been accountable to an extent for this *volte face*. Anyway when we were exchanging presents just before judgement day, he presented me with a copy of *Madhuchhander Matramala* (a translation of some Vedic hymns supposed to be unravelling the mysteries of life and death). The question erupts not out of just an idle curiosity what was Bhagat Singh thinking on life, death, God and allied subjects? Fortunately, the editor of *Pratap* Jullundur, Virendra was in that jail and he has recorded an event which throws direct light on the subject.

Just the day before the hanging, the Sikh chief warder Chatter Singh approached Bhagat Singh. Chatter Singh was given re-employment in the jail department after retiring as havildar from the British army. Knowing that Bhagat Singh had only a few hours to live, as a devout Sikh he thought it is his duty to help him prepare properly for the next world. According to his religion Chatter Singh was doing a very pious work. He went to Bhagat Singh and said, 'My son, death, the journey's end is round the corner. I am just like your father. Listen to me.'

Bhagat Singh was a little surprised, he asked, 'What is the matter?'

Advice of Chatter Singh

Chatter Singh said, 'I have only one request to make. The end is very close. Now you take the name *Wahe Guru* and read *Gurbani* (Sikh Gita). Here I have brought the *Gutka* (the little book) for you.'

Bhagat Singh let out a laughter and said, 'Old man, I would gladly comply with your request, but now that the journey's end is very near, if now I pray to God, people would say that Bhagat Singh was chicken-hearted. I never prayed, and now that I am feeling the icy breath of death on my neck if I started praying people would misunderstand me. It would be better to let me go my own way. I might be abused because I am an atheist and do not believe in God, but nobody would say that Bhagat Singh was dishonest and flinched at the sight of death.'

This report coming from very reliable source confirms the fact that Bhagat Singh did not put on his scientific socialism as a shirt worn only on the platform like our communists. He remained true to dialectical materialism, which is as much a part of socialist philosophy as the head is a part of the body. It is a daily happening in India that persons claiming to have a monopoly of Marxism, in matters of religion conduct ir their private life like their forefathers. Of course, when asked they say they do not believe in the Sikh, Muslim or Christian rites, which they only perform to appease their senile parents, wife or some such person. But Bhagat Singh refused to behave like a Sikh even in the face of death.

This is accounted for by the latest research on him. Sohan Singh categorically writes : "In discussions with him, I found that Bhagat Singh did not believe in any religion. Some Arya Samajists have claimed after his martyrdom that he was an Arya Samajist. Some Sikhs have claimed he was a Sikh. In fact he was neither. 'I am an ordinary human being, that is all,' he would say."

This coupled with his conversation with the Sikh Warder, proves conclusively that Bhagat Singh was an atheist and remained so even inside the condemned cell.

Prannath had given to him a book by Lenin or on Lenin. Years later I asked Prannath to confirm, but he could not recall whether it was a book on Lenin or by Lenin. When asked to mount the scaffold Bhagat Singh was reading this book. He continued his reading and said : 'Wait a while. A revolutionary is talking to another revolutionary.' There was something extraordinary in his voice which made the excutioners wait otherwise befuddled as they are with drink (officially the excutioner was given his thirty pieces of silver and a bottle of wine during British rule) backed by brute-force, they hardly care for anybody.

Khudi Ram

Bhagat Singh continued reading. After a few moments he flung the book towards the ceiling and said, 'Let's go.'

While Khudiram had climed the gallows with a copy of the *Gita* slung round his neck and Ashfaq had gone to mount the gallows on the 19th of December 1927, with a copy of the *Quoran,* Bhagat Singh was lost in a book by Lenin or on Lenin. The trio Bhagat Singh, Sukhdev and Rajguru were hanged together. Bhagat Singh was in the middle, Sukhdev was on his right and Rajguru on his left. It is said that Bhagat Singh recited this couplet before going to his death :

Dil se na niklegi markar bhi watan ki ulfat
Meri mitti se bhi Khushboo-e-watan aegi.

'Even after death the love of motherland shall linger in my mind. My dead body shall emit the fragrance of my motherland.'

After he had sung the couplet he told the magistrate with a smile, 'You are really fortunate that you are witnessing how Indian revolutionaries march to their death.'

After this they were hanged and they became history.

All the martyrs before and since Bhagat Singh have been hanged the morning, but in the case of these three an exception was made and they were hanged at 7.33 in the dusk on the 23rd of March. This was carried out to maintain secrecy, but the ordinary prisoners of the jail raised slogans. Fearing that if the bodies were taken out of the jail gate, some hiding scout of the revolutionaries might notice, the high wall was breached at the back of the jail and the bodies were taken out for summary disposal to Ferozepur. There under cover of darkness a collective pyre was prepared. After some time, the half burnt bodies were thrown in the waters of the Sutlej. After the police party had left, the villagers came to learn of dead bodies burnt with the connivance of the local police, they hit upon the truth. They retrived the bodies from the river, made a pyre and cremated them properly according to their own conception. When I visited the place some 30 years after the occurrence, there were some villagers who remembered everything and they showed me the spot.

Death and Reaction

The news of these hangings was retaliated with strikes and protest meetings all over the country. The *hartal* at Kanpur took rather an ugly turn. A few days earlier, on the death of Muhammad Ali (The death was natural, he was not hanged or beaten to death), some Muslims had called for *hartal,* but Hindus had not responded. The Ali brothers were topmost leaders in 1921, but since then, Shaukat Ali had turned into a rank communalist (his famous dictum—'In my eyes the worst Muslim is better than the best Hindu, Gandhi'), Muhammad Ali, however, had only separated from the national mainstream.

The Muslims of Kanpur refused to join the *hartal* at Bhagat Singh's death. At this some youths began force the Muslim shops to close. The agents provocateur came out to create trouble. Some policemen disguised as ordinary Muslims travelled very swiftly on tongas through the populous parts of Kanpur publicizing Muslims were being killed. It was completely untrue, but this started the fracas. By evening of the 23rd of March, fifty people were wounded, on the 24th and the 25th it grew into a huge riot.

The forces of reaction triumphed. What could be the first glow of revolution got converted into a fratricidal riot. The police did not act. Ganesh Shanker Vidyarthi who had rescued many Muslims from Hindu areas was assassinated in a Muslim area while rescuing Hindus. His dead body was discovered after 4 days. It was recognised because he had worn Khadi clothes. From his pockets was found an article on the Karachi Congress. Thus India lost one of her bravest sons. His death finally proved that the solution of the religious problem through sloppy sentimentalism and hypocritical mutual admiration could not succeed. But conventional leaders, including Gandhi, had nothing else to offer, that is why the problem still persists in independent India.

The striking power of the waves let loose by Bhagat Singh's supreme sacrifice, was very much reduced by these riots. Imperialism scored a great victory at Kanpur.

Bhagat Singh in Communist Eye

One of the accused remitted in the Lahore case was Ajoy Ghosh. Later on, he became the secretary of the CPI (then united). For many years, till the day of his death he held its supreme position. He wrote about Bhagat Singh. Here is an extract :

"I think I met Bhagat Singh for the first time some time in 1923. Then I was fifteen. Bhagat Singh was also, I believe, of the same age. Batukeshwar Dutt of Kanpur introduced me to him. Bhagat Singh was tall and slim. He was rather clumsily dressed. He appeared to be very shy and spoke with great effort. He was not smart and seemed to lack self-confidence. He was a typical village boy. At that time I did not find anything remarkable about him. When Bhagat Singh left, I conveyed my evaluation to Dutt.

I met him the second time before long and we had a longish talk. Those were the days when we used to dream of revolution, childish dreams they were. It so appeared that revolution was round the corner, might take just a few years, that's all. But Bhagat Singh was not so complacent. I do not now remember his words, but he again and again referred to the prevalent somnolence and apathy in the country. He said that the path of awakening the masses bristled with difficulties. This meet confirmed the impressions created during the first interview.

Our conversation devolved on the past attempts to bring about revolution. We talked about the martyrs of the 1915-16 period. But as soon as the name of Kartar Singh came, Bhagat Singh became altogether a different man. Bhagat Singh had not met Kartar Singh, nor had I. Kartar Singh had been hanged when we were children. But we both knew that at the age of 19, he had become the undisputed leader of the group of men that had come from the USA to spearhead the revolution. This group contained such stalwarts as Sohan Singh Bhakna, Baba Rur Singh, Prithvi Singh Azad. Kartar Singh was a fearless freedom-fighter and a first class organiser. Friend and foe, all admired him. When somebody admires the idol you have loved and cherished for a long time, it gives you real pleasure. So when Bhagat Singh praised him, I was very pleased because he happened to be my idol as well. Immediately I felt something like love oozing within me towards Bhagat Singh. By the time Bhagat Singh left Kanpur, there was a strong bond of friendship between him and me. I however never spared him for what appeared to be a streak of pessimism in him.

In 1928, a young man burst into my room and wished *namaste* to me with a lot of flutter. I wondered who this fellow was. Well, it turned out to be no other than Bhagat Singh. But this was a different Bhagat Singh, very different from the one I knew. Here was a tall, well-built, handsome man with crimson lips and soft glittering eyes. We talked and I came to the conclusion that he had not only grown in years, his mind had also matured.

Now he was one of the two leaders of our party. The other leader was Chandrashekhar Azad. The goal of our party had become to establish a socialist society. The structure of the party had also changed. At the apex was the central committee of the revolutionary party, next came the provincial committees consisting of representatives from the district committees. All decisions were arrived at democratically. The members of the party were bound to obey all the decisions.

With regard to the main task, as to how to fight for freedom and socialism, our immediate strategy remained the same. That had undergone no change, and it was the method of armed group action. It was our considered opinion that there was no alternative but the revolutionary methods with which to fight the system that had bound us hand and foot. The idea was to strike at selected nerve-centres of the government again and again and thereby release the blocked energy of the masses, which when released would sweep away imperialism. At that stage, the idea was to join the mass upsurge, work, as its armed vanguard and give the torrent of lava, a socialist direction.

At that period and after, all those who met Bhagat Singh, have testified to his sharp intellect. His words forced conviction. Not that he was a good conversationalist, but when he spoke, all resistance seemed to liquefy *vis-a-vis* a clear path thought through to the end. We talked till 'night's candles were burnt out and jocund day stood tiptoe on the far flung horizon'. When we went out together for a stroll, and I saw the sun shedding its first shafts of light, it appeared to me that a new grey dawn was breaking.

Such was the conception of socialism those days. Eminent public leaders had forfeited our trust. Their legalistic methods, their empty boast to explode the system from within and change the raven of imperialism by painting its feathers, annoyed and irritated us. As a contrast, we wanted to present ourselves as models to forge a new pattern of leadership. Socialism was our ultimate goal. This was to be materialised after capturing power.

Bhagat Singh was singularly free from the symptoms of a traditional terrorist leader. We had serious differences of opinion and there were some stormy conferences. Bhagat Singh had to adopt certain paths and take up certain actions, which he, left to himself, would not have adopted or taken up. His was a restless soul. He lacked the quiet repose of Chandrashekhar Azad. Sometimes Bhagat Singh would flare up and hit hard at waverers, but seldom did he hurt anybody's feeling. If ever, in spite of this, he hurt somebody, or he thought he had, he came out with such profuse and sincere apologies that it was impossible to be sore with him. By nature he was loving, specially towards people who were unhappy or ill. He was free and frank in his behaviour. The inner structure of his mind ruled out all triviality.

He was crazy about books. As a prisoner he spent all his time in studying socialism. He was perhaps the first among us to be drawn towards socialist ideas. He was a confirmed atheist and untouched by the religious beliefs of his predecessors in the revolutionary movement. It would be however sheer exaggeration to say that he had become a full-fledged Marxist, but impelled by his studies, the discussions that we all had, and the stormy events that were happening, for instance the Sholapur rising, the Peshawar upheavals leading to the brave mutiny by Grahwali soldiers under the leadership of Chandra Singh, he began to emphasise more and more on this point that our 'armed action' should be in conformity with, and form an integral part of the needs and demands of mass action.

Impact of Soviet Union

"We were great lovers of the Soviet Union. The studies in prison made this love penetrate deeper. We sent greetings to the Soviet Union on Revolution day (Nov. 1930) in which we extolled successes and victories of the Soviet people and pledged support to her against her enemies."

This evaluation by Ajoy Ghosh, when he was the all powerful secretary of the CPI (not yet split), is tantamount from the viewpoint of understanding the revolutionary movement and its great leader Bhagat Singh. It clarifies communist thinking also. Though he extolled Bhagat Singh to the skies, Ajoy Ghosh had a dig at him that he could not be agreed upon as a full-fledged Marxist. The question is, if he was not a Marxist, who is? Ajoy Ghosh hit at him from a pedestal, at that time a monolithic body, but now torn into many fragments. Even if we forget this, it may be queried : is a party, confined to parliamentary activities entitled to call itself Marxist-Leninist? Can we call such people communists, who put on the sacred thread, call the Mulla, pundit, padri and granthi to sanctify their marriage, death and birth? Is it essential that revolution in every country should exact the same pattern as the 1917 revolution? Was not the 1917 revolution itself an unorthodox revolution, and is it not a fact that give it credence. Lenin had to invent the weakest link theory, unfamiliar to the two great founding fathers of scientific socialism? What about the Chinese Revolution? Did it happen the orthodox way, even granting that the 1917 way was the orthodox one? And what about Cuba? Did communism come there through the communist party? In reality, the Cuban communist party limped behind Castro, who was nearer to Bhagat Singh and Chandrashekhar Azad than any Indian communist believing only in parliamentary work can be. Is it not a fact that all communist parties in developed countries have gone for the comfortability of parliament-arianism, although few parties have unhesitantly admitted this by abandoning loyalty to the dictatorship of the proletariat. Of course, since the Chinese Revolution the term 'proletariat' was redefined to encompass the full gamut of the toiling masses.

These are basic questions. There are other questions that are not that fundamental, but they are still important. For instance, did Mao continue to be a Marxist in spite of his ultra patriotic foreign policies? What is going to be the volition of history? Marxists (and not their enemies) have only themselves to thank for the confusion that has engulfed the world to socialism. Ajoy Ghosh had no knowledge all this, but he should have been less arrogant while writing about a man, who dragged him from his petty-bourgeois existence, and made him man of substance. Bhagat Singh's services to socialism is greater than that of any Indian. Even now 'Inquilab Zindabad' is the battle cry of all leftists in India.

Whether one likes it or not, Bhagat Singh has become the epitome of the fight for socialism more than any person or party has.

Mistakes of Sohan Singh Josh

Sohan Singh Josh, a great freedom-fighter, writing some three decades after Ajoy, had committed almost the same mistakes in evaluating Bhagat Singh. The mistakes committed in this regard by Ajoy may be forgiven, but events of the last thirty years, specially trends in Euro-Communism should have made Sohan Singh humbler.

8

Proceedings in Privy Council

The Privy Council further demonished the cause of Indian revolutionaries. Revolutionary Bhagat Singh epitome, had lost all interest in legal proceedings after the Tribunal's verdict. But he was pushed, that a petition for special leave to appeal to the Judicial Committee of the Privy Council in London would surely yield of political advantage, whatever its eventual fate might be. The Defence Committee, especially its members Lala Duni Chand and Dr. Gopi Chand Bhargava, were very expectant on moving the Privy Council. Same thought lawyer Pran Nath Mehta and a counsel of national eminence, Motilal Nehru. He delivered a message from his sick bed in Shimla. He was to die on February 6, 1931 just five days before the Privy Council did not even give it to a regular hearing.

Opening of Petition

Like in any other petition to the Privy Council, issues of fact were eschewed. The only issue was the legality of the Ordinance. It is unlikely that Bhagat Singh's counsel, the young D.N. Pritt, K.C., actually knew about his client's popularity in India or the political significance of his trial. To him, it was just another banal brief in the Privy Council where only legal issues are contested. He had not quite made the transition "From Right to Left", the sub-title of his *Autobiography*

Though published in 1965, it gives no reference of Bhagat Singh at all. Incidentally, his colleagues were also joined as parties to the petition. The petition was heard on February 11, 1931, four months after the Tribunal gave judgment, by a Board consisting of Viscount

Dunedin, Lord Thankerton, Lord Russel of Killowen, Sir George Lowndes and Sir Dinshah Mulla.

Luckily a full transcript of the argument can be availed in the National Archives of India. Rather than consign it to the ghetto of an Appendix, it is given here in full. The reader who is not interested in them can turn the pages.

D.N. Pritt, K.C., Horace Douglas, C. Sidney Smith instructed by Messrs. Douglas Grant & Dold, appeared for the petitioners.

A.M. Dunne, K.C. and W. Wallach, instructed by the Solicitor, India Office, appeared for the Respondent.

View's Pritt

Pritt: May it please your Lordships. In this case I appear with my learned friends Mr. Horace Douglas and Mr. Sidney Smith for the Petitioners, and my learned friends Mr. Dunne and Mr. Wallach appear for the Crown. If we can make good to your Lordships the proposition which we seek to advance, I hope I may submit with some confidence that it is a case that does not meet with the usual difficulties.

Viscount Dunedin: I think you may take that. It would strike at the whole jurisdiction. What you have to make out is that Section 72 does not authorise what was done.

Pritt· Yes, my Lord. Possibly the best thing will be to go straight to Section 72 and submit my arguments to your Lordships on the effect of that section. It is a section which has been in the statute for some time; it is a section of an Imperial Act of Parliament; there is no doubt whatever of its force and validity, but I do not think anyone would deny that it creates a somewhat striking power, and is one, at any rate, which any Court will construe with care.

Viscount Dunedin: It creates an absolute power.

Pritt: Yes, when the conditions are fulfilled.

Viscount Dunedin: Yes, I do not suppose Parliament has ever done anything more absolute than in passing the old Acts of Attainder.

Pritt: No, my Lord. The power it creates is a limited power of delegated legislation: "The governor-general may, in cases of emergency, make and promulgate ordinances for the peace and good government of British India or any part thereof, and any ordinance so made shall, for the space of not more than the months from its promulgation, have the like force of law as an Act passed by the Indian Legislature; but the power of making ordinances under this section is subject to the like restrictions as the power of the Governor-General in Legislative Council to make laws".

I do not think I need trouble your Lordships with the words after the last semi-colon. The substance of the matter here is in my submission, that before any ordinance can be valid three things must happen, and at least two of those are of some importance to this Petition. In the first place, there must be a case of emergency, whatever "emergency" may mean ; the second is that the ordinance must be an ordinance falling within the description that it is an ordinance for the peace and good government of British India or some part thereof ; and the third point is that it must in addition to being for peace and good government, fall within the restrictions of the legislative powers of the Indian Legislature which I think are to be found mainly, if not wholly, in Section 65.

My Lords, these three points fall into two classes, the first is that something must happen before the power comes into force at all ; and secondly, when it has come into force, that is to say when there is an emergency and the Governor-General may do something, there are two limits, so far as we are concerned, to what he may do. May I state my submission in outline, in relation to this very striking power. My submission firstly is that if the exercise of the power be challenged, it is necessary to establish affirmatively that there is a case of emergency ; it is not for the Executive, if I may so describe the Governor-General, to say there is an emergency ; it must be proved ; like any other question of fact lying at the root of a jurisdiction, it has to be established before the Courts, in my humble submission.

Viscount Dunedin: You mean really the Court is to have the power of reviewing the view of the Governor-General that there was a case of emergency?

Pritt: I do not put it in that way ; I would put it in that way if I were forced to do so. I put it in this way : the Courts in British countries are places where the facts are decided. At the root of the Governor-General's right to make an ordinance lies in every case the question of fact : Was there an emergency? If it becomes material to know whether there was an emergency or not, that is a matter which has to be proved before the Court.

Viscount Dunedin: Is it your proposition that before the Governor-General can promulgate an ordinance he would have to bring a declaratory action in the Courts for a declaration?

Pritt: No, my Lord.

Viscount Dunedin: What do you mean by "the Courts".

Pritt: I mean this, my Lord, that anybody, however eminent, who has power to act when certain facts exist, must make up his mind whether they exist or not, and then act, and that when his power is challenged and it is suggested that those facts did not exist, the question whether those facts exist or not is a question like any other question lying at the root of any jurisdiction and must be decided by the Courts.

Viscount Dunedin: Your contention comes to this, that this Board, which is the only place to which you can come, shall have an inquiry into the facts and review the view of the Governor-General that there was a case of emergency. That is what it comes to, is it not?

Pritt: In the same sense as happens when any other executive makes up its mind that there is a riot and exercises powers which it has when there is a riot, and which it does not have when there is not a riot, and then subsequently at their leisure the Civil Courts decide whether there was a riot or not.

Viscount Dunedin: I do not know quite what you mean by that. I am not aware of any clause in an Act of Parliament like Section 72 which has to do with riots.

Pritt: Not in an Act of Parliament but it is a question that often arises in English common law when the Civil Executive applies to the Military

Lord Thankerton: You say this is a pure question of fact. I should have doubted that. Surely the trouble about an emergency is what it may lead to, as much as, if not more than, what has already happened. Does not this assume somebody having an opinion not as a question of fact?

Pritt: It is a very difficult question of fact.

Lord Thankerton: I should have said it was a question of opinion.

Pritt: Even a question of opinion is a question of fact.

Lord Thankerton: It is so treated by the Courts, I agree ; but that leads to a consideration as to who is the proper person to judge of it, on the construction of this section ; it is not the ordinary question of fact.

Pritt: The state of a man's mind is as much a fact as the state of his digestion.

Lord Thankerton: This is a question of administration, is it not?

Pritt: In my humble submission, Section 72 is not a matter of administration ; it is a matter of substituted legislation.

Lord Russel of Killowen: What is the test to be applied in ascertaining whether an emergency exists?

Pritt: The usual test as to whether Johnson has told a lie, or drove a car negligently.

Lord Russel of Killowen: This seems to be more a question of opinion. The question is : Who is best qualified to form an opinion?

Pritt: That brings me back really to my submission. I am putting my submission in two ways : firstly, that merely construing that section, the words "in cases of emergency" meant not that the Governor-General is the sole judge as to whether there was an emergency or not, but that there had to be in fact an emergency. The second limb that I am going to put on that is this. A proper method of construing one section of a statute is to see what words it uses in other sections, and a comparison of this section with half-a-dozen other sections in this Act makes it, in my submission, overwhelmingly clear that the Imperial Parliament, when conferring this very great power by Section 72 on one individual, however eminent in the Executive of British India, was deliberately refraining from entrusting to him the right to decide, either as fact or opinion, whether there was an emergency or not.

Sir George Lowndes: I should have thought there was a personal element here.

Pritt: Many personal elements have to be decided by a Court afterwards. There is a personal element in every running-down case. May I call your Lordships' attention to Secton 67(b) of the Government of India Act ; "Where either chamber of the Indian legislature refuses leave to introduce, or fails to pass in a form recommended by the Governor-General, any Bill, the Governor-General may certify that the passage of the Bill is essential for the safety, tranquillity or interests of British India or any part thereof". Those are plainly words that leave the matter in the hands of the Governor-General alone. Then it says the Bill shall become an Act by certain means which I need not trouble your Lordships with. Then sub-section 2 says : "Every such Act"— that is the Bill turned into an Act—"shall be expressed to be made by the Governor-General, and shall, as soon as practicable after being made, be laid before both Houses of Parliament, and shall not have effect until it has received His Majesty's assent". Then lower down your Lordships see : "and upon the signification of such assent by His Majesty in Council, and the notification thereof by the Governor-General, the Act shall have the same force and effect as an Act passed by the Indian legislature and duly assented to". Then in case the matter has to be dealt with so swiftly that even this is too slow, we get the proviso : "Provided that where in the opinion of the Governor-General a state of emergency exists which justifies such action, the Governor-General may direct that any such Act shall come into operation forthwith". Perhaps I can put the matter shortly in this way : There are at least eight other passages in that Statute of varying strengths and varying kinds. I do not pretend that I have not given your Lordships the best of them, but there are others as good and others not much worse, in which it is shown overwhelmingly that the Imperial Parliament, when it wants to entrust a matter to the Governor-General, has sufficient command of the English language to be able to put it beyond the range of doubt. Section 72 has existed for a long time, and some of the other Sections in which the sort of thing is dealt with have existed for a considerable time, and my first submission to your Lordships accordingly is that the Governor-General has power here to substitute himself to a certain extent and for a short period of time for the legislature in order to move more swiftly than the legislature can in Legislative matters . . .

Viscount Dunedin: I quite understand the point, but I must bring you to this: What is the remedy according to you?

Pritt: The remedy, in my humble submission, is a remedy for the Crown.

Viscount Dunedin: Is it not a remedy for the subject?

Pritt: The remedy for the subject is that when an Ordinance is sought to be applied to him, he shall submit an argument to some of His Majesty's Courts, or if one is being established by the Ordinance, I think there is authority for the proposition that he may submit it to that tribunal or he may submit it to another tribunal and say : Here is the Crown doing something which I say it has no power to do.

Viscount Dunedin: Assuming we grant leave to appeal, what would you say to the Board when the appeal was heard?

Pritt: I should say to the Board three things. The first thing I should say to the Board is : I challenge this Ordinance ; it is made under a definite limited power ; I say that the conditions of the exercise of the power do not exist, and never have existed.

Viscount Dunedin: What would happen after that?

Pritt: My submission on the whole of the facts would be this : The power is limited ; in order to show that it has been validly exercised and that the conditions are fulfilled, there must be some proof that there was a case of emergency. I have challenged that, once before this very tribunal and once before the High Court at Lahore, and in neither instance did the Crown adduce one title of evidence that there had ever been a case of emergency.

Viscount Dunedin: Then you would say that the matter must be gone into, I suppose?

Pritt: I am not sure I should not take a higher line and say : The

Crown having had two opportunities to establish that they had this power because there was an emergency, and having refrained on both occasions from adducing any evidence . . .

Viscount Dunedin: The Ordinance had been promulgated long before this?

Pritt: Long before what, my Lord?

Viscount Dunedin: Long before the matter came into Court.

Pritt: This Ordinance was promulgated six or seven months after my clients first stood their trial.

Dunne: That is not the point.

Viscount Dunedin: It was promulgated before the trial took place before the special Tribunal?

Pritt: Yes, my Lord.

Viscount Dunedin: That is all that was done, is it not?

Pritt: As soon as that was done, we challenged it by *habeas corpus* proceedings, and the Crown adduced no evidence of any description.

Viscount Dunedin: And you failed on that?

Pritt: We failed on that, I think I ought to tell your Lordships at once that when the matter came before me I took the view, on behalf of my clients, which may be right or wrong, that they really ought to present to your Lordships at some stage an appeal from that decision. That was put in train at once and leave is now being applied for to the High Court at Lahore to appeal from that Judgment, and ultimately, if your Lordships think fit to grant us leave to appeal here, then either by the High Court at Lahore granting me leave, if it thinks right, or by me asking your Lordships in a supplemental petition if the High Court does not think right to grant me leave and your Lordships thought right to grant it, then ultimately by consolidation the matter would come before your Lordships in the dual form, namely, an appeal from the Judgment in the *habeas corpus* proceedings and a direct appeal from the decision on the Tribunal.

Coming back to the substance of the matter, I should most certainly submit on behalf of my clients that the Crown, having twice had the opportunity of establishing a case of emergency and not having even attempted so to do, that the decision of the Court ought to be declared by your Lordships to be entirely void, whereupon the condition of my clients, as I understand it, would be be that my clients would be people as to whom there had been a preliminary hearing before the Magistrate, if that is the right description at Lahore, which was entirely void and they would be people whose trial was entirely void , and they could, if it was thought right, be re-arrested and tried according to the ordinary process of law which was mysteriously interrupted at the beginning of last May.

The second submission I should make to your Lordships, if I was granted leave to appeal and the substantive appeal came on, would be this—I am still only dealing with the emergency and not with the other difficulties which I desire to raise—let it be granted that I am wrong in asserting that it is for the Governor-General to establish that there was a case of emergency, or at any rate, let it be granted that I am wrong in asserting that it is for the Governor-General to establish that by evidence, and let me approach it in the way which one of the Courts below approached it at one stage and say : I see a statement by the Governor-General ; the Governor-General is so important a person that if he says something in his Gazette, I will take it as evidence. It was not put in that crude fashion, but that is the substance of what one of the Judges said in the *habeas corpus* proceedings. Then I should submit to your Lordships' Board that we have only to look at the Governor-General's statement to come to the conclusion that there was no emergency.

Lord Thankerton: That is to say, we are to come to the conclusion that the Governor-General was wrong?

Pritt: When he said there was a state of emergency, he may not have regarded it as a matter of opinion.

Lord Thankerton: The preamble of the Ordinance gives the reasons, does it not? You say he should not have come to the conclusion that there was an emergency?

Pritt: It is not the preamble. One must be very accurate here. The preamble does say something about an emergency. It appears in the same number of the Gazette as a statement by the Governor-General ; but in my very humble submission, in spite of the eminent position of the Governor-General, the statement by him proves nothing.

Viscount Dunedin: Either you look at his statement and say : Those are his reasons and he has come to a wrong conclusion that there was an emergency ; or else you say : Those are not his reasons : I do not know what his reasons were ; how can I say whether there was an emergency or not in the opinion of the Governor-General? Which do you say is the correct construction for the purpose of this argument?

Pitt: I put it alternatively. In the first place, I say there must be proof of an emergency ; secondly, if it is suggested that is evidence, then I say, when it is looked at, there must be some limits to the word "emergency", and that he can only act within those limits. May I put another alternative : One or two Courts in India, for reasons which I confess I do not follow as a matter of logic, have laid down expressly that it is for the Court to make up its mind and to investigate the questions of fact whether there is an emergency or not, but the Court has sufficiently investigated that when it has come to the conclusion that there is some evidence on which the Governor-General could decide, and I should submit to your Lordships, if leave to appeal was granted, that there was no evidence. This depends upon a consideration of the facts of the case and a consideration of the meaning of the word "emergency", and the question of the meaning of the word "emergency", although important and lying at the base of the whole matter, is not the whole argument that I would desire to put before your Lordships. I rely very much upon the definition of the power, or rather the definition of the power to legislate under circumstances of this sort, that it must be for the peace and good government of British India. I do not presume to challenge the proposition that "the peace and good government of British India" is a very wide phrase, but at some stage in my submission to your Lordships I do want to put it very strongly that this particular Ordinance is a privilegium of a very terrible description ; whether it could possibly conduce to peace is a matter of some difficulty ; that it could conduce either to good government or to government at all, I would invite your Lordships to consider very carefully indeed. My submission is that on the true construction of Section 72 it is plainly intended to empower the Governor-General in cases of general emergency or cases of a particular emergency area, or whatever it may be, to pass what may fairly be called legislation, but this is legislation which I think in every Roman law country and jurisprudent would indignantly deny to be legislation at all.

Lord Thankerton: Why?

Pritt: Because it is a privilegium. It makes no law that and has to obey, except the civil servants of the Crown and the members of the Tribunal. It lays down no liberty to any man to anything ; it lays down no provision by way of criminal law or anything else that any man shall not do anything.

Viscount Dunedin: What about the old Acts of attainder? What did they do?

Pritt: They were passed by the supreme Imperial Parliament.

Viscount Dunedin: Certainly.

Pritt: This is not ; this is dedicated legislation, and all that the Governor-General can do is to make and promulgate Ordinances for the peace and good government of British India or any part thereof, which are to have the force of law for six month. That is a privilegium, and I submit that cannot in any view be called legislation at all for peace, order and good government.

Lord Russell: Do you say that under Section 65 of this Act the Indian Legislature could not have passed an Act in these terms?

Pritt: Section 65 is not the only Section which has to be looked at in order to discover the power and restrictions of the Indian Legislature, but it is much the most important. I concede reluctantly that the Indian Legislature could have done this, but then the Legislature is allowed to legislate within clauses (a) to (f), whether it is for the peace, order and good government of British India or not. It is, in my humble submission, right to bear this in mind, that what this Statute actually does is this. It says : Here are a number of men ; they are all in custody ; they are not running about ; they are under trial ; that is to say, preliminary proceedings are being carried forward against them on specific charges. They have at the moment the right of citizens in British India to have a *prima* facie case made out against them, and before they are tried to know what that case is. They have a right to be tried before the ordinary Sessions Judge with assessors or a jury, and after the trial to appeal to the established High Court at Lahore, with which Court this Ordinance cannot interfere; that is another point to which I will come in a moment. The authorities say by this privilegium, in which there is not a word about other men, not a word about other offences, not a word about means of preserving law and order and peace and good government, we say that these particular individuals shall be deprived of the right to know the case against them, shall be deprived of the right to have a *prima facie* case made against them, shall be deprived of the right of trial before a Sessions Judge and a jury or assessors, shall be deprived of the right to go to the High Court at Lahore on appeal ; and we say they shall be tried before a special tribunal without knowing what the case is against them except as and when it comes out of the mouth of approvers or independent witnesses, as the case may be. At any moment the tribunal may change its personnel, and when they come to the end of the case, it may be that these people will be sentenced to death without appeal by three gentlemen who, by reason of the changes in personnel, may none of then have seen a single one of the witnesses, and they may sentence these men to death on evidence of approvers whose demeanour they never have had the opportunity to observe. I submit to your Lordships that on any reasonable meaning of the word "legislation" this is not legislation at all.

Assessment of then Existing Legislation

Lord Thankerton: Why is it not legislation? You may think it is bad legislation. You have admitted that under Section 65 the Indian Legislature could have passed such an Act. Would you have said that was legislation?

Pritt: I should have said that to an Englishman brought up with the idea of Parliaments with unlimited powers and of subsidiary Parliaments with very limited powers, that that would be an administrative Act disguised in the form of legislation, but which is perfectly lawful, but when one comes to a Section which does not say the Governor-General shall be invested with all the legislative powers of Section 65, but does say that he may make and promulgate Ordinances for the peace and good government of British India, that means that the Governor-General may make legislation which provides what people ordinarily call law ; which provides something which applies to more than one person or one group of persons. Legislation that it shall be unlawful to wear a particular kind of hat that is insulting to one's fellow citizens would be legislature ; but an administrative Act disguised as a piece of legislation dealing *ex post facto* with the trouble which has already arisen in the case of the certain individuals who are to be tried for specific offences, in my humble submission, if legislation is used in any ordinary sense or if it is used as power to make and promulgate legislative Ordinances for the peace and good government of the country, my clients ought to be given the opportunity to put before this Board on a full appeal the argument that such an Ordinance is invalid and cannot fall within the words "Ordinances for the peace and good government of anything".

The third point is important, but less important and perhaps less clear, namely, that the restrictions imposed by this Act upon the power of the Indian Legislature to make laws must also be proved. Your Lordships will probably know that in one case that has been challenged on the broad proposition whether this type of ordinance offends against the unwritten law or constitution of the United Kingdom of Great Britain and Ireland. I do not think I can advance that argument to your Lordships ; that seems to be precluded ; but there is another ground here, and that arises out of the *consideration of Section 84* and a later one. I think *Section 113*. Section 65 is the main section imposing the power and placing restrictions on the power. Section 84 is in a department called "Validity of Indian Laws". The only one that matters here is ; "A law made by any authority in British India and repugnant to any provision of this or any other Act of Parliament shall, to the extent of that repugnancy, but not otherwise, be void". That is partly an enabling section, because it prevents repugnancy destroying the whole thing, but in my submission the effect of that is this : If any act of the British Indian Legislature be challenged, and therefore in any ordinance under Section 72 be challenged, as operating repugnantly to any provision of this Act of Parliament, it will be void. My submission is that this is repudgant to the provisions of this Act of Parliament, it will be void. My submission is that this is repugnant to the provisions of this Act of Parliament because it deprives the High Court at Lahore of Jurisdiction in the matter. May I refer your Lordships to *Section 113:* "His Majesty may, if he sees fit, by letters patent, establish a high court of judicature in any territory in British India, whether, or not included within the limits of the local jurisdiction of another high court, and confer on any high court so established any such jurisdiction, powers and authority as are vested in or may be conferred on any high court existing at the commencement of this Act ; and where a high court is so established in any area included within the limits of the local jurisdiction of another high court, His Majesty may, be letters patent, alter those limits and make such incidental, consequential and supplemental provisions as may appear to be necessary by reason of the alteration." My submission on that point, whether it be sound or not, can be put comparatively shortly. It is simply this : The right to confer jurisdiction on what is now the High Court at Lahore is committed by this Imperial Statute to His Majesty to be done by letters patent. If the Indian Legislature, being a subordinate Legislature, seeks by any Act of its own to deprive the High Court at Lahore, established by His Majesty's letters patent, of jurisdiction, in whole or in part, the argument is the same. It is offending against Section 113, which has conferred upon someone else, and someone higher, namely, His Majesty, by the executive act of letters patent to create the High Court. This particular ordinance, in order to be valid, has to be such as not to infringe Section 113. If this particular ordinance took away the whole jurisdiction of the High Court at Lahore, it would, in my humble submission, equally offend against Section 113.

Sir George Lowndes: Is that provided for specifically in the Act?

Pritt: There is something about it in the letters patent ; I have not found anything in the Act. Section 65 is the general section which gives the power to make laws. It is suggested to me that Sir George Lowndes may be thinking of Section 106. My suggestion about it is that Section 65 and Section 84 have to be read together. Section 65 confers a very wide, but nevertheless not universal, power on the Indian legislature, and then Section 84 says : "A law made by any authority in British India and repugnant to any provisions of this or any other Act of Parliament shall, to the extent of that repugnancy, but not otherwise, be void."

Lord Russell of Killowen: I am not sure that I follow your repugnancy yet. Where is the repugnancy?

Pritt: The repugnancy, I suggest, is this : Whereas His Majesty alone can create the High Court at Lahore, or limit, or amend, or alter, or take away from its powers, before this ordinance was passed the High Court at Lahore had jurisdiction to hear my clients on appeal, and that has been taken away by the ordinance which had said they shall not have any appeal.

Lord Russel of Killowen: The ordinance has constituted a special tribunal to try particular people.

Pritt: Yes

Lord Russell of Killowen: Is that repugnant to section 113? I do not see it.

Pritt: In my submission, yes, because my clients, when the ordinance was passed, were people who were being prosecuted on charges that were being formulated in the ordinary course, and the High Court had jurisdiction at the moment to hear an appeal, and the ordinance has entirely destroyed that exceedingly important portion of the jurisdiction of the High Court at Lahore.

Sir George Lowndes: The section I was thinking of is section 65, sub-section 3, which limits the powers of the Indian Legislature. It cannot abolish a High Court. That clearly suggests that it has power to limit the jurisdiction of the High Court.

Pritt: My submission, in answer to that, would be that the Indian Legislature cannot abolish any High Court existing when the statute was passed, neither can it interfere with the operation of section 113, which says that His Majesty can appoint a new High Court and deal with its jurisdiction.

I ought to refer, because this matter was sufficiently in the minds of the draftsmen of the letters patent, to a very few words in the letters patent which establish the High Court at Lahore ; they were made on 21st March, 1919. It is a relatively recent High Court. The following words were put in : The last paragraph, which is No. 37, says : "We do further order and declare that all the provisions of any of our letters patent" etc. (reads paragraph). So it is quite plain that the Crown, as an executive Act, has sought in the letters patent to authorise the Governor-General to do that which, in my submission, if I am right, he cannot do, and that which, if I am right, in my submission, the draftsmen of the letters patent thought there might be some difficulty about doing. My submission is that nothing in clause 37 of the letters patent can affect the position, for the reason that the *Crown by letters* patent cannot create, or alter, or modify the power of the Governor-General or the Indian Legislature under the various sections of the Government of India Act.

Sir Dinshah Mulla: Is not that the same as clause 44 of the letters patent at the Calcutta High Court of 1862?

Pritt: I imagine that it must occur in at any rate any recent letters patent. I will find out for your Lordship.

Sir Dinshah Mulla: I wanted to know whether there was any distinction between the two. One is a very old High Court and the other is a new one.

Pritt: Clause 44 in the Calcutta letters patent reads as follows : (reads same). It is textually the same. I suppose that letters patents of the Calcutta High Court have been redrawn.

Sir Dinshah Mulla: The Calcutta letters patent are of 1869, and what is done is to substitute the sections of the Government of India Act of 1915 in the case the Lahore High Court.

Pritt: Yes ; that is obviously what has been done. This clause was substituted for the original clauses by amending letters patent of 11th March 1919. I am obliged to your Lordship for guiding me in the matter.

Now may I put before your Lordships some of the authorities upon the subject of the powers of the Court to investigate the question whether there was a case of emergency. There is no very direct English authority, although there is one which I think it would be right to refer your Lordships to, but there are several in India, where the matter has been expressly discussed, and the trend of Indian decisions is that the Courts have power to investigate that question, and must investigate it. They must investigate the question and see whether there was any reason on which the Governor-General could arrive at his conclusion.

Viscount Dunedin: Were these cases which arose under Section 72?

Reaction of Pritt

Pritt: One of them was this very *habeas corpus* case, and another arose under the same section. The particular one that I want to draw your Lordships' attention to is as recent as the 1st September last, and was a case in the High Court of Bombay, which dealt with section 52.

Sir George Lowndes: Is that the Sholapur case?

Pritt: Yes. This is a case where there was legislation. There were riots on a widespread scale in Sholapur.

Lord Thankerton: That does not matter for this point.

Dunne: We have prints of that judgment. (Handing same).

Pritt: I want to refer to the judgment of Chief Justice Beaumont, and I will begin where he quotes the section. A few lines after the quotation of the section, after discussing the Defence of the Realm Act and the state of siege in France, he says : "As the question in this case, in my judgment, turns upon this section, I will quote it in full." I have already read that to your Lordships. "It is to be noticed that the section applies 'in cases of emergency'. The question whether the determination as to the existence of an emergency is an administrative act to be decided by the Governor-General alone, or whether it is a question of fact which can be inquired into by the Courts has been discussed by the High Court of Lahore in the case of *Desraj* v. *Emperor*, and the learned Judges who decided that case differed upon the point. In my opinion the judgment of Mr. Justice Bhide is correct, and the question whether an emergency exists or not is one of fact which the Courts can inquire into. But inasmuch as the Governor-General is the person who must, in the first instance, decide whether or not there is an emergency upon which he ought to act, and inasmuch as he may frequently have information which, in the public interest, he may be unwilling to disclose, and which no Court can compel him to disclose, I think all that the Courts can do is to enquire whether there is evidence upon which the Governor-General may reasonably conclude that an emergency exists. If that question be answered in the affirmative, there is an end of the matter."

Lord Thankerton: That involves an inquiry into what the Governor-General does not want to disclose.

Pritt: Perhaps, May I submit several points in answer to what the learned Chief Justice says. There is in the first place the Governor-General: he may disclose to the Court what he thinks is enough.

Viscount Dunedin: The first point is whether the judgment of Mr. Justice Bhide is correct. Does he give any reasons?

Pritt: No, my Lord, I do not think he gives reasons.

Viscount Dunedin: Therefore there is no argument upon that.

Pritt: It obvisously was very fully argued.

Viscount Dunedin: I am not saying there was not an argument before him, but there was no argument in his judgment except to say : "I think

Mr. Justice Bhide's judgment is correct". Therefore it does not help us upon that point.

Pritt: Only to this extent, that the argument that leaps to the mind, though I may be wrong, is adopted by this learned Chief Justice.

Viscount Dunedin: It does not help us, except the fact that he says so.

Pritt: That is so.

Viscount Dunedin: I do not think you need go into this matter.

Pritt: If your Lordship pleases. Then the judgment of Mr. Justice Madgavkar contains a certain amount of argument. I confess I find it a little difficult to follow, because while he is concurring it seems to me to be rather against me than for me, and therefore it is natural, and inevitable, that I must read it. The passage I am referring to is at the top of page 6. He says : "On the third point"—that is this point— "I agree with the reasoning and the conclusions of the learned Chief Justice, and have little to add".

Lord Russell of Killowen: There are no reasons of the Chief Justice at all.

Pritt: They may have been given interlocutorily. "Unlike legislation in India, the validity of Statutes of Parliament cannot be questioned in the Courts of British India. Section 72 of the Government of India Act empowers the Governor-General to pass such ordinances in cases of emergency. It is argued for the petitioners that the omission of any such words as 'in the opinion of the Governor-General' after the word 'emergency' suffices to enable us to consider whether there was such an emergency as to justify the passing of the Ordinance and further to examine also its provisions to see how far they make 'for the peace and good government of British India'. Two learned judges of the Lahore High Court have considered the former question in the case of *Desraj* v. *Emperor*. Their difference of opinion seems to me more apparent than real. Section 72 as a whole hardly empowers the Courts to consider whether the Governor-General was right or wrong in his conclusion that an emergency existed, much less up examine how far the provisions of the Ordinance tend to the peace and good government of the country. That responsibility the statute has laid on the Governor-General and not on the Courts. Unless the Governor-General thought that there was an emergency, and he alone under the section is the judge thereof, he would not promulgate the ordinance to meet that particular emergency. The statute does not require that the Legislative Assembly should not be sitting as a necessary precedent to the exercise of the power of passing an ordinance. Therefore the fact that in some cases the Act of Indemnity has been passed by the Central Legislature and not by way of ordinance by the Governor-General is immaterial".

Viscount Dunedin: That goes to another point, does it not?

Pritt: Perhaps it does.

Lord Thankerton: The next passage rather deals with your argument. He points out that there is no law against it.

Pritt: There is no law in England against a privilegium.

Dunne: There is another passage on page 11 dealing with the third point.

Pritt: I am obliged to my learned friend. "The third point on which our decision really rests has been dealt with in detail in the judgment of the learned Chief Justice. I have already held that the ordinance is within the power of the Governor-General, and that it is not open to us to examine its provisions and whether, it at all, they go beyond the necessities of peace and good government, within the meaning of Section 72 of the Government of India Act" ; and yet he concurs, as I understand it, in the judgment which says the exact opposite. It is fair that I should read it. Then Mr. Justice Blackwell says, on page 13 : "It was contended by Mr. Thakore for the applicants that no case of emergency had been established. I do not agree with this contention. The reasons which moved the Governor-General are set out at the end of the Ordinance. On the materials placed before him the Governor-General was in my opinion clearly entitled to conclude that an emergency had arisen. I therefore think it unnecessary to decide whether the Court is empowered to enquire into the question whether in emergency existed, or whether that is a matter solely for the determination of the Governor-General. There has been a difference of judicial opinion upon this question in the Lahore High Court (see *Desraj* v. *Emperor*, A.I.R. 1930 Lahore, 781). I incline strongly to the view that the Court is entitled to enquire into the matter. Assuming that it is, the Court is not in my opinion entitled to enquire into the question whether the facts placed before the Governor-General were accurate or inaccurate. The Governor-General must obviously act promptly, and may sometimes have to make up his mind on information which may afterwards be found to be erroneous. In considering whether there was a case of emergency within the meaning of Section 72, the Court in my opinion is only entitled to require to be satisfied that facts were placed before the Governor-General which, if true, might reasonably lead him to conclude that an emergency existed."

Viscount Dunedin: The only way to do that would be by examining the Governor-General.

Pritt: May I draw your Lordships' attention to something that I think I mentioned when I was reading the Chief Justice's Judgment? The Governor-General is in this position. The matter is challenged and it is said that there was no emergency which justified his making the Ordinance. He cannot be compelled to come into Court ; he can please himself and he may do one of three things. The first, which he would be very reluctant to do, is to say : Never mind the public interest ; I am challenged ; I will give you every fact. If that were his only course, there would be a difficulty. His second course would be to say : I can reconcile the general public interests and the particular interest of maintaining the Ordinance ; I will show you quite enough to prove an emergency without showing you everything I know.

Viscount Dunedin: In order to do that he would have to be made a party to the case?

Pritt: If it is in the direct criminal proceedings, it would be the Crown, or if it is in the *habeas corpus* proceedings it would be the Crown again. The Crown, having access to public information, on applying to whatever Department is proper, would be supplied with such evidence and information as the Department thought proper. The Crown in England often has to do the same thing. The third course which the Governor-General could adopt is a course which is adopted by the Executive in this country whenever a difficulty arises. He can go to his Legislature and say : I had to act in an emergency which I say is an emergency ; I am not going to publish my facts to the Court in the disturbed state to this country at present. Give me an Act of indemnity.

Lord Thankerton: If it is an Act of indemnity, it is either at the time of the emergency or long after.

Pritt: Long after.

Lord Thankerton: I cannot understand the opinions of two of the Judges in this Bombay case. It may be that the reasons cannot possibly be disclosed. Do you say if the Governor-General does not disclose the reasons, the Ordinance is bad? If he does disclose the reasons, it may prove another emergency. The Court must either be seized of the whole of the facts or none of them.

Pritt: I respectfully agree.

Viscount Dunedin: Have you any other authority besides this that you can show us?

Pritt: Perhpas your Lordships ought to see the decision in this very *habeas corpus* case.

Viscount Dunedin: I think we know that. One judge said there was no inquiry at all ; the other judge said that an inquiry was possible, but that he thought that the people had put themselves into such a position as to show that there was an emergency.

Pritt: Yes, and I think they relied as an alternative on the Governor-General's own statement. May I say in answer to Lord Thankerton I see the difficulties of the Executive. It would be impertinence on my part to say that I sympathise with them. The answer is : I did not draft this Constitution. This Constitution has said, in my humble submission, in the plainest possible terms that the Governor-General may do this very striking thing in cases of emergency, and he may do it in cases where he is of opinion there is a state of emergency for any time. Before he does it, there must be a state of emergency. That is the kernel of the case.

I was inclined to think that some of the English cases threw some light on the matter, but I do not want to weary your Lordships with them if it is thought that they do not. Your Lordships remember the line of cases under the Defence of the Realm Act, one or two of which went to the House of Lords. This covers two points of my argument ; it covers the question who is to decide a question of fact like this question of whether there is an emergency, and also the question of what is legislation in the direction of peace and good government.

Viscount Dunedin: We will listen to any case you choose to give us, but I do not myself see how any case would be much use, unless there was something equivalent to Section 72, which, so far as I know, there is not.

Pritt: I agree, and that is why, even when a number of my clients have been sentenced to death, I hesitate to read them. It is a true analogy, but the words may be still so different that it may not be of much use. I must put before your Lordships why I say it is an analogy. The analogy is complete in this sense. I submit they are both cases of subordinate legislation, and they came from the same body. In the one case, the Imperial Parliament has said certain persons may pass subordinate legislation for securing the safety of the Realm and for the better prosecution of the war—I have forgotten the exact words for the moment—in the other case, the same Imperial Parliament has said in cases of emergency certain persons may pass legislation for the peace and good government of British India. The essence of the cases on which I wanted to rely—indeed, perhaps it is sufficient to state it—is that there is an efficient body, the High Court of the Court of Appeal and, I think I may say, the House of Lords in this country, dealing with the Defence of the Realm legislation to see whether the legislation passed falls within the four corners of the Section of the Imperial Statute.

Viscount Dunedin: Obviously.

Pritt: The analogy is this : It is the duty of whatever court becomes concerned with the Lahore Case to construe whether the legislation passed by the Governor-General to establish this particular Court falls within the four corners of Seciton 72.

Viscount Dunedin: Nobody doubts that.

Pritt: The question is : Is there a case of emergency, and is it legislation for peace and good government?

Lord Russell: The analogy would be if you were able to say that this Statute exceeded the power of the Indian Parliament?

Pritt: That is only one limb.

Viscount Dunedin: It is only the argument that you have given us over again?

Pritt: Yes ; I suggest that that argument is supported by some English authority. I think I can fairly leave these cases.

Viscount Dunedin: I do not think they help us at all. One is perfectly willing to concede you the proposition that obviously it must be within the four corners of the Section.

Lord Russell: It must be *intra vires*?

Pritt: Yes, and the *vires* depends on whether there is an emergency, and whether the legislation is for peace and good government.

Viscount Dunedin: That is your argument?

Pritt: Yes.

Viscount Dunedin: We are much obliged to you.

(Counsel and parties were directed to withdraw and after a short time were again called in.)

Viscount Dunedin: Their Lordships need not trouble you, Mr. Dunne. They are unable to advise His Majesty that leave to appeal be granted in this case for reasons which will be given later.

The reasons were given on February 27 in a judgment by Dunedin.

In brief, Pritt argued that before he could promulgate an Ordinance, the Governor-General had to establish affirmatively as a question of fact that an "emergency" did exist. Dunedin simply did not appreciate the point when he asked the preposterous question whether the Governor-General had to bring a civil suit in the courts for a declaration before making the Ordinance. It was a conditional power and fulfilment of the condition—existence of an emergency—had to be established if any one challenged the legality of the Ordinance. Pritt revealed that he had advised his clients to come to the Privy Council in appeal from the High Court's judgment in Des Raj's case, delivered seven months earlier in July 1930. Justice Bhide's judgment might have helped the petitioners.

But this Board would not have altered its opinion. Dunedin's brief judgment showed that the consideration that weighed with him was the finality of the Governor-General's view. He was the sole judge as to the existence of an emergency. Even in the judicial clime of 1931, it was an extreme view that Dunedin propounded. "It is more than obvious that that someone must be the Governor-General and be alone. Any other view would render utterly inept the whole provision. Emergency demands immediate action, and that action is prescribed to be taken by the Governor-General. It is he alone who can promulgate the Ordinance."

Pritt's Contention that the G-G's opinion was open to judicial review was dismissed out of hand. "In fact, the contention is so completely without foundation on the fact of it that it would be idle to allow an appeal to argue about it."

Dunedin went so far as to hold that the Governor-General did not have to give any reasons in support of his action : "Their Lordships must add that, although the Governor-General thought fit to expound the reasons which induced him to promulgate this Ordinance, this was not in their Lordships' opinion in any way incumbent on him as a matter of law."

Chamier and Mitchell

Watching the proceeding before the Privy Council in London was the Legal Adviser to the Secretary for India, Sir Edward Maynard Chamier. He had held the office since 1917 and knew India well. He had served as government Advocate in the North-West Frontier Province as far back as in 1875, in Oudh as Judicial Commissioner, and as Chief Justice of the Patna High Court (1911-15). He knew the legal world in India and in London, in so far as it touched India. Hence the significance of an air-letter he dashed off to D.G. Mitchell, the Joint Secretary in the Law Ministry. Mitchell hastened to forward it to the Home Secretary, H.W. Emerson, on February 24. This suggests that Chamier wrote as soon as the Privy Council dismissed Bhagat Singh's petition.

The letters, now resting in the National Archives tell their own tale :

24th February

My dear Emerson,

I enclose a copy of an air-mail letter I have just received from Sir Edward Chamier. Crerar will be interested.

Yours sincerely,
D.G. MITCHELL

Copy of an air-mail letter received by me today from Sir Edward Chamier.

My dear Mitchell,

I was agreeably surprised to find that Lord Dunedin presiding over the Board which heard the petition in the Lahore Conspiracy Case—*with any other President I think the petition would have been admitted to a regular hearing*—but Dunedin took a very strong line from the start and carried the others with him not that Lowndes (or Saunders?) and Mulla wanted any "carrying". They evidently felt that in the end the petition must fail and it was useless to prolong the agony.

I will send you with their "reasons" a transcript of the shorthand notes—you may be interested to see exactly what line the board took .

Yours sincerely,
E. CHAMIER

9

The National Martyr

Lord Irwin was born on 16th April 1881. It is ironical that as England celebrate his 100th Birthday, India mourns Bhagat Singh's 50th death anniversary who died on the 23rd March 1931. Nobody, including Gandhi, could earn him mercy.

Bhagat Singh was not the first to be hanged in India's long history of martyrs. Nor was he the last. There had been thousands of executions before and after him. Khudiram Bose, Madanlal Dhingra, Kartar Singh Sarabha, Ashfaqullah Khan and Ramparsad Bismal are a few names in the sea of countless patriots in the pre-Bhagat Singh period who kissed the gallows with revolutionary song on their lips. There have been hundreds after Bhagat Singh who accepted the hangman's noose as a wedding garland. Life for them was a bride and death the bridegroom who comes to whisk her away.

In the post-Bhagat Singh period we witness the 29-year old Mahavir Singh Rathore of Punjab National Bank, Lahore 'dacoity' fame who died at Port Blair on May 17, 1933 as a result of forced feeding when milk intruded into his lungs and became poison, the 22-year old coast battery-man at Madras who dreamed he was caressing the gallows only to realise later on that he was actually doing so on September 17, 1943. It almost amounted to crucification. And many more who died unheard and unsung after adding fire to struggle for independence. The corpse of Bhagat Singh, however, always stood between the British empire and India. What is special about this particular corpse and what would have happened if Bhagat Singh's life was spared? In the same historical strain it may be observed that Lord Irwin was not the first Viceroy of India who never felt moved by the hangings of the patriots. Lord Chelmsford before and Lord Wellingdon afterwards were harder nuts to crack and refused outright to commute death sentences in several cases under powers specially vested in the Viceroy for the purpose.

The question, therefore, that arises is as to why Bhagat Singh's case caused an unusual uproar and a sensation which was unprecedented. Even in Sholapur case, Peshawar case and Bombay cases, the demand for commutation of death sentences was not let out of the province concerned and limited to only intellectual classes. In case of Bhagat Singh the agitation was nation-wide and on all-India basis which was supported by Burma at that time.

In no other case the demand for saving his life was so total, universal and overwhelming. In fact, the whole nation was electrified and the demand transformed into a popular movement where the men of letters and those without letters participated with equal vigour and enthusiasm, in which the most helpless peasant and the most self-confident politician of the day took equal interest. Even women with wailing babies-in-arm and famished mouths crying for food had assembled in front of the Lahore Central Jail and performed what in Punjabi is known as *'Siapa'* (Beating the Breast) asking for nothing but mercy. Those who had never seen Bhagat Singh wanted to see him once—just once. Analysing the back-numbers of the newspapers and magazines it appears as if there was a political earthquake and if Bhagat Singh and his comrades were not commuted the British empire would crumble the very next day and that the revolution was round the corner.

Let us first have a glance at the contemporary records to know what was peculiar with Bhagat Singh's case which did not exist before? Writing editorially by way of comment in its issue dated March 26, 1931, three days after the hangings, *the Tribune*, Lahore stated : "No criminal case within living memory had made such a tremendous sensation in the country, and in no previous case had so strong and so universal a demand been made for the commutation of the death sentences. . .

The reason is not far to ask for. The circumstances of the case, the succession of hunger strikes, martyrdom of Jatindranath Das, the protracted and more or less farcical proceedings in the Special Magistrate's.Court, the part played by the Police and the Executive in those proceedings, the Ordinance, the ex-parte proceedings before the Special Tribunal constituted under it and one or two extremely regrettable incidents in that court, and all the rest of them, not excluding the well known fact that the three prisoners had to be last refused to make any petition for mercy, had invested the case with a peculiar character."

No, Mr. Editor. That is not everything. There is something more that touches the heart, is something else which trickles the emotion. It was not a 'criminal' case and that makes the whole story different.

Addressing a public meeting at Delhi the same day Subash Chandra Bose asserted that Bhagat Singh was not a person but a symbol, he symbolised the spirit of revolution that had gripped of the country. The same evening, i.e., March 26, 1931, the Viceroy made a more detailed reference to Bhagat Singh's execution in his farewell speech at the Chelmsford Club dinner.

The 49-year old Lord Irwin who had completed his five years term in India and was about to return said : "I have been told that the Government of India and I myself have made Mr. Gandhi's task far harder by failure to commute the sentences recently passed upon Bhagat Singh and his companions. I can well believe that our action has at this juncture been a real difficult for Mr. Gandhi and those associated with him, and I owe it to Indian opinion generally that I should take this opportunity, in a few words, of placing them in clear possession of my own thought. I take full responsibility for the decision at which Government arrived. I know no heavier responsibility that rests upon the shoulders of a Viceroy than the decision of whether he should or should not make use of his special power by way of commutation or remission of sentences. As I listened the other day to Mr. Gandhi putting the case for commutation forcibly before me I reflected, first of what significance it surely was that the apostle of non-violence would be earnestly be pleading the cause of devotees of a creed so fundamentally opposite to his own. I reflected also upon the quality of the responsibility that falls on those in whose hands it lies and whose duty it is to decide finally whether their fellow men should live or die. And I am free to confess that I should frankly regard that responsibility as an intolerable one to any man to support, unless he guided his conduct by adherence to certain very clear and definite principles. What should those be? First of all, he must satisfy himself that no facts have been brought to his notice which were not before the sentencing tribunals and which might suggest a possible miscarriage of justice. There was nothing of this sort in this case, and it is significant that none of the petitions in any form, directly or indirectly, suggested that the prisoners were other than guilty of the crimes alleged against them. For the rest, I conceive it right that I should have regard, in the exercise of clemency, to the actual merits, as I can judge them, of the case before me. On these principles I from time to time, on the advice of my Council, concur in or remit death sentences that have been imposed. But I should regard it as wholly wrong to allow my judgement on these matters to be influenced or deflected by purely political considerations. I am well aware of the interest taken by large numbers of people in the fate of Bhagat Singh. But I could discover no argument by which commutation of that sentence could have been justified that would not have involved, if justice was to be equal, the commutation of all other sentences involving the death penalty. For I could imagine no case in which, under the law, the penalty had been more directly deserved. I have seen it suggested in the Press that, even supposing commutation was impossible, it was highly undesirable that the executions should take place on the eve of the Congress meeting at Karachi. I was fully alive to these considerations, and I will state with complete frankness the principal reason which led me to think the suggestion of postponement was not one that my Government could possibly accept.

To suggest to Congress that there was after all a chance that the sentence would be remitted, whereas I should have in my own mind been clear that the sentence must be carried out as soon as the Congress had concluded, seemed to me—as it would have to you—a wholly indefensible proceeding. I am quite prepared to think that it would be made the immediate atmosphere at Karachi easier, but only at the cost of enabling Congress to say with justice that it had been treated by the Viceroy and by the Government with complete lack of candour. For those reasons I felt that the action suggested to me was impossible."

There is no evidence to document that the Viceroy who was otherwise an astute politician bravely weathered the storm and felt lonely after the execution of Bhagat Singh as has been conceived from some of Irwin's apologists.

As this juncture, to apprise the reader about the Gandhi Irwin Pact would be appropriate. It took place in 1931 and Lord Irwin would persuade Gandhi to take part in the 2nd round table conference. On April 12, 1931 Gandhi met the Viceroy along with other delegates bound for the Round Table Conference to London. On April 13, the Viceroy left Delhi for good and got into the same boat to London on April 18, 1931 which had carried his successor, Lord Wellingdon two days before. Gandhiji again met the Viceroy at Bombay on April 15. They had a heart-to-heart talk but it is not known whether Bhagat Singh was on their agenda. When Lord Irwin celebrated his 50th birthday on April 16, Gandhi was still in Bombay. He sent roses to Irwin.

Let us now turn to other sources and seek our answers. Allan Campbell Johnson, the biographer of Lord Irwin, in his book, *Lord Halifax*

(1941) has this to say : "Two days later (April 13, 1931) he left New Delhi for the last time amid the usual scenes of splendour and was given a magnificent send-off. During these moments of abdication he must yet have known the full majesty of power. In the enthusiasm and devotion of this person was the real reward for the reproaches and calumnies he had to face in carrying out in five years the duties of a lifetime. If this simple upright man had indeed betrayed India Lord Rothermere would have done well to study his popularity before holding him up to contempt in the Daily Mail."

Johnson continues : "Up to the end, therefore, he (Irwin) demonstrated his uncanny capacity to extract concessions from the little man who to everyone else has always seemed the most perverse of negotiators, but who to Irwin was pliable and conciliatory."

For his excellent services in India Lord Irwin was promoted to the post of Foreign Secretary while Gandhi was taken into custody again on his return from the Round Table Conference.

Let us shuffle the pages of Nehru's *Autobiography* (1936) to unfathom the reasons of Bhagat Singh's popularity : "Terrorists have flourished in India, off and on, for nearly thirty years, and at no time, except in the early days in Bengal, did any of them attain a fraction of that popularity which came to Bhagat Singh. This is a patent fact which cannot be denied; it has to be admitted. And another fact which is equally obvious, is that terrorism, in spite of occasional recrudescence, has no longer any appeal for the youths in India.

Bhagat Singh thus did not become popular because of his fact of terrorism, but because he seemed to vindicate, for the moment, the honour of Lala Lajpat Rai, and through him of the nation. He became a symbol; the act was forgotten, the symbol remained, and within a few months each town and village of Punjab, and to a lesser extent the rest of northern India, resounded with his name. Innumerable songs grew up about him, and the popularity of that the man achieved was amazing."

According to Mr. Manmath Nath Gupta in the chapter 'Communist Evaluation of Bhagat Singh', in his book *Bhagat Singh and his Times* (1977) Bhagat Singh was a symbol but of another kind. To use his words: "whether one likes it or not, Bhagat Singh has become the symbol of the fight for socialism more than any person or party has."

Bhagat Singh, in fact, was much more than a symbol. He was a visionary with dreams, the madness of a Spinoza, the halo of a superman. He was neither a dead mental principle nor an empty political vow.

For the Indian people Bhagat Singh was a emblem of bravery and courage. As the time passed even Mahatma Gandhi praised Bhagat Singh without hesitation. "It is impossible to assess his courage. Hanging has placed a crown of bravery on these youngmen. Wherever words of praise have been said about these youngmen I agree with it. We must appreciate their sacrifice, bravery and unbounded courage, though we may not use our courage the way they used it."

Bhagat Singh was a mark of a new and a better and a proud India. The deeply moving story of his life and the more inciting story of his death has made him an extraordinary personality of the 20th century, a lion among men who knew neither defeat nor death. At the time of execution he was, as he always was, an ordinary son of the soil, a man devoid of power, property or position, bereft of any academic or literary distinctions, devoid of any scientific, intellectual or spiritual attainments. Yet the whole country bowed and acknowledged his selfless sacrifice and paid homage to him as they had not paid to any mortal or martyr before or after.

A flashback of the ancient heritage of his country he was a symbol of the 'Shakti' of India, its solidarity and its strength. When he sang with his companions the *'Bande Mataram'* in the crowded court of Lahore Central Jail, it was not the physical 'Shakti' of this country he instigated, but the timeless and eternal India, her soul and spirit which was worshipped by an awakened humanity. The new resurgence deliberated through Bhagat Singh who thundered and burst over his enslaved motherland like an avalanche. As a creative political thinker Bhagat Singh holds a very high place in the Indian history. The constitution of the Hindustan Republican Association which he started will exhort every reader and scholar of political thought that Bhagat Singh was neither a thin-blooded revolutionary nor an arm-chair political dummy but a serious thinker who conceded his country a new charter of freedom, a new Magna Carta based on social justice and economic equality, a non-sectarian, non-exploiting order at peace with itself and the world.

By his own example he asserted that no weapon in the arsenals of the world is so dreadful as the will and the moral courage of men and women determined to attain of freedom which Tilak said was man's birthright. The declaration of freedom flames with his eloquence.

Driving through miles of mustard and maize and mangoes on Phagwara-Nawanshahr road there is a small village called Khatkar Kalan, a little ahead of the 27th milestone from Phagwara in Jullundur district. This is Bhagat Singh's ancestral village to which he must have been carried in the arms of his mother but where today stands his statue unveiled on

March 23, 1973 by Shrimati Indira Gandhi, the Prime Minister, which retrospects everybody of Lincoln's Gettysburg address on November 19, 1863, and the price that has been paid for our freedom. There stands Bhagat Singh imploring his mother to prepare a *BasantiChola* (The Yellow Robe) for him for that is the colour which the revolutionaries put up in this land of sorrow before going to the gallows. There he stands as a monument of heroism illumining the mind of man, exalting his heart, ennobling his life and beckoning him on to the realisation of his destiny on history's long road to freedom.

With his highly sensitive profile and expressive eyes, with an unbelievably calm face Bhagat Singh's name after 50 years comes to the mind like a gentle dew that falls unseen and unheard and yet brings into blossom the fairest of roses, striking a responsive chord in every heart, expelling all that could not be absorbed, absorbing all that could not be expelled, abated but not slain. A giant who stole the spark of the angels to kindle the forest fires. Bhagat Singh symbolised a new idealism that set everybody thinking, a new surge and thunder whose music led the slaves to salvation.

Bhagat Singh was a flutist, a Pied Piper of Punjab whose freedom tunes mesmerised everyone who hypnotised the whole of India with his emanating charm and haunting melodies. In the long struggle of freedom Bhagat Singh is like Shelley's 'Prometheus Unbound' longing for a reign of love and a society where 'thrones, altars, judgement-seats and prisons are things of the past and Man remains

Sceptreless, free, uncircumscribed, but
Man
Equal, unclassed, tribeless and nationless,
Exempt from awe, worship, degree, the
King
Over himself ; just, gentle, wise but Man.

Baba Ram Kishan started his Kuka movement or the Namdhari movement whose founder was Baba Balik Singh Namdhari after he opposed the First Anglo-Sikh War at Mudki, on December 22, 1845 at the age of 29. He believed more than others that the Punjab army was an army of lions led by jackals. As the winter sun rose the Punjab skies and the war was declared by the beat of the drums this man consigned his gun and his uniform into the river Sutlej and got engaged in cultivation. He spent next 25 years of his life in the Punjab villages creating a climate which breeds revolutions. He started well with the peasantry but soon he got diverted into the bylane of religion.

Rani Jindan, the youngest wife of Ranjit Singh, had also asked for Balak Singh's blessings when she challenged Sir John Lawrence, the British Resident at Lahore for wrongful annexation of a region of Punjab as a result of the Battle of Sabraon. Barring the first onslaught of British imperialism in Punjab she told Lawrence to come out openly and fight with the Punjabis instead of inciting one against the other. In a letter dated August 7, 1847, the Rani wrote to the Resident : "Why do you take over the kingdom by underhand means. Why don't you do it openly"? Used, misused and abused by her own countrymen ; insulted, humiliated and exiled by the Britishers she first ran away to Benares, then searched for asylum at Kathmandu and later died at Kensington in UK on August 1, 1863 Her last words were : "Donot let my bones rot in this inhospitable country. Take them back to India". Popularly called as the Lahore tigress Rani Jind Kaur was the first woman freedom fighter of Punjab who came out of her veil, addressed large congregations, invoked the soldiers to revolt against the Britishers and restore the territories illegally annexed by the East India Company. Baba Balak Singh died in 1862 but left behind a 'Kook', a cry, in this case the cry for independence. For Ram Singh the 'Kook' became a condition of existence. Soon he gave it a concept and dressed it in economic terms.

Kuka's : An Inspiring Chap

The Kukas lead a life of austerity and abstinence. A contemporary historian, Maulvi Ghulam Bhikh Jullundhuri speaks in his 'Tarikhi-i-Wakri': "They shun every evil as sin : stealing, adultery, drinking. Meat eating is absolutely forbidden. He who becomes a 'Kuka' is supposed to lead a life of total abnegation. Their motto is : 'Be ready to die, have no desire for life and think yourself to be as humble as dust. Put the interest of your country above everything else. Drive out the foreigners who are polluting your motherland. Then and then alone you are entitled to be called a 'Kuka'.

Baba Ram Singh was a great organizer. He raised enormous funds and conferred excellent military training on his disciples. He even despatched a mission to Kathmandu for military training and urged the Maharaja of Jammu and Kashmir to oblige a few hundreds for rifle training, mountain climbing, sword-play. In fact the 'Vanar Sena' of Maharaja Ranbir Singh was mainly constituted of the 'Kukas' of Punjab. They dressed in white and their style of tying the turban was also different. They had their own Gurudwaras and appointed 'Soobas' (Governors) who collected donations and inducted young boys. Within a few years several thousands of youngmen had been enrolled in the organisations. Baba Ram Singh toured extensively in Punjab, J&K, UP and Central India to seek more recruits. The secret reports of the period describe him a revolutionary who seek interacted with people in a language they readily understood. 'He talks to them of their land and water taxes. He spreads discontent, disaffection and arouses in them the spirit of patriotism'. When Ram Singh visited Anandpur Sahib, Amritsar and Lahore he was accompanied by a very huge number of followers riding on horses, singing hymns, carrying white flags, like a disciplined army.

At Ludhiana and Malerkotla huge congregations took place where the number of people who harked at him was tremendous. The Sikh institution of *'Langer'* (Common meal) served as a convenient platform for the organisation. Wherever he went the feeling of antipathy for the English went on soaring high.

Each harvesting season of Punjab was Ram Singh's greatest opportunity. It was during this period that he had complete influence over his listeners. The simple peasants of Punjab looked at him as a new hope. They believed that Guru Gobind Singh had returned on the earth and that the days of plenty of Maharaja Ranjit Singh would soon come back to them. Baba Ram Singh told them that God and nature allotted land to the tillers, no man could snatch it away from them. Baba Ram Singh was not a common man. He was a movement. Namdharis, as the Kukas are generally known, were no clan. They were a concept. One major resolution with them was the banning of cow-slaughter.

The British Government began to take notice of the doings of the Kukas as early as 1861. Within two years their 'Diwan' was banned by order of the District Magistrate of Ferozepur. Bhaini Sahib, the centre of Kuka activities, was put under strict vigilance. By 1867 the movement had gained so much influence that the Commissioner of Ambala Division had to recommend the immediate arrest of Baba Ram Singh and ban the entry of Kuka boys into the Police and the Army. "It is my thorough belief", wrote the Commissioner, Mr. Taylor, 'that these lads mean war sooner or later, and I strongly recommend my Government to be beforehand with them". It was also reported that the Maharaja of Jammu was raising a Kuka regiment. In a letter to Lord Lawrence, Mr. Donovan, a railway officer, wrote : 'Let us rule with a rod of iron, knowing they are heathens and a godless people. The heart of every Briton burns when we see the ingratitude of the blacks. The plant is yet tender and can be bent at pleasure, thereafter it will not yield. This case should be dealt with in a doubly severe manner than the Fenian insurrection."

It is often thought, and rightly so, that if the Kukas had organised themselves a little earlier than 1857, the Sikhs would not have given support to the East India Compay in Great Rebellion. In July 1871 the Kukas pounced upon the butchers of Amritsar and killed a number of them outside Lahore Gate. A few months later they attacked the butchers of Raikot. In both instances, the Government was unforgiving in dealing with the Kukas, whose leaders were too feeble against the British military machine and their informers'. Many were arrested and hanged. By then the movement had acquired a distinct political arena. In the words of Mr. MacNabb, the new Commissioner of Ambala "the Soobas I have seen are young and daring looking men. Whatever may have been the intentions of the leaders of the sect at the beginning, the tendency is now distinctly political. Everything points to this. Ram Singh has no pretensions to be a saintly 'fakeer'. He visits you attended by half a dozen horsemen. He is followed by scores of men on foot, he comes into your room, surrounded by a court like a prince. He and his people are dressed in exquisitely fine clothes"

But it was at Malerkotla that the Kukas wrote history in 1872. A comprehensive and a detailed attack was planned on Malerkotla, Nabha, Jind and Patiala.

It was also decided to demolish the rail link between Ambala and Ludhiana. The Kukas captured the fort of Malodh without difficulty and marched in procession, like forces of victory, to Malerkotla two days after the *Maghi* festival i.e. January 15, 1872. The treasury was the first target. Here they had access to a lot of booty and wasted their time inside the palace. This gave breathing time to the British Government. A special Gurkha contingent was brought to crush the rebellion. Forces were also deployed from Patiala. A battle ensued at Rur, a village few miles from Malerkotla. The Kukas were quashed with a very heavy hand. On January 17, sixty five Kukas were blown off by canons which was witnessed by thousands of troop and spectators 'to teach them a lesson', at a place called 'Kukian da Kalar? One was torn limb by limb. Baba Ram Singh was sent to Rangoon. There he died 13 years later in 1885 at Mergui in prison.

A rumour was spread that the Baba had escaped to Russia to organise an invasion from there. The Malerkotla executions are singular in history. Even the conscience of the new Viceroy, Lord Mayo, was pricked at this barbarity. He immediately suspended Mr. Cowan, the then Deputy Commissioner of Ludhiana. At the same time a ruthless search for every Kuka started in the province in every temple and shrine. The gurudwara at Bhaini Sahib and the ailing father of Baba Ram Singh were not spared.

Bhai Santokh Singh, in his *Satgur Bilas*, has recorded an inspiring passage of dialogue between a Kuka prisoner and an English officer. "Why did you rebel"? enquired the blue-eyed Firanghee of Kuka Hira Singh. The blue-turbaned Kuka, whose eyes shone like diamonds, replied : "We do not want Firanghee Raj. We want our own Raj. Until your Raj is over or is finished, we will continue to rebel. We shall take heads and give heads. We shall be born again and again to annihilate your power". Hira Singh was shot to death the following morning.

The Kukas now looked forward to Russia for help. There is documentary evidence of the epistles exchanged between Baba Budh Singh and the Russian Governor of Turkestan. In 1883 the British Government intercepted some secret messages and turned even more ruthless in their treatment to the Namdharis. The situation took a unexpected turn when in 1887, the exiled Maharaja Dalip Singh, the surviving son of Maharaja Ranjit Singh, landed in Russia. Sooba Bishen Singh travelled all the way to Russia to hold discussions with the banished Maharaja, but nothing concrete came out. Dalip Singh's promised return to Punjab and the expected trumpling of the British government of Punjab turned out to be a mere dream. Yet there were rumours everywhere that Baba Ram Singh's spirit had entered Dalip Singh's body.

Dalip Singh died in a Paris hotel a frustrated man, With him also was buried all hopes of Punjab's liberation with Russian help. That happened on October 22, 1893. The Kukas, however, continued to be kept eyes on and suspected. The police-cum-vigilance post set up at Bhaini Sahib in 1872 kept functioning till 1922 when it was withdrawn under great national pressure.

One of the most patriotic people Punjab has produced, the Kukas inscribed an inspiring chapter in the history of the freedom struggle. Truly a people's party, they aim was to establish socialistic order in the most democratic sense of the term. Challenging comparison with the Ironsides of Oliver Cromwell, the Kukas recapitulated the brave memories of Akali Phoola Singh Nihang's *Suicide Squads* of the days of Maharaja Ranjit Singh.

Though politically a failure, the Kukas expounded a great influence on the social, religious and moral and political life of Punjab after the Great Rebellion. The Kuka movement, like all movements of freedom and patriotism died out leaving only a flicker behind. In such revolutions, the death of one is the birth of another. A very difficult time was ahead for the freedom fighters. The British authority was now fully established, yet a fear was lurking all around that something was boiling beneath the soil. Punjab had tasted the Molasses of freedom after eight centuries of slavery and within less than half a century they were again enslaved. After Ram Singh the Punjabis had to search for another leader but there was none in sight. The wait this time was longer as per the Punjabi proverb that when a sinner takes on to fasting Allah makes the day longer.

The *Nayi Hawa*

With the dawn of the 20th century a new wave called 'Nayi Hawa' swept the country particularly the Punjab and the Bengal. Writing on April 30, 1907, i.e., five months before the birth of Bhagat Singh, Sir Denzil Ibbetson, the Lieutenant Governor of the Punjab and its Dependencies depicts in his famous political minute :

"Everywhere the people are sensible of a change of a 'new air' (Nayi Hawa) which is blowing through men's minds, and are waiting to see what will come of it. But in the east and west in the province the new ideas are confined to the educated classes, and among them, in main, to the pleaders, clerks and students. As the centre of the province is approached, however, the feeling in the towns grows stronger, and there are greater signs of activity and unrest. In the cities of Amritsar and Ferozepur there has been an attempt on the part of Lahore agitators to arouse feelings of disloyalty which has apparently met with considerable success in Ferozepur, though it has not been so successful in Amritsar. In the towns of Rawalpindi, Sialkot and Lyallpur, an active anti-British propaganda is being openly and seculously preached. In Lahore, the capital of the province, the propaganda is virulent and has resulted in a more or less general state of serious unrest."

Bengal was reeling under equal discontent. The Sedition Committee Report said that *Jugantar*, a Bengali newspaper daily poured forth poison. Answering a question in the House of Commons, Lord Morley stated on June 6, 1907 that within a month 28 meetings were held in the Punjab and only five discussed ostensibly agricultural grievances, the rest 23 were all purely political.

The sudden realisation by the Indian youths that they were being deliberately kept unarmed led to the rushing purchase of arms without license. When the Government learnt about the situation, kept a stricter vigilance on arms sale. The revolutionaries had to establish factories for the manufacture of bombs and other ammunition. Thus a class of people had come forth which did not have faith in the path of petitions, pleadings and prayers.

It was in this atmosphere that a boy was born at Banga, Tehsil

Jarranwala, district Lyallpur, on September 27, 1907 and it was the above philosophy which was nurtured by the boy's father, Sardar Kishen Singh and his uncles Sardar Swarn Singh and Sardar Ajit Singh. In fact when the child was born to Kishen Singh's wife. Vidyavati, his father and his two uncles were in custody for revolutionary activities.

Lala Lajpat Rai was in Mandalay jail but the 'Nayi Hawa' blowed from house to house and hut to hut as if the walls had ears and breeze tongues. It was the time when even the peasant women of Punjab witnessed the sickle of the new moon from their green fields. They no longer cursed their 'kismet' but joined their menfolk in the struggle to modify it.

One such product of the 'New Wave' was Madan Lal Dhingra, a Lahore lad who had joined the University College at London in 1906 and watched the Indian scene from abroad boiling with anger every time the news came of an Indian Youth being hanged or transported. During the three years he studied engineering, he also got trained in the use of fire-arms. Dhingra short into prominence by assassinating Col. William Curzon Wylie, Political ADC in the India Office at a gathering in the Imperial Institute, London on July 1, 1909. Dhingra shot five bullets and Willie died on the spot.

Son of a staunch loyalists, a Civil Surgeon at Gurudaspur, Madan Lal had himself wrote the new India's character of freedom when he was a student at Lahore. In London he was present at the secret meetings of the revolutionaries and had pledged that he would avenge his country's humiliation at the hands of the Britishers. At the time of commiting this daring crime Madan Lal was hardly 22. The boy made no effort whatsoever to escape. In a melee when other people ran to safety he raised his voice and declared with unusual firmness and clarity that no one should fear him because he had accomplished his job.

When some spectators called him 'murderer' he objected and said he was a patriot working for the emancipation of his motherland from the alien raj. Displaying no sign of nervousness before an agitated crowd he said : "I am perfectly justified in what I have done. The English would have done the same thing had the Germans been in occupation of England".

"The only thing I want to say", he told the Magistrate, "is that I did not wilfully murder Lalkaka, the Indian Parsi doctor. I saw him advancing ; he caught hold of me and I only fired in self-defence". Dr. Lalkaka died of Dhingra's sixth bullet. Madan Lal was over-powered, seized, grappled with, arrested and remanded in police custody for a week beginning July 2, 1909.

During this time Madan Lal mostly kept awake and was busy preparing down the text of the statement which he carried in his pocket before advancing to the guilotine. He had indeed revised and rehearsed it a number of times in the prison of Pentonville. Each time he read it his face shone and his eyes became red. He went on rehearsing it till his excitement subsided and he could recollect his statement with a composed mind. On July 2, the following morning, a cable was sent by the Commissioner of London Police to the Director of Central Intelligence, Simla seeking particulars and character antecedents of Dhingra.

The cable's text read as follows : "Sir W. Curzon Wyllie murdered at eleven O'clock night of the 1st July by Madan Lal Dhingra said to be the son of civil surgeon of Goordaspur. A Parsi named Cowas Lalcaca also died soon after. Shall send particulars next mail." The Bengal police was more worried lest Dhingra should turn not to be a Bengali.

Veer Savarkar who was in London and who eulogised Madan Lal for his daring patriotic action was manhandled and forcibly thrown out of the India House meeting which was organised to denounce Dhingra and his deed.

Virendranath Chattopadhya, brother of Sarojini Naidu who later carried an award 10,000 on his head also admired Madan Lal's heroic deed. In a letter published in *The Times* Londan, he said : "The catalogue of coming assassinations will probably be a long one and the responsibility for its length will have to be laid at the door of those, who instead of espousing the cause of Indian freedom, wish to hold India in the interest of British".

But the father disowned the son. Losing no opportunity to forward to the Governmeat about his loyalty and his long meritorious services to the Crown spanning over two decades, he addressed to Sir Dunlop Smith, the Private Secretary to the Viceroy, Lord Minto, a letter in which he stated : "The whole family expresses its deep abhorrence of the horrible deed of this mad son of mine. I assure you that I am not so much sorry for the loss of my son as I am of the killing of the two innocent men and proving a disgrace to this family which has always been so loyal and grateful to the Government for its numerous favours". On July 7 the two elder brothers of Madan

Lal, Mohan Lal and Bihari Lal sought personal interview with Sir Dunlop Smith and gave a written declaration : "That we shall not consider Madan Lal as a martyr as the Extremists would desire, we look upon him as a lunatic and his act as a detestable act".

But Madan Lal was not tried as 'lunatic'. He was tried as 'murderer' at the Old Bailey Court on the 23rd day after the assassination, i.e., July 23. The decision to sentence him to death was snapped in less than 23 minutes. It was also decided to send him to the hanging rope 25 days later, i.e., on August 17, 1909. There was none to defend him. Madan Lal ignored the mock proceedings with the contempt they deserved.

When the Judge finished reading his judgement, Madan Lal raised his voice and said : 'I am proud to have the honour of laying down my humble life for my country. But remember we shall have our time in days to come." On the gallows on August 17 he prophesed his act as 'a humble revenge for the inhuman hangings and deportations of patriotic Indian youths". In a prepared statement he added : "I believe that a nation held down by foreign bayonets is in a perpetual state of war. Since open battle is rendered impossible to a disarmed race, I attacked by surprise ; since guns were denied to me I drew forth my pistol and fired. Poor in wealth and intellect a son like myself has nothing else to offer to the mother but his own blood and so I have sacrificed the same on her altar". The Irish press hailed Madan Lal a hero. So did the Egyptian paper published from Cairo, *La Patrrie Egyptienne* which predicted the collapse of the British Empire in another forty years. The Labour Members of the Parliament stated that the Conservative Government comprehended the language of bullies only.

Mrs. Annie Besant said : "More Madan Lals are the need of the hour". Virendranath Chattopadhaya started a monthly magazine in Madan's memory' It was printed by Madame Cama from Berlin and was named 'Madan Talwar' (Madan Sword). Soon it became the embonhevee of the views of the Indian revolutionaries abroad. At home the reaction was mixed. While Pandit Madan Mohan Malviya in his Presidential Address at Lahore described Madan Lal's act as 'detestable crime' the general masses of India treated him as a martyr and his act as memorable and symbolic in Indian history. Madan Lal's last earthly wish was : "I may be reborn of the same mother and I may-re-die in the same Sacred Cause till the Cause is successful". To make the above Cause successful the contribution of the Ghadar Party cannot be overruled. A considerable number of Indian population had migrated, in search of better careers, to countries such as Canada, USA, Singapore, Malaya and Hong Kong. Most of them were of peasant stock from Punjab and in general were very enterprising people. However they got very shabby treatment there by the authorities regarding wages and work and housing facilities and other living conditions. Already an apartheid existed in USA against the Negroes and it was applied on Indians too. The racial discrimination was most obvious like public places like hotels, buses, parks and theatres. During the first decade to the 20th century the racial laws in Canada and USA were made more racial. The Indians looked to the British Consular authorities for redress but nobody cared to help them.

Indians Abroad

But something had to be done. The 'Nayi Hawa' had reached the Punjabi peasants abroad. Sohan Singh Bhakna, Lala Hardyal, Bhai Kesar Singh, Bhai Parmanand and Pandit Kanshi Ram gave push to the movement of uniting the Indian residing in America. A meeting was organised at Astoria in Oregan on the *Baisakhi* day, i.e., April 13, 1913 and the Union of the Hindustani Workers of the Pacific Coast was created. This was the forerunner of the Ghadar Party. It was at Astoria that the Indians abroad agreed that the object of their Association would be to end the British rule in India through armed revolution and instate a free government based on the principles of liberty, equality and fraternity. The headquarters of the new movement were located at *Yugantar Ashram* at San Francisco. They had their weekly magazine, also called *Ghadar* published in Urdu, Hindi, Punjabi, Marathi and Bengali. Some issues of *Ghadar* of Novemberes 1913 elucidate the conditions of squalor and misery of Indians abroad. On the eve of the First World War an incident occurred which altered the course of the Ghadar Party. In the history of the freedom movement the incident is known as 'Komagata Maru'. Originally the name of a Japanese ship which Baba Gurdit Singh of Singapore chartered and sailed to Canada with 400 Indian immigrants on board to meet the objections of the Canadian Government which had passed discriminatory immigration laws against the Indians, Komagata Maru became a numeration of revolution. Only 22 passengers were allowed to set foot at the port of Vancouver in Canada. The passengers ignored the immigration laws and decided to stay in the ship. For two months a cold war took off between the immigrants and the Canadian authorities. When the Canadian Government did not give in Baba Gurdit Singh sailed towards India. At Hong Kong and Singapore also where the passengers had their homes the ship was not allowed to enter port. Their real difficulties, however, started when they finally reached Budge Budge port at Calcutta. The secret reports of the British Government described the passengers as dangerous revolutionaries due to which they were despatched to Punjab by special train under police escort. At Calcutta itself a clash took place between the police and the passengers 18 of which were killed by police bullets. A large number of them were wounded. Baba Gurdit Singh and few others escaped. All the newspapers of Calcutta highlighted the incident and there was considerable anguish. In Punjab the incident almost created belligerent conditions.

One immediate consequence of the incident was that the Ghadarites decided to return to India in batches from San Francisco in Japanese ships called Tosha Maru and Mishima Maru. Onroute they met the Indian troops at Singapore, Penang and Hong Kong and apprised them of their future programme. At Lahore, Amritsar and Lyallpur they were given rousing receptions. It was at this juncture that the activities of the Ghadar party were taken over by Rash Bihari Bose.

The Ghadarites also established anti-British Secret Cells in almost all the cantonements of Punjab. They also provoked the Indian troops stationed at Meerut, Allahabad, Benares and Lucknow. February 25, 1915 was fixed as the General Uprising Day. It is said that if this uprising had succeeded the Britishers would have left India much earlier. Planned on more organised lines than even the 1857 rebellion the 1915 revolt was foiled in the bud much before the scheduled time because of a highly organised espionage on which the British administration banked. Kirpal Singh Brar was a paid spy whom the British Government had installed in the heart of the Ghadar party in that he was member of the inner cabinet. As such all the activities of the party were known in advance to the Home Department. The result was that very large numbers were transported for life to Andamans, Mandalay and elsewhere, Many of them passed away in the jails because of tortures by the police. The armed forces disaffected by the Ghadarites were disarmed, their ring leaders court-martialled. By the Monsoon time in Punjab in 1915 the whole movement was crushed and completely restrained.

That was the time when Bhagat Singh, a boy of seven summers, was desperately trying to identify on the map of India places red with the blood of revolutionaries. Each time he scribbled something on his geography exercise book his lead pencil wavered between Meerut, Delhi and back to Lahore, the cities which had changed the course of history more than once. A child who used to 'sow rifles' instead of corn in his father's farm was so petrified particularly, at the execution of his hero

Kartar Singh Sarabha on September 13, 1915, that he pledged to his mother that if he did not see his country free he would sacrifice his life on the gallows following Kartar Singh's footsteps. At nine he completed his elementary education at Banga and joined the DAV High School at Lahore.

Sarabha's last words, on the gallows, were : "My only ambition is to see my country free. All that I did had is this objective. I have never done anything out of hatred for any person, nation, religion or race. I only desire one thing—independence. This is my only dream".

It is said Kartar Singh's grandfather came to see him in the condemned cell on his ultimate day and asked him to apologise : "You are dying for people. Nobody cares two pence for you". Kartar Singh raised his voice and said : 'Death is death. We all shall have to die'. Then he mentioned a name and asked : 'Where is he?' 'He died of plague' : replied the grandfather.

'And he'?, he mentioned another name.

'He died of cholera'.

'And he'?

'Of TB'.

'So you are grieving', Kartar Singh replied laughingly, 'that I am not dying of plague or cholera or TB. Is this death not better than all those deaths'?

For a boy of Bhagat Singh's feelings who carried Kartar Singh's photograph in his pocket there was no choice. He had chosen death : not death by disease but death on the gallows. This is what he promulgated in his public speech at the 11th death anniversary of Kartar Singh which *Naujawan Bharat Sabha* celebrated in 1926 before a life-size portrait of Sarabha paid tribute with blood by the two great women revolutionaries of the time : Durgavati and Sushila Devi, the wife and the sister of Prof. Bhavaticharan Vohra. They also played a very tantamount role in the future revolutionary activities of Bhagat Singh.

Another woman revolutionary of India who fought the British bullets both in India and abroad was Madame Bhikaiji Cama who, at 46, in 1907, the year in which Bhagat Singh was born attended along with Sardar Singh Rana, the International Socialist Conference at Stuttgart, Germany and delivered a moving speech. Displaying for the first time the historic tricolour flag, she said: "This flag is of Indian Independence. Behold, it is born ! It is already sanctified by the blood of martyred Indian youths. I call upon you gentlemen to rise and salute this flag of Indian Independence." The delegates rose and saluted the flag.

After the Conference Madame Cama reached New York and

delivered another memorable address : "Our best men are deported or sent to prisons like criminals, and there they are flogged so that they have to go to hospitals. We are peaceful, we do not want a bloody revolution, but we do want to teach the people their rights and throw off despotism."

On her return to London, she delivered one of the most daring speeches in November, 1908 : "Three years ago, it was repugnant to me even to talk of violence as a subject of discussion ; but owing to the heartlessness, the hypocricy, the rascality of the Liberals, that feeling is gone. Why should we deplore the use of violence when our enemies drive us to it? If we use force it is because we are forced to use force. How is it that the Russian Sophy Pervoska and her comrades are heroines and heroes in the sight of Englishmen and Englishwomen while our countrymen are considered criminals for doing exactly the same thing for the same cause? If violence is applauded in Russia why not in India? Tyranny is tyranny and torture is torture wherever applied. Success justifies any action. Successful rebellion against foreign rule is patriotism. Friends, let us put aside all hindrances, doubts and fears."

Madame Cama tremendously influenced the mind of Bhagat Singh: A great orator, she roared like a lioness and shooted away the British CID officials who were literally petrified at the mere mention of her name. Popularly known as 'Mother of Revolution' she asked her countrymen to overthrow the foreign rule : "Learn to shoot straight because the day is not fat when you will be called upon to shoot the English out of the land which we love so passionately."

This is exactly what Bhagat Singh did when he grew up.

There could not be any more heinous crime than the Massacre at 'Jullianwala Bagh', on the 13th of April 1919, at Amritsar. Bhagat Singh was just 16 years of age then.

"This ground was hallowed by the mingled blood of about two thousand innocent Hindus, Sikhs and Mussalmans who were shot by the British bullets on 13th April, 1919." So runs as inscription at the Jallianwala Bagh, Punjab's Gattysburg in the holy city of Amritsar.

The 49-year old Gandhi had just come back from South Africa and was a total amateur to the Indian political scene. He declared his intention of launching a Satyagraha. The two Rowlatt Bills had hit the stands in the Spring Session of the Imperial Legislative Assembly.

The District Magistrate, Amritsar, had summoned Dr. Saifuddin Kitchlew and Dr. Satyapal and kept them in an unknown detention. There were meetings, processions and jathas. Two persons died and several injured as a result of police firing. The tension in the town was so great that the whole city was handed over to the army authorities. In all 1650 rounds were fired. General Dyer's claim that not a single bullet was wasted was more than borne out by the number of human beings killed.

Asked by Mr. Justice Rankin, the Enquiry Commissioner in the Punjab Disorders Enquiry Committee whether he took any measures to attend to the wounded, General Dyer, the 'Hero' of the outrage, replied : "No, certainly not. It was not my job. The hospitals were open and they could have gone there."

Brigadier General Reginald E.H. Dyer, an India-born British army officer recorded in his diary : "I thought I would be doing a jolly lot of good." According to the Hunter Commission Report there were 1516 casualties accounting for 1650 rounds. Jallianwalla Bagh, says the report, "is a rectangular piece of unused ground covered to some extent by building materials and debris. It is almost entirely surrounded by walls and buildings The entrances and exists to it are few and entirely imperfect. At the end at which General Dyer entered there is raised ground on each side of the entrance. A large crowd had gathered at the opposite end of the Bagh and was being addressed by a man on a raised platform about 150 yards from where General Dyer kept his troops : 25 Gurkha soldiers from Nepal and 25 Baluchis from Baluchistan armed with rifles, 40 Gurkhas armed with knives and two armoured ears."

It was a sacred day for the Sikhs and Hindus, a secular festival for all Muslims and non-Muslims including Punjabi Christians. It was the *Baisakhi* of the Punjab and thousands of turbaned Sikhs and Hindus and Muslims in 'Tahmids' had gathered at Amritsar to celebrate to sing and dance round their rich harvest. A 'Mela' was to follow as usual every year, on the outskirts of the city but this year the climate was smelly with the activities of the revolutionaries. The visiting parties from the neighbouring village found Amritsar very different and dull. In fact the whole town was angry at the arrest of Gandhiji, Dr. Kitchlew and Dr. Satyapal.

The Bagh is not really a Bagh but a 'Maidaan', devoid of tree and water, where grass does grow but no birds sing. Nearly 20,000 people had accummulated there and the speaker was Hans Raj who was telling the anxious crowd the implications of the arrests. While he was speaking two files of soldiers ran into the Bagh from the Jallianwalla bazaar side through the narrow lane. There were English soldiers also with them. The sepoys knelt down and aimed their rifles at the crowd. In the twinkling of an eye, there was firing, noises, melee. Hans Raj shouted from the dias asking his listeners not to run and keep calm : "Keep calm : they are only firing blanks."

When General Dyer heard this he ordered with equal force "Fire down at them, why are you firing high." It was about 5.30 in the evening and the sky was clear. Punjab fields had yielded a very rich harvest and flavour of *Snogra* and *Sirson* had filled the air. Although firing continued only for ten minutes its echoes on the neighbourhood were felt even after ten hours. All eye-withnesses have affirmed that the firing was directed towards the gates through which the people were escaping. An old man who rushed the Bagh to search for his nephew describes : "On reaching the garden, I found my nephew's body riddled with bullets. His skull was broken. There was one shot under his nose on the upper lips, two on the left side, one on the left neck, and three on the thigh and some two or three on the head."

Aftermath of Jallianwala Bagh

Within minutes the Jallianwalla Bagh was drenched in blood. There were corpses all around. Some bodies were discovered from the drains. Blood flowed like drain water. Soon the darkness covered the city like an old blanket. In the words of Rattan Devi who became a widow that evening, the sight of the dead was hairraising, the whole scene catastrophic. The brave woman spent hours to identify her dead husband, wailed and spent the night all alone in a solitary jungle where she had dragged her husband's body away from the British eye, and waited for a charpoy to take him home to do the last rites. "It is impossible for me to describe what I felt. Heaps of dead bodies lay there, some on their backs and some with their faces upturned. A number of them were poor innocent children. I was all alone the whole night in the solitary jungle. Nothing but the barking of dogs, or the braying of donkeys was audible. Amidst hundreds of corpses, I passed my night crying and watching." Since the whole Bagh was over-flowing with blood there was scramble for dry places which were rare, the entire, 'Maidaan' wet with human blood. The hero of the massacre further told the Hunter Commission : "My mind was made up as soon as I came along in my motor car. I had made up my mind that I would do all the men to death." The Enquiry further revealed that he did not consider any warning to the crowd to disperse them necessary, that he did not also think necessary to talk to the Deputy Commissioner nor was the Deputy Commissioner present at the site. General Dyer concluded his evidence by saying that he considered Jallianwalla Bagh shooting a duty. . . a horible duty." "I wanted to teach them a lesson so that they might not laugh at me. I would have fired and fired longer, if I had the required ammunition I had taken an armoured car but found that the passage to the Bagh could not admit it and so I left it behind. I thought I should shoot well and shoot strong so that I or anybody else should not have to shoot again." In a telegram General Dyer's action was approved by Sir Michael O' Dwyer : "Your action correct. Lt. Governor approves." When the news of the massacre reached Calcutta, Subhash Chandra Bose took oath with a pistol in his hand, in a public meeting to shoo out the British from the Indian soil forcefully.

There was in the crowd, a confectioner of a nearby village who had come to sell sweets and see the Mela at Amritsar. Hearing that there was a public meeting at the Bagh he decided to venture there before setting up a stall at the fair. According to his relations, Mewa Singh's body was harboured all over bullets and bullet-marks. Blood came out of his skull as if a shower. Scores of students of local colleges were exterminated too. For the people of Amritsar this was the most unforgettable Baisakhi in their living memory. The great killing, according to Dr. Raja Ram, the author of monograph entitled "The Jallianwalla Bagh Martyrs" published by the Punjab University, was pre-planned and thoroughly pre-meditated, The book gives in details the names of all those who died on that fateful *Baisakhi* including the biographical sketches of some of the principal martyrs compiled from of official files and documents hitherto unavailable to the students of history. Coming in the wake of the 'Ghadar' and the 'Home Rule' movement the Amritsar massacres were another nail in the British coffin. The statement of the Lt. Governor, Sir Michael O' Dwyer that the "firing was to create a moral effect, though from a military point of view," provoked only laughter.

All other documents and contemporary evidences are united in their verdict that the Amritsar massacres were unprecedented in the history of mankind. While there was open revolt in Punjab, the wave of anger gripped the whole country. Motilal Nehru gave a clarion call to the nation to respond to the voice of the 'Lacerated heart of the Punjab."

The Government also retaliated. Military courts were set up everywhere in the state. These courts tried 852 men out of which 582 were convicted. Hundred were executed. Evey *Punjabi* became a soldier, every house turned into a fort. Secret societies were formed, everywhere there was talk of independence and 'Inquilab.' The more the oppression the more intensity the movement gathered. Jallianwalla Bagh was globally regarded as the most heinous crimes of the British Government on the unarmed peasants of Punjab. The massacre was followed by the Martial

Law and a reign of terror folled in the land of five rivers. At Lahore aeroplanes bombed and machine-gunned the rebels.

Martial Law was imposed in the districts of Gujranwala, Lahore, and Amritsar. A new type of flogging was introduced. K.C. Ghosh in the "Roll of Honour" says : "Thousands of students were forced to walk sixteen miles a day for roll calls : students and professors numbering hundreds were arrested and detained. School children between five and seven were compelled to attend parade and salute the British flag. Owners of property were ordered to bear the responsibility for safety of the Martial Law posters stuck upon their property. An entire marriage party, without having the least knowledge of any provision of Martial Law was flogged publicly. Six boys of Islamia School, Lahore, simply because they happened to be big, were flogged and no other reasons were adduced anywhere. To humiliate the people, open cages were constructed and placed in central places where arrested men, some very respectable, were confined like so many ferocious animals. Novel punishments like crawling order, the skipping order and others unknown and undreamt of in any law, civil or military, were freely practised on the innocent and the guilty alike. Persons were handcuffed and roped together. Hindus and Muslims were handcuffed in pairs with the object of demonstrating the consequences of Hindu-Muslim unity. This shocked the conscience of the entire country. The people's anguish was voiced by Rabindranath Tagore in his immortal letter to the Viceroy renouncing his knighthood as a protest against the massacre of the innocents at Jallianwalla Bagh. The All India Congress Committee met on 20-21 April, 1919, at Amritsar. The Annual Congress Session also took place in Amritsar. At Gujranwala there was serious trouble. Railway Station was burnt on April 14, 1919. A Railway Bridge was also burnt. The main Post Office was set on fire, the Munsiff's Court was razed to dust. The Telegraph Office, the Dak Bangalow, 'Katcheri' and a missionary school were also set ablaze. At Kasur and Wazirabad there were similar occurrences. At Lahore there was shooting and firing. Calcutta burst out in anger. In Amritsar more than two persons were not allowed to walk on sidewalks. 'Langars' (Free food kitchens) were forbidden. Electric fans were forfeited from the houses of citizens for the use of British soldiers. Anyone on suspicion was made to crawl on the belly. Flogging became more than common. There was all night curfew suspended only for a few hours in a day. All tongas (hackney carriages) were ordered to assemble at a place outside the town. The students of various college in Lahore were asked to report 19 miles away from their college, daily for a month. When the Martial

Law Notice was seen torn in the Notice Board of one college the whole staff and the Principal were arrested, taken to the fort under military escorts, hand-cuffed and detained in Lahore fort, and made to crawl and sleep on the floor without any water to drink or food to eat. A village headman was publicly flogged, then tied to a tree and an iron cage put around it. Summary Courts and Special Tribunals were the order of the day. While Col. Johnson specialised in Martial Law administration in Amritsar, Col. O' Brien administered it in Gujranwala, Captain Doveton in Kasur and Mr. Borworth Smith at Sheikhupura. As a sort of jibe at Hindu-Muslim Unity these Martial Law Administrators hand-cuffed and chained Hindus and Muslims together and put them in the same cage. Even wedding and funeral parties were flogged. Parades of naked persons were quite common. Even prostitutes were brought to witness the floggings. A huge punitive fine was imposed on the whole town. A reign of terror was unleashed and a wave of anger spread like wild fire. Udham Singh who shot and killed Sir Micheal O' Dyer, 11 years later, in a public meeting at Caxton, England and avenged the Jallianwalla massacre was only 16 at this time, an eye-witness to the bloodiest day of India's history. Among the dead which he saw were 41 boys and a baby seven weeks old.

On hearing the news of the massacre Bhagat Singh did not go to his school but took a train to Amritsar and visited the spot. There the boy stood for several minutes in deep trance, picked up some earth from the soil, rubbed it on his forehead, carried some of it in his phial. During his return journey he tightened his grip on the phial when the conductor asked him for the ticket. When he reached home that evening his sister asked him for the meals and the share of mangoes she had kept for him. Bhagat Singh who relished mangoes more than anything else kept fast that night. When asked why he kept fast he took his sister aside and showed him the blood-stained holy earth. According to his family members he paid tribute with fresh flowers to the holy earth every morning, investing new life in the garden's dust, taking new inspiration from the rounded orchard. One early morning he went to the river Ravi and pledged that he would colour its waters with the colour of his blood, which would merge with the five streams of the Punjab to create what he called the Freedom's Flood.

General Dyer boasted to the Punjab Governor that he salvaged Punjab for him. But history is a slippery maiden. It seldom obliges. The coming events showed that Dyer might have 'saved' Punjab for his immediate boss but he lost India for his distant masters and far-away countrymen. In a soul stirring poem Sarojini Naidu predicted the doom of British rule in India. So did Lenin from Soviet Union in his letter dated April 10, 1920 addressed to the Editor of *Amrit Bazar Patrika* which landed in the hands of British police.

For Gandhi Jallianwalla Bagh was no less than Government's madness in that it did not spare even the journalists and editors. Mr. B.G. Horniman, Editor, *The Bombay Chronicle* who condemned Government's action was deported. To fill the popular gap Gandhi was appointed the Editor of *Young India*. Babu Kali Nath Ray, Editor, *The Tribune*, Lahore was taken into custody. On July 21, 1919 Gandhi issued a Press Statement asking for the suspension of Civil Resistence Movement and demanding a Commission of Inquiry in the Punjab happenings. "I have been accused of throwing a lighted match", he wrote. "If my occasional resistence be a lighted match, the Rowlatt Legislation and the persistence in retaining it on the Statue Book is a thousand matches scattered throughout India". Gandhi entered Punjab on October 17, 1919 when the order against him was annuled. Pandit Motilal Nehru and Jawaharlal Nehru were already there. Purushottam Das Tandon and C.F. Andrews joined. It was at this point of time that Hunter Commission was appointed to inquire into the happenings in April earlier in the year.

The Congress Session sat at Amritsar in December 1919. It resolved to build a memorial at Jallianwalla Bagh in the memory of those who laid down their lives. The Bagh itself was acquired for the Nation. The Special Committee appointed to inquire into the inhumanities stated that the 'admissions made by General Dyer before the Hunter Commission established beyond doubt that the action of the 13th April was nothing but cold-blooded, calculated, massacre of innocent, unoffending, unarmed men and children, unparalleled for its heartless and cowardly brutality in modern times".

The Amritsar Congress passed 50 Resolutions covering a wide range of subjects starting from woes of the Third Class Railway Passengers to the recall of Lord Chelmsford. In a crowded session attended by nearly 50,000 persons Gandhi arose as the unacknowledged leader when he spoke on the Resolution condeming mob frenzy : "There is no greater Resolution before this Congress than this one. The whole key to success in the future lies in your hearty recognition of the truth underlying it, and acting up to it. I agree that there was great provocation given by the Government in arresting Dr. Kitchlew and Dr. Satypal and in arresting me who was bent on a mission of peace at the invitation of Dr. Satypal and Swamiji — these troubles would not have arisen. But the Government went mad at the time ; we went mad also at the time. I say, donot return madness with madness, but return madness with sanity and the whole situation will be yours".

The Hunter Commission's Report was published on May 28, 1920. The All India Congress Committee met at Benares on May 30 and recorded the nation's ire on its findings. The action of both General Dyer and Sir Micheal O' Dwyer was condemned. Though General Dyer was stripped of his command and thereby perhaps lost his pension a sum of £ 20,000, it was collected by the British community in India and presented to him publicly. A sword was presented to him by the British ladies for having protected their honour in an alien land. In London a public reception was arranged where he was exhorted as a hero. While this was being done in England, Duke of Connaught, the Uncle of King George was on an errand to India to assuage the pain of Indian hearts. In a public meeting, inaugurating what is today called Connaught Place in Delhi, he said: "I have reached a time of life when I most desire to heal wounds and reunite those who have been disunited. An old friend of India, I appeal to you all—British and Indian to bury alongwith the dead past the mistakes and misunderstands of the past to forgive where you have to forgive and to join to hands and to work together to realise the hopes that arise from today". Later, when the Punjab tragedy was raised by a resolution in the Supreme Council, Sir William Vincent, the Member who led the debate from the Government side deeply regretted the atrocities committed on the innocent people at Jallianwalla but managed to get the clause on deterrent punishment nullified. The result was that neither appeal of the Duke of Connaught nor the regret of the Home Member, Sir William Vincent could improvise the situation which remained as tense as ever.

The result was that when the Reform Bill was introduced in the British Parliament the following Manifesto was adopted by the British Committee of the Indian National Congress in England : "It is time that the British public had a clear vision regarding India, where, through the folly of the Government, a cloud bigger than a man's hand has already gathered threatening to break into a storm, the dimensions of which no one can forsee".

On the midnight of July 31st, 1920, Lokmanya Tilak passed away expressing complete platitude over the British attitude and disapproving their so-called measures to soothe the Indians. It was at this juncture that Gandhi who had rendered loyal services to the British cause during the First World War found it unbearable to remain moderate any longer. He returned his gold medal, 'Kaiser-i-Hind' as well as his Zulu War Medal. In a letter dated August 2, 1920, he wrote to the Viceroy : "Your

Excellency's lighthearted treatment of the official crime, your exoneration of Sir Micheal 'O Dwyer and Mr. Montague's despatch, and above all your shameful ignorance of the Punjab events and callous disregard of the feelings betrayed by the House of Lords have filled me with the greatest misgivings regarding the future of the empire, have estranged me completely from the present government and have disabled me from tendering as I have hitherto tendered my loyal co-operation".

To bring the Jallianwalla tragedy to its logical conclusion another story must be related briefly. It is said when General Dyer was testifying before the Hunter Commitee on November 19, 1919 that he did not waste many British bullets in the firing, a 21-year old Punjabi youngman of peasant stock was harking from behind the closed doors and the drawn curtains. On hearing this, his blood boiled and he took oath that he would avenge the massacre of the innocents, that he too would shoot well and strong and waste no British bullet. For the right moment, however, the man had to tarry for 21 more years, seven of which he spent in London, first as an engineering student and then as an engineer. On March 13, 1940, at 42, when the man got his opportunity, he used only one bullet and killed the killer of thousands recklessly. The ammunition recovered from this man was 21 year old. The gun was American, the bullets British. He also had on him a knife which he did not use. His diary bore ample evidence to corroborate the date, in fact the day, since when he was waiting for his victim. And now when he avenged himself in the Tudor Room of the Caxton Hall he felt he was free from all fetters. So he offered himself to the police. His name was Udham Singh.

When the corpse of Sir Michael O' Dwyer was being removed Udham Singh said that he nursed no personal grudge against his victim but he simply happened to be the Governor of Punjab at the time of Jallianwalla tragedy. My grudge is against the system he represented. I don't mind dying under a system where millions are starving. It was my duty to do so for the sake of my country. I donot mind dying. What's the use of waiting until you get senile. I do not mind what sentence is given to me : ten, twenty, or fifty years or be hanged".

Born on December 26, 1898 at Sunam his parents had left him to god while he was young. He was, therefore, brought up in an orphanage at Amritsar. As a boy he was arrested for making an inflammatory speech as soon after Jallianwalla Bagh massacre occurred. Later he went to America and took part in the Ghadar movement. On his return to India he set up a shop in Amritsar which had a sign board : "Ram Mohammed Singh Azad".

So when he subsequently went to London to study engineering he was popular to his revolutionary friends by that name. Accordingly when the Judge wanted to know whether he was Udham Singh he replied : "My name is not Udham Singh. My name is Ram Mohammed Singh Azad", Ram for Hindus, Mohammed for Muslims, Singh for Sikhs and Azad for the freedom of India.

After a mock trial and detention Ram Mohammed Singh Azad was assigned on the gallows and joined Bhagat Singh on June 12, 1940. His last words on the gallows were the same as uttered earlier by Madan Lal Dingra at Pentonville prison, London on August 17, 1909 and later by Bhagat Singh at Lahore Central Jail on March 23, 1931. Death made no conquest of these martyrs for now they live in undying fame.

Appendix I

Bhagat Singh Legend

September 27, 1907 (9.00 a.m.)	:	Born at Village Banga, Chak No. 105, Tehsil Jarrawala, District Lyallpur (now in Pakistan).
October 1, 1907	:	Father Kishen Singh and Uncle Ajit Singh released from Lahore and Mandalay (Burma) Jails respectively. Another uncle, Swarn Singh, also a revolutionary, released on bail from Lahore Jail.
August, 1910	:	Swarn Singh died at the age of 23 of Tuberculosis developed as a result of working as bullock in Central Jail, Lahore.
September, 1911	:	Admitted into District Board Primary School, Banga.
May, 1912	:	Joins DAV High School, Lahore.
April 13, 1913	:	Formation of Hindustani Workers at Astoria at Oregan (USA).
August, 1914	:	Ghadar Movement launched by Punjab Peasants returning from USA and Canada.
September 13, 1915	:	Kartar Singh Sarabha, Bhagat Singh's hero, hanged at 20 for revolutionary activities.

April 13, 1919	:	The Tragedy of Jallianwallah Bagh, Amritsar.
April 20, 1919	:	Visits Jallianwallah Bagh, Amritsar.
August 1, 1920	:	Death of Bal Gangadhar Tilak.
July, 1912	:	Joins National College, Lahore, founded by Lala Lajpat Rai and Bhai Parmanand and affiliated to Qaumi Vidyapeeth.
April 1921	:	Passed Intermediate Examination.
September, 1921	:	Leaves College under Mahatma Gandhi's call to boycott educational institutions ; goes to Kanpur and starts his underground activities.
July, 1924	:	Worked as Head Teacher, Shadipur, District Aligarh.
October, 1924	:	Organised Relief Measures during the flood in rivers Ganga and Jamuna.
January 15, 1925	:	Returned to Lahore at the instance of Hasrat Mohani to attend to his ailing grandmother.
July 8, 1925	:	Warrants issued in connection with Jaitu Morcha, but escaped arrest.
August 9, 1925	:	Kakori Train Hold-up case.
September-Oct. 1925	:	Worked as Staff Reporter *Veer Arjun*, a Hindi Paper, at Delhi.
March 13, 1926	:	Founded *Naujawan Bharat Sabh*a at Lahore.
December 12, 1926	:	Assassination of Swami Shradhanand.
October 23, 1927	:	Arrested in Dussehra Bomb Case, Lahore.
December 17, 1927	:	Ramparsad Bismal, Ashfaqullah Khan, Roshan Singh and Rajinder Nath Lahiri, Kakori revolutionaries, hanged.
June, 1928	:	Founded Hindustan Republican Army. (The Auxiliary Wing of HRA).
August 8, 1928	:	Organised a meeting of Hindustan Republican Army, revolutionary wing of Hindustan Republic Association at Ferozeshah Kotla Ground, Delhi. Declared Independence and Socialism as India's goal. Sixty prominent men revolutionaries and five women revolutionaries attended the meeting.
October 30, 1928	:	All party demonstration against the All-white Simon Commission at Lahore. Lala Lajpat Rai injured by the beatings of Mr. J.A. Scott, Superintendent of Police, Lahore.

November 17, 1928	:	Lala Lajpat Rai dies in hospital.
December 4, 1928	:	Punjab National Bank dacoity at Lahore.
December 17, 1928	:	J.P. Saunders, Assistant Superintendent of Police, Lahore, shot and killed. Bhagat Singh's dramatic escape to Calcutta by train, dressed as 'Sahib'.
December 25-31, 1928	:	Congress Session at Calcutta.
April 8, 1929	:	Throws Bomb in the Central Legislative Assembly, Delhi, scattered red leaflets and courts arrest.
May 7, 1929	:	Trial in Assembly Bomb case starts.
June 6, 1929	:	Historic Statement in the Court.
June 12, 1929	:	Judgment pronounced in Assembly Bomb Case. Sentenced to transportation for life.
June 15, 1929	:	Starts Hunger Strike in Central Jail, Lahore, to improve the jail facilities of political prisoners and under-trials.
June 30, 1929	:	Celebrated as Bhagat Singh Day throughout India.
July 10, 1929	:	Trial in Lahore conspiracy case begins at Lahore ; Bhagat Singh tried as co-accused.
September 13, 1929	:	Death of Jatin Das on 63rd day of Fast at Lahore Central Jail.
September 20, 1929	:	Kishen Singh files Petition.
December 25-31, 1929	:	Congress Session at Lahore.
December 31, 1929 (Midnight)	:	Jawaharlal Nehru unfurled the Flag of Independence on the banks of Ravi.
October 7, 1930	:	Judgement of the Special Tribunal, Lahore.
February 6, 1931	:	Death of Pandit Motilal Nehru.
February 10, 1931	:	Privy Council rejects Petition of Bhagat Singh.
February 11, 1931	:	New Delhi inaugurated by the Viceroy. The imperial extravaganza cost Rs. 14, 46, 71, 678.
February 18, 1931	:	Public Memorial to Viceroy.
February 27, 1931	:	Chandrashekher Azad killed in gunfight, Alfred Park, Allahabad.
March 5, 1931	:	Gandhi-Irwin Pact signed.
March 23, 1931	:	Died on the gallows with Sukhdev and Rajguru in Central Jail, Lahore at 7.15 p.m.
March 23, 1931 (Midnight)	:	Bodies taken to Hussainiwalla, near Ferozepur on the banks of Sutlej : Half burnt bodies of

		three martyrs thrown in the river. The site has been obtained from Pakistan in 1950 in exchange of other territory. It was formally inaugurated in 1968 when a *Samadhi* was raised there. Bhagat Singh's mother, Smt. Vidyavati attended this function.
March 24, 1931	:	Complete Hartal (strike) in Punjab, Bengal and U.P. At Kanpur, Ganesh Shankar Vidyarthi, an old associate of Shaheed Bhagat Singh was killed saving Muslim brethren and while preventing violence.
March 25-31, 1931	:	Congress Session at Karachi.
March 26, 1931	:	Farewell to Lord Irwin at Chelmsford Club, New Delhi.
March 31, 1931	:	Death of Shyamaji Krishna Verma.
July 1932	:	Arjun Singh, Bhagat Singh's grandfather died.
August 15, 1947	:	Ajit Singh, Bhagat Singh's uncle, a great revolutionary, who had lived abroad as political exile, died at Dalhousie.
May 30, 1951	:	Death of Sardar Kishen Singh, Bhagat Singh's father.
June 1, 1975	:	Death of Smt. Vidyavati, Bhagat Singh's mother. Died at Willingdon Nursing Home, New Delhi.

10

Could Gandhi Have Saved Bhagat Singh?

Could Gandhi do much more for Bhagat Singh with the tremendous reputation he enjoyed? People all over the country longed to save Bhagat Singh, Sukhdev and Rajguru from the gallows. The general outlook is that Gandhi spoke about them to the Viceroy at a personal level—not at the level of the political fact—and his request was turned down. But the actual situation is not so simple as we shall presently see.

"Before we delve deeper, may I, as a comical interlude, mention a related episode (alas, an imaginary one) written by Jitendranath Sanyal in his Hindi book on Sirdar Bhagat Singh. Jitendranath, coming from the famous Sanyal family, was implicated in the Lahore Case, but was acquitted. Immediately after his release, he wrote, "I think, the premier ever book on Bhagat Singh, which was a roaring success. Batuknath Agarwal of Mirzapur republished it after the book had been out of print for nearly 4 decades. Jitendranath Sanyal was requested to revise it, which he gladly did. At the instigation of a person who posed that he had salvaged a fact from the archives, he made certain additions". These paragraphs were added :

Gandhi and Irwin, the Viceroy

"Now it is well-known that the Viceroy, Lord Irwin, had conceded to Gandhi's request and had passed orders commuting the death sentences to transportation for life. The Punjab government was to be telegraphically informed of this order and the Chief Secretary had actually sent the amended order, but the Home Secretary had advised the Post Master General to delay the transmission of the message. In the meantime the Punjab government was told that the revolutionaries should be executed on the 23rd of March, so that the Viceregal order which was being sent by post would become infructuous. This explains why they were hanged at 7 in the evening, a most unconventional time for hangings in India. There were unprecedented demonstrations to save the young men, and the agitation was ripening into a movement. Now it is well-known, that as a result of this mounting force of the movement the government had commuted the sentences."

There is no doubt regarding it that this ingenuous story is very drawing and reads like a thriller, but alas, it is pipe dream of the author's friend, who misled him into thinking that he was making a scoop. Had it been that way, Lord Irwin as well as Gandhi would have exposed it some time or other. Now let us come to terms with actual facts. Writes Sitaramayya :

"Anyway Lord Irwin was unable to help in the matter, but undertook to secure a postponement of the execution till after the Karachi Congress. The Karachi session was to meet in the last week of March, but Gandhi himself stated to the Viceroy that if the boys should be hanged, they had better be hanged before the Congress, than after. The position of affairs in the country would be clear. There would be no false hopes lingering in the breasts of the people. The Gandhi-Irwin Pact would stand or fail on its merits at the Congress and on the added facts that the three boys had been executed."(*History of the Indian National Congress,* p. 744).

In this matter posterity is going to be more severe with Jawaharlal Nehru. Subhas Bose, who had an inside knowledge, writes candidly :

"At this juncture the responsibility of Pandit Jawaharlal Nehru was very great. Besides being the president of the Congress, he was the only member of the Working Committee, who could be expected to understand and advocate the left wing point of view and his refusal would have been sufficient to prevent the final acceptance of the pact by the Mahatma and the W.C. Unfortunately he gave in and so the pact was approved by the W.C. and the next day March 5th, the Mahatma and Lord Irwin put their signature to it. When the publication of the pact created an uproar in the country, Pt. Nehru came out with the statement that he did not approve of some of the terms of the pact, but as an obedient soldier he had to submit to the leader. But the country had regarded him something more than an obedient soldier."

Reaction of Subhas Bose

Subhas Bose goes on :

"Pressure was brought to bear on the Mahatma to try to save the lives of the young men and, it must be admitted, he did try his very best. On this occasion he ventured the suggestion that he should, if necessary, break with the Viceroy on the question, because the execution was against the spirit, if not the letter, of the Delhi pact. I was reminded of a similar incident during the armistice between the Sinn Fein party and the British government, when the strong attitude adopted by the former had secured the release of an Irish political prisoner sentenced to the gallows. But the Mahatma who did not want to identify himself with the revolutionary prisoners, would not go so far, and it naturally made a great difference when the Viceroy realised that the Mahatma would not break on that question." (*Indian Struggle*, p. 232).

According to Tendulkar, Gandhi when approached by hecklers after the hangings said, "I pleaded with the Viceroy as best as I could. I brought all the persuasion at my command to bear on him." (*Mahatma*, Vol. III, p. 79).

D.P. Das, who has gone very deep into the archives, opines that the story given by Lord Irwin and Gandhi, individually and collectively, is far from the whole truth. Thus Gandhi said he tried his best as an individual and Lord Irwin corroborated it publicly. The record preserved in our archives, says D.P. Das, portrays a different picture to the whole episode. But before we reveal this let us see how, many years later when Lord Irwin had become Lord Halifax, he cooled in the same version as was agreed upon between the two. Lord Halifax wrote in his memoirs :

"Mr. Gandhi said that he greatly feared that unless I could do something, the effect would be to destroy the pact. I said that I would regret that, no less than he, but would be clear to him there were only three possible courses. The first was to do nothing and let the execution proceed, the second was to change the order and grant Bhagat Singh reprieve, the third was to hold up any decision till after the Congress meeting was over. I told him that I thought he would agree that it was impossible from my point of view to grant him his reprieve and that merely to postpone decision and encourage people to think that there was such a chance of remission was not straightforward and honest, the first course alone was possible in spite of attendant evils."

Halifax then gives details as to the depth into which the subject was discussed. He proceeds :

"If the young man was hanged, said Mr. Gandhi, there was likelihood that he would become a national martyr and the general atmosphere would be seriously prejudiced."

In the course of the talk, Gandhi asked Lord Irwin, as the latter reveals :

"Would your Excellency see any objection to my saying that I tried for the young man's life? I said that I saw none, if he would also add that from my point of view he did not know what other course I could have taken. He thought for a moment, then finally agreed and on that basis went to Karachi . . . and I was told that he was roughly received. But when he had opportunity he spoke in the sense agreed between us." (*Fullness of Days*, pp. 149-150).

Quoting the above from Lord Halifax, D.P. Das asks, "Can the testimony of a reminiscing Viceroy, who remembered all these almost thirty years after the event, be relied upon without disrespect to him?"

The question sounds rather foolish, but it is not that foolish, when one reads what follows. Das goes on :

"Then there was the testimony of another competent observer Allan Campbell Johnson, in his book *Lord Halifax* written and published in London in 1943, which referred to an understanding between Gandhi and Irwin that Bhagat Singh should not get any reprieve. This is certainly a grave charge which has so far gone unchallenged in books on Gandhi published later in India. Johnson wrote :

Views of Emerson

'Sir Herbert Emerson, the Home Member, who was called upon to play a prominent role in Delhi negotiations, records listening with amazement to Irwin and Gandhi after the agreement had been reached by them that Bhagat Singh must be executed, engaged in a prolonged discussion not as between two statesmen, on political implication of terrorism, but as between two saints on the sanctity of human life'." (*Lord Halifax*, p. 313).

Mr. Das is rightly surprised that the implication of this serious charge against Gandhi has not been refuted by anybody, although there are individuals and organisations, very well funded by certain trusts, whose only engagement is to build and maintain the father figure of Gandhi.

Das asks a very pertinent question : "If we dismiss the evidence of Johnson on the ground that it was mere hearsay, how could we accept the contention of the Indian authors? The Indian authors also depend either upon the public pronouncements of Gandhi and Irwin or upon the gossip of their friends, who might have heard from close associates of Gandhi about the attempts by him to save the life of Bhagat Singh. Surely one gossip does not disprove another."

Views of D.P. Das

Das continues : "What is the evidence now left out yet to be examined? The Gandhi-Irwin negotiations which culminated in the formulation of the Delhi Pact were started in February 1931. The terms of the settlement were published in the Gazette of India of March 6. Usually no one else was present when the two spoke to each other in close confidence in the Viceregal House in New Delhi. Sometimes Herbert Emerson, Home Secretary (not the Home Member as Johnson mentioned him to be) would be called in for drafting the clauses of the settlement. (It was this Emerson who gossipped to Johnson)."

It is well-known that the public posture assumed by a statesman or a diplomat is often diametrically opposed to his own-private opinion or even facts. Das therefore went searching the archives, and he discovered, "Lord Irwin had left a detailed account of the day to day discussions he had with Gandhi. The minutes are a valuable guide to future historians, writing on this aspect of our national liberation movement. The Bhagat Singh' question was raised by Gandhi on February 18 with Irwin. Irwin wrote in his minutes :

Delhi Pact

'In conclusion, not connected with the above (talks of Delhi Pact) he mentioned the case of Bhagat Singh. He did not plead for the commutation (of the death sentence). But he did appeal for the postponement in the present circumstances.' (File No. 5-45/1931 KW 2, Home Department, Political Branch in the National Archives of India).

"On March 19 Gandhi had again some discussion with Irwin in the course of which he mentioned the case of Bhagat Singh. This is Irwin's minutes :

'As he (Gandhi) was leaving, he asked me if he might mention the case of Bhagat Singh that he had seen in the press the intimation of his execution for March 24. This was an unfortunate day as it coincided with the arrival of the new president (of the Congress) in Karachi and there would be much popular excitement. I told him that I had considered the case with most anxious care, but could find no grounds on which I could justify to my conscience commuting the sentence . . . He appeared to appreciate the force of this argument and said no more'." (*ibid*, Minutes, dated March 19).

Das goes on : "On March 20 Gandhi had a meetings with Herbert Emerson, who in his note to the Viceroy, recorded what were Gandhi's feelings in the Bhagat Singh case. He wrote that Gandhi 'did not seem to me to be particularly concerned in the matter. I told him that we should be lucky if we got through without disorder and I asked all that he could do to prevent meettings being held in Delhi during the next few days and to restrain violent speeches. He promised to do all he could." (File No. 33-1/1931, Home Deptt., Political Branch, National Archives).

Even to the casual reader, it will be apparent what Das very rightly concludes : "The public posture of Gandhi and Irwin is at variance with the facts contained in the files of the Home Department of the time. Irwin notes that Gandhi did not plead for the commutation of the death sentence, but pleaded for the postponement of the execution. How is it that while in private they discussed a question with a particular motivation, a different impression was sought to be created in the public mind?"

Apart from the above disturbing question, which defies any answer, how to throw light on the fact that Gandhi, the leader of a movement, which had declared complete independence as its motto could assure Emerson that he would restrain violent speeches by Congressmen after Bhagat Singh's hanging? Here are some more skeletons that Das pulled out of the accounts of history.

Emerson and Gandhi had discussed on the morning of March 20 just three days before Bhagat Singh, Rajguru and Sukhdev were hanged.

A letter from Emerson on that very day requested Gandhi to restrain Subhas Bose from holding a publilc meeting in the evening of the same day. This is Gandhi's reply in full :

1, Daryaganj,
Delhi, March 20, 1931.

"My Dear Emerson,

Thank you for your letter just received. I know of the meeting you refer to. I have taken every precaution possible and hope that nothing untoward will happen. I suggest that there should be no display of police force and no interference in the meeting. Irritation is likely to be there. It will be better to allow it find vent through meetings etc.

Yours sincerely,
Sd. M.K. Gandhi"

(FA/ 21/ 1931, Home Deptt., Political Branch, National Archives).

The whole episode, now that it stands fully dissected, is bound to pinch the nostril of any careful reader. The Congress hand-out to history supported publicly by such stalwarts as Nehru and Bose stands exploded and shattered. Perhaps even Nehru and Bose were duped, at least they were not aware of the full facts.

The two protagonists enacted a successful drama in public, but Irwin although playing on stage his agreed-upon-part in the drama up to the last, did not or could not bluff his masters. So he wrote the whole truth in the minutes, a copy of which, it may be presumed, was being sent telegraphically to London. Irwin had good reasons to deceive the Indian public, he could collude in this gladly, but to his bosses in London, he had to convey the real lucid truth in all its aspects. In his autobiography, Irwin could have exposed the whole truth, but either the Lord's memory failed him in his old age or like Casabianca he maintained his public posture to the very last. In any case we have two versions of the same affair written by him, one written on the same day, on the spot, for his bosses and successors to see, the other written two decades after the events. His reports on the spot are further accentuated by other supporting contemporary evidence. It is prominent from Gandhi's own letter to Emerson that he was not at all emotionally involved in the imminent hanging of the three youths in the way in which as a whole India, including Nehru and Bose, were. He seems to have been mortally embarrassed and harassed that such a thing should have cropped up when he was on the brink of tasting the first fruits of an event, which he considered a victory.

He was not even willing to harness the death sentences and originate them for a purpose as other public leaders had done before him. He did not want to say to the Viceroy like those leaders 'Listen to me or else...' It is not very hard to assess why he was so apathetic. Firstly as we have seen, he was by nature antagonistic to the very idea of revolution and thereby to revolutionaries. Secondly the tremendous amount of publicity which Bhagat Singh was receiving could not have exactly lightened Gandhi's heart. Apart from this he was absolute that India was at last, at the end of its travail and he did not like all this at this juncture, which was not only a disquieting nuisance to him, but seemed to be depraving him of his hard earned glory.

D.P. Das does not go very deep into the causes of Gandhi's love-hate (or is it only that of hate) relation with the revolutionaries. He reacts in his own way to the dual role played by Gandhi in regard to the commutation of Bhagat Singh's (throughout Bhagat Singh includes Sukhdev and Rajguru) death sentence. He says :

Gandhi's Responsibility

"It will be rash to run into a cynical conclusion about Gandhi. What was his motive in playing a dual role in the crucial days of February-

March 1931? The civil disobedience movement launched in 1930 had reached a high peak which disturbed the British power. They offered to negotiate with Gandhi, which Gandhi reciprocated. Their negotiation culminated in the Delhi Pact, which he wanted to save at any cost. Churchill's 'naked fakir' epithet was flung at Gandhi at this time and also against Irwin as the capitulator to Congress party. Similarly Gandhi was under pressure from leftist elements in the Congress for disowning the pact.

Gandhi wanted to save the pact from being wrecked. He genuinely believed that the Delhi Pact was much more important than the lives of one revolutionary here and another there. Bhagat Singh and his comrades were the tragic cases that arose at the time, which almost stood between a settlement with Irwin by Gandhi.

Gandhi had no difficulty in making his choice or option. In the light of his understanding, the course he took was the only one available in the circumstances. It is true it led him to the path of small deception for a cause which he considered noble and patriotic. Moreover, there was no serious reason for him to be particularly concerned with the Lahore case, which was the symbol of the cult of violence quite inimical to the principle he cherished.

There is no lack of precedents in ancient Indian history and our religion of taking resort to small lying or deception for the sake of noble objectives. There was the case of Yudhishtira of Mahabharata before him. Yudhishtira applied a phonetic variation in uttering a truth which amounted to a most blatant lie to undo the Kuru commander-in-chief Dronacharya. If this could be excused by the ancient Hindus including modern purists, Gandhi's public statements on Bhagat Singh should not be taken seriously. Take the case of the murder of Bali, the monkey king in the 'Ramayana', by Rama. Even the murder was justified on grounds of policy or statecraft.

So Gandhi's deception should not make us cynical about him. Nor should the discovery of his deception for a cause considered noble by him be taken as an indication of any absence of nobility by him. Let the Bhagat Singh episode be just a spot in his career and a condonable spot. Have not we condoned the spot in the moon, Yudhishtira and Rama?"

Can any condemnation of Gandhi be worse than the defence so naively offered by Das, obviously a Gandhi fan? In dealing with the political aspect where Gandhi is supposed to have indulged in 'small deception' we will see that even that way it was a great blunder. The soft spoken Lord Irwin wanted to stem the tide of revolution, and he succeded.

He was to leave shortly after this, to make way for Lord Willingdon, who could say, as he almost said that, he was not bound by the pact. By that time the revolutionary tides in the country had receded and the Congress leaders like King Canute could not order the tides back as they found later to their great dissappointment.

Before we proceed further, let us have a closer look at the Gandhi-Irwin Pact excluding Bhagat Singh and the revolutionaries. An incident in 1930, which is in a way unprecedented in the whole history of our struggle for freedom, will illustrate what I have to say. I quote from *The History of the Indian National Congress* by Sitaramayya :

"An incident of importance took place in the Frontier Province, which deserves to be described here. In the course of the repression adopted in the province, some Garhwali soldiers were asked to fire upon a meeting. They refused to board the lorry brought to take them, in order to fire upon a peaceful and unarmed crowd. These soldiers were therefore court-martialled and given long sentences ranging from 10 to 14 years."

He adds : "The release of these prisoners became the bone of contention between Congress and Government in the final negotiations of March 1931."

We have already seen what Gandhi did or failed to do for Bhagat Singh. But the case of the Garhwali prisoners belongs altogether to a different category. They were not revolutionaries, believers in the cult of revolution. Indeed, they had staked their life in the service of non-violence. Neither Nehru, nor Bhave, nor even Gandhi himself risked standing a firing squad for the cause of non-violence as they showed. These convicted ex-soldiers were the most precious fruits that the tree of non-violence—as advocated by the Buddha, Mahavira, Christ, Tolstoy and Gandhi—could bear. Mercenary soldiers trained and paid to shoot at people, in this case harmless and unarmed, refusing to obey the shooting bout and as a consequence inviting the death penalty, what could be a worthier cause for Gandhi to plead before the Viceroy? This was the cause of non-violence, which Gandhi professed to adopt more than any other cause.

Contrary to the report of Sitaramayya, the release and reappointment of these prisoners never became the cause of contention between the Government and the Congress. Did Gandhi insist on their release as a condition of the Pact? If he did, on what moral grounds did Gandhi agree to retreat on this point? We have nothing substantiating this from any source. B.R. Nanda, who has written a book on Gandhi, draws a complete blank on this aspect. In a footnote (obviously a passing after-thought), he mentions the case of Bhagat Singh, but he does not bring forth the case of the Garhwali prisoners. Either he failed to catch the importance of this affair, or he thought that this was a ticklish question which even his intellect could not solve, so it was better to allow posterity to devour it. In either case, he proved himself unworthy of the mantle of a historian. His loyalty should have been to posterity and not to the symbol of a clique.

So how could posterity overlook such a gross lapse on the part of the architect of the theory of *satyagraha*, because it is there in the Pact itself? The Viceroy did not leave this matter to chance or simply slur over it or bypass it.

The Pact is very positive on this point and exposes the abject climb-down, to which Gandhi was drawn into to by the soft-spoken Lord Irwin.

The Pact clearly states—

"(12-iv)—Prosecutions, if any, against soldiers and police involving disobedience of orders will not come within the scope of this provision.

(13-iii)—Soldiers and police, convicted of offences involving disobedience of orders—in the very few cases have occurred—will not come within the scope of the amnesty." (*History of the Indian National Congress*, pp. 741-2)

It is difficult to say what will be the volition of history on Gandhi as far as his dislike to Bhagat Singh is concerned, but his indifference to the release of the Garhwali prisoners on this occasion as a part of the pact, will always be seen by some as a stain on Gandhi.

After the hanging of Bhagat Singh, Gandhi should have yoked the revolutionary spirit born out of it, to the strengthening of the struggle, but this he did not pursue, because he perceived that the battle had been won. He was to be disillusioned very soon. History is bound to say that he was fooled by the Viceroy.

11

Judging the Revolutionaries

The most common practice of awarding death by British courts to revolutionary youths was nothing new to digest. It was as quaint as the establishment of the British Government in our country. Numerous youngmen kissed the gallows showing a smile on their faces. As the goal was supreme and indeed one i.e. to attain complete independence for the motherland, they competed with one another to prove their mettle in the best patriotic spirit they could show. The martyrdoms of Khudiram Bose, Madan Lal Dhingra, Kartar Singh Sarabha, Ashfaqullah, Ramparsad Bismal and many others were epitomes for the younger patriotic generation which stepped into their shoes with unquestionable sincere fervour.

There had been much resentment ; sympathy and excitement on the eve of the hangings of these revolutionaries. That had engulfed regional level or provincial level. But in case of Bhagat Singh and his comrades, the agitation, sympathy and fervour attained at an all-India proportion. The press deliberated in the shape of headlines, editorials, comments and speeches by leaders of all-India fame. Men, women and children ; peasants in villages ; workers in farms and factories, students in schools and colleges, intellectuals including teachers, lawyers and doctors—all spoke in a single voice of sympathy for them. It was something very unique in the history of our country.

Bhagat Singh's extreme sacrifice at a time when British imperialism was well ensconced in our country made him a heroic symbol amongst the youths of India. His sense of virility, his style and way of living, his writings, statements and speeches and also his acts of defiance against the British Raj transformed the story of his short career, unequivocably colourful and eventful, a legend and a role model for the restless youthful spirits which played their role, in some way or the other, when he was no more on the scene. He had tremendous ability. He was audaciously brave and fearless. Subhas Chandra Bose called him a true symbol of Indian revolution. 'He symbolizes the spirit of revolt that has taken possession of the country'.

'Like a meteor Bhagat Singh appeared in the political sky for a brief period. Before he passed away, he had become the cynosure of millions of eyes and the symbol of the spirit and aspirations of a new India, dauntless in the face of death, determined to smash imperialist rule and raise on its ruins the edifice of a free People's State in this great land of ours.'[1]

His revolutionary career stands as a lasting lighthouse to the patriotic element of India. Undoubtedly he had an extraordinary vision and an energetic youthful charisma which proved a potential challenge to the British Raj. Imbued with the patriotic fervour mixed with the revolutionary spirit, he had prepared himself sedulously for a life which was actually meant for any kind of a sacrifice for the noblest cause of the attainment of freedom for the country. Indeed his determination, grit, fortitude and fearlessnees were unequalled in the history of India.

'Bhagat Singh was not only one of India's greatest freedom fighters and revolutionary socialists, but also one of its early Marxist thinkers and ideologues.'

Jawaharlal Nehru gave appropriate tribute to his ideology, working of mind, patriotism and supreme sacrifice. 'Bhagat Singh did not become popular because of his act of terrorism, but because he seemed to defend the honour of Lala Lajpat Rai and through him, of the nation.

He became a symbol, the act was forgotten, the symbol remained, and within a few months each town and village of the Punjab and to a lesser extent the whole of northern India echoed with his name. Innumerable legends grew up about him and the popularity that the man achieved was something amazing.'[2] The very fact that it was an alien Government that had deep roots on our soil since the establishment of the British East India Company's rule in the eighteenth century and also a reality that it had become not only difficult but an impossible agenda to get them out of our country, had created an aversion, anger, hatred and dissatisfaction with the British rule. The early history of freedom struggle in one way or the other since the first war of independence in 1857 and the subsequent serious but infrequent attempts made at various levels as the anti-British measures to achieve the cherished aim for India showed that there was no much headway to the finality of the goal.

Whereas the dawn of twentieth century brought about some administrative and constitutional reforms at some levels to satisfy the growing demands of the leaders of the Indian National Congress, they were thought to be as 'tiny drops in the large ocean' in the shape of our political demands.

Role of Young Patriots

The style of discussion, appeal and mendicancy was substituted for by direct action and application of revolutionary methods by numerous youths who differed with the cult of 'slow moving' non-violence. The main aim of the youths who were quick, active, agile and violent in their thought and action, was to achieve results without showing patience. This type of model looked well, satisfying and feasible in their theoretical framework and they did succeed for sometime in this regard, but the proposition of achieving the desired goal appeared to be difficult, ticklish, hazardous and in many ways full of risks, even of lives.

The defiance of British imperialism in twenties and thirties with violent means and methods was indeed to ask for personal risks and unheard troubles for the families from police and British bureaucracy. Illegal methods of arrests and convictions were commonplace and the punishments meted out were indeed very stern and drastic.

The supreme sacrifices of numerous youths from different provinces of the country during the freedom struggle are great. There anti-British liberation movement was launched in spite of their own sufferings, tortures, whipping and flogging by police, tribulations and sacrifices. They were erudites educated in any university in the formal sense of the world. They in fact never felt the need to receive a traditional type of education imparted in the colleges and universities under the British Raj.

This type of educational policy, they thought, would enforce in them the slavish and subservient mentality which would make them good professional persons useful mainly for the British administration. So this kind of education and the institutions run under the British bureaucracy were not only discouraged but were greatly hated by them. A new kind of model developed in the educational field. It was the setting up of a chain of national institutions with main emphasis on national heroes and their achievements as well as constructive work. The admission into these institutions could not provide any hope for a better career or a bright prospectus in their lives, but they just joined them as a serious protest against any type of system founded, organised and administered by the British Raj. By acting thus these youths indeed sought no formal permission of their parents or guardians.

It seems quite obvious that such were their independent decisions or some of them did act under the influence of a few renowned and dedicated teachers imbued with patriotic zeal and fervour. The impact of the teachers of National College, Lahore was immense. Their ability, scholarship, dedication and missionary zeal had set a splendid example for them to follow and chose the line of action which was much dear to the cause of the country.

The patriotic fervour and selfless style of work with which these teachers functioned had created a new method of education preparing the students to become better Indians than to serve the *Raj* in a subservient way. Indeed, their consistent teaching was that failures of any kind must be met with courage and fearlessness in this world.

It is a remarkable feat on the part of revolutionaries to start national institutions—the parallel educational centres in various parts of northern India. The teachers working in these institutions were men of ability, scholarship and missionary zeal. They functioned with a small income. The national fervour and revolutionary excitement which they inculcated in the minds of the new generation with their practical examples, brought about a new system in the field of education.

The dull and drab lessons in various disciplines were substituted by disciplines which trained them completely to serve the cause of motherland, which was the need of the hour. Undoubtedly, this kind of association of the youths with the dedicated band of teachers greatly broadened the mental faculties of the former and enabled them to take a wider view of human life.

Slavery or bondage was the word detested by these youths and they prepared themselves for a cause which would one day break the shackles of dependence under a colonial Government. Besides the literature, a part of their curriculum, opened new vistas of knowledge for them which they used intelligently to achieve their cherished object in the spectrum of the anti-Raj activities.

'The National College of Lahore embodied the educational thinking of Lala Lajpat Rai. But all these institutions had two very great handicaps. There was lack of the right kind of textbooks and there was shortage of good teachers. Then what was the prospect for students, who would graduate from these institutions? Some good teachers were found for the college at Lahore. Jugal Kishore who had returned with a foreign degree agreed to forego all prospects and sink or swim with the new movement. He was installed as the principal. Bhai Parmanand, another savant and stalwart of the public life of the Punjab, nicknamed Devtaswaroop, the

Godly, also joined him. He had been implicated in a revolutionary conspiracy and was sent to the Andamans with a life sentence.'[3]

Majority of these youths were in their teens and at one stage or the other, they said all to revoir their institutions in order to do the political work in the villages and towns. The pamphlets and literature they distributed amongst the people and the arguments they went through with numerous youths of various regions who joined the revolutionary struggle at a later stage, obviously shows how much knowledge they possessed about the outcome of the revolution.

They were much impressed by the Russian and Italian revolutionary patriots, their thinking, doings and above all the marvellous success they had been able to achieve. They were also impressed by their political dogmas of liberty, equality and fraternity. This kind of model had top priority in their long-drawn revolutionary programme. Indeed, 'Long Live Revolution' was the slogan by each and every one of them during their speeches, private dialogue as well as at the time when they went to gallows. It is, however, an important phase of Indian nationalism and inseparable part of the freedom struggle launched in our country. This style had contributed in its own way as it clearly brought about a permanent nightmare in the British minds in India as well as in England.

With the passage of time, it became difficult for the British to crush these elements totally and they did prove as obstacles in the smooth functioning of the administrative machinery of the Government. The flaring proof of this kind of nightmare in the form of an assessment of the work of these revolutionaries and their achievements in various regions of India is lying in the private and official correspondence of British Viceroys in India with the Home Government. The very fact that their subordinates occupy a significant place in their private and official papers, concede a definite, concrete and significant credo to their anti-British activities in India. It also shows the degree and magnitute of apprehensiveness in the minds of the British bureaucracy in India.

The incessant revolutionary work by these youths required first-rate organisation of the whole scheme. It required dedicated workers who could implement the programme, big or small, in an efficient manner. They were meticulously trained in the art of maintaining absolute secrecy taking care that they were not entrapped by a policeman or a government official. And to maintain this in the best possible way, they disguised when they sniffed any kind of danger from the police. Such type of ability was very tactfully, intelligently, shrewdly, fearlessly and successfully shown by Sardar Bhagat Singh at a number of occasions when the police were very much at his trail.

There were occasions when he saw eye to eye with a policemen in a *mela,* on railway station or in a railway train. He eluded them in such a way that they could not recognise him or overpower him. This was mainly because he was tall, had an enviable physique and, above all, he was bold and fearless as a person.

When the broad-day light murder of a young British police official, Saunders, occurred at Lahore, the policemen of all the local police stations, the personnei of the Criminal Investigation Department and other police agencies were strictly alerted to search each and every corner of the city. These government agencies had gained so much of momentum in their investigations that it had indeed become an daunting task for Bhagat Singh and his associates who committed murder of Saunders to hide themselves and brew plans to escape from the clutches of the government.

To leave the city at an early date was the best kind of safety for these revolutionaries. The way Bhagat Singh disguised with the help of Durga Bhabi and others who eluded the police in a masterly manner, adds to their credibility and shows how they could face these risks at a time when thousands of policemen had combed the whole city. As a matter of fact by his consistent, unbroken and unbending opposition to the British Government, Bhagat Singh created an enviable and glorious tradition of highest degree of patriotism which unchallengedly placed his stature, aims and objects, philosophy of life and, above all, his anti-British doings to achieve the cherished goal of independence for the country, at a higher stature amongst the generation of revolutionaries and martyrs who laid down their lives with fevour and smile on their faces. Obviously, for the maintenance of this kind of tradition based on self-respect, honour and patriotism, they had to undergo numerous kinds of physical sufferings, spent sleepless nights and got through such hardships which could have broken the spirit and determination of a common man.

The motto was to keep the torch burning once it was lit by him and his associates.

'Bhagat was a revolutionary of the highest class. Human life was sacred to him. Saunders was not murdered because he was a British. It was to show the nation's agony over the heinous crime of hurling lathi blows at Lala Lajpat Rai, while he was leading the peaceful procession against Simon Commission. . . The action of the revolutionaries was two-fold. Firstly, to gain sympathy from the public at large for the revolutionaries which hitherto had been unresponisve to the revolutionaries. This was fine piece of propaganda as Lala Lajpat Rai was a universally respected leader. Secondly, this was to show to the bureaucracy that there was a party which would repay 'Tit for Tat' and should know what things were to come for them in due course. The action was solely directed against the system and not against any individual.'[4]

Gandhi's View

Manmathnath Gupta reminisced thus, "...the revolutionaries caught the eye of the masses all right. Taking the statistics, for instance, in 1930, in Bengal alone, there were, in two or three jails, some two thousand revolutionaries. Keeping this apart, every year, some fifteen or twenty volutionaries were jailed and hanged, about a thousand men were exiled to the Andamans and so on. Of course, the ordinary masses could not join to pay tribute directly into a secret movement, because they were not wanted there, but no revolutionary movement can thrive without their sympathies... When Jatin Das died, six lakh people were there in Calcutta around his body. Thus revolutionaries had approached the masses in a different manner . . . The revolutionaries did not long for personal publicity, but, on such occasions as the Assembly Bomb Case, or Bhagat Singh's Lahore Case, or the Kakori Case and our hunger strike in jail, together they always wanted publicity, because without publicity, without appeal to the masses, without the coming of the masses to help them, they could not succeed in anything."[5]

Durga Das Khanna recapitulates, 'They appeared to me very sincere and men of integrity and high calibre who would not profess what they would not be able to follow themselves. They were not after power or pelf. They were not in the movement for gaining any personal benefit. They were there to sacrifice their lives for the freedom of India.[6]

It may be interesting to know about Bhagat Singh's programme in jail. Probably, he never bothered about his execution. His main interest there was to go through new literature that came his way. Whosoever met him, found him very busy reading one book or the other. And often, persons meeting him used to pass on new books for his study. He thus could avail books from various libraries[7] and friends.

On 3rd June 1930, Bhagat Singh wrote a letter to Jai Dev Gupta asking him to provide him some articles which were needed by him in the jail. This indeed shows his taste and love for certain things which personified simplicity. '. . Also, please send one white shirt, chest 34, with a Shakespearen collar and half sleeves...Send two langots for bathing and exercise, made of some soft cloth, a few soap cakes for washing clothes, also some badam (almonds) and Swan ink bottle.'[8]

Bhagat Singh was also greatly influenced by a famous classic *Ninety-Three* by Victor Hugo—a work which elaborated upon the French Revolution. 'It has rather about 30 page introduction. That introduction was taught to us by Prof. P.C. Mehta for about two months, and in that period he gave a vivid description of the French Revolution. This book impressed him very much ; it made his character.' Other literature which moulded his thoughts consisted of *Mewar Patan*, *Anand Math*, *My Fight for Irish Freedom*, *Bandi Jivan*, *Mother*, *Heroes and Heroines of Russia*, *Three Musketeers* and other revolutionary books.[9]

His leanings towards Soviet Russia were so deep-rooted that he not only studied, time and again the model of revolution brought about in that country in 1917, but also greatly valued the deeds of their leadership which were anti-Czar in character. To an extent that he and his associates also sent their greetings to the Soviet Union in 1930 on the occasion of the anniversary of the November Revolution. This kind of felicitations showed the bent of minds of Bhagat Singh and other revolutionaries and the great change for which they had been aspiring to install in India. Besides, Bhagat Singh exhorted inspiration from Guru Gobind Singh because it was he who used to say : *Chidiyan noon baaz naal ladaoon, tud Guru Gobind Singh Kahalaon.*

In a melodious voice, Bhagat Singh used to sing in the jail-room.

Maan mera rang de basanti chola
Issi rang mein rang ke Shiva ne
Maan ka bandan khola
Maan mera rang de basanti chola.

Personality

Bhagat Singh had a magnetic personality. He was amiable, temperate and considerate to others. He was a fluent orator and a prolific writer. He made the well-known slogan *Long Live Revolution* and repeated it again and again till it became a household slogan. He had great intellect who could, with his keen insight, judge character of a person or a situation.

Always frank and jovial, he inspired his colleagues with highest degree of patriotic zeal and fervour. He always showed will, resolve and determination and never went for any kind of weakness or irresolution in the body politic of his organisation. He condemned the faint-hearted and wobblers and showed contempt for those who lived a luxurious live of official favour. By doing so, he was lucid in his mind that the sacred cause of the country would never suffer, at any rate, for their want of support.

As a Student

As a student, Bhagat Singh put on a simple dress—a *kurta*[10], *pyjama*[11] and *pugree*[12]. He was neither robust nor lean. He never liked to be fat. He had a desire to become robust but there was a deficiency in him. When he was a child, his mother was taking him to her parents, he fell from the horse and broke his two ribs above the heart. These ribs healed but they remained a curse to him as his chest could not expand.

He, indeed, wanted to be a broad-chested man. He also had acquired the chest expanders and did numerous exercises. Bhagat Singh had finer fellow feelings. He was very simple in his habits. He did not have any fancies.

As the leader of the party, he could not afford to have rich food. He was a very reserved type of boy from the school days. He played no game but he regularly practised *dand-baithak*[13] and running. He had remarkable intelligence and assiduously mastered each and every detail of the revolutionary work assigned to him.

Besides he was excellent as a speaker who always expressed his ideas with earnestness, passion and sincerity. At times he exhibited anxiety and restlessness and had become very keen to achieve the desired goal in the minimum possible time. And this kind of behaviour tinged with a well-chiselled political ideology always got for him a remarkable success in his mission which took numerous shapes at different places. Bhagat Singh wielded a powerful pen. He had expressed the inclination of his inner feelings which are devoutly patriotism personified. His patriotic verses in simple and chaste Punjabi language tell of his anti-British feelings which greatly influenced the young minds during the twenties and thirties. The beauty of his verses was that they were meaningful and also depicted the plight of a common Indian. Besides it contained the reality and philosophy of life of an ordinary peasant.

He did not favour the idea of committing dacoities. The same kind of feeling was shared with Chandra Shekhar Azad. But the dire necessity for money to execute their various kinds of plans forced to resort to this kind of thinking and action.

'Terrorism, armed action against the enemies of the people, we were convinced, was indispensable to a rouse the nation. But, clearly, terrorism by itself could not lead to freedom. In what channels and by what means was the mass movement unleashed by terror to be directed, what sort of Government would replace British rule? These questions, vaguely formulated were slowly asked in our ranks.'[14]

Manmathnath Gupta admitted in an interview about the paucity of resources amongst the revolutionaries. And this was indeed a great hindrance with them which proved a sort of handicap in the quick and speedy implementation of their schemes in various regions.

'Weaknesses were many, but they came together with the situation. That means, those weaknesses we could not comply' for instance, finance. Now, again and again, it happened that a group was formed consisting of a hundred young men in a district, of only such young men who had the capacity within five minutes notice to be ready to leave their homes and kill and be killed. The first problem then that faced them was money. So, for money they committed dacoities, train hold-ups, and naturally when they did that, they were arrested, as these were found out. Many a times, it so happened that revolutionary movement got complicated in this dacoity stage ; it could not go beyond that in many cases, and, again and again it had to give in. In certain cases, they tried other methods also. For instance, in Bengal, they tried to produce counterfeit currency notes ; that also did not work... During the First World War, they tried to solve this problem by accepting money from Germans, but that also did not succeed because the Germans did not win.'[15]

Their agitation took the form of hunger strike, non-appearance in the court of law, refusal to seek advice from any legal expert, raising of revolutionary slogans in the campus of the jail, defiant attitude towards jail authorities, battling against handcuffs—all led to the ex-parte justice without any kind of defence witnesses.

Thus the principal accused led by Bhagat Singh showed impetuousness, intelligence and precocity. At one stage, Sukhdev recalled with a sense of satisfaction, 'It was a good thing that everything came to light to the people. Dear Brother, I consider my arrest as good luck only for this reason."[16]

By his supreme sacrifice, Bhagat Singh attained the stature of legend and a symbol for the nation. The newspapers, bulletins, magazines and journals greatly eulogised his sacrifice at a point of time when the British imperialism was undoubtedly at its peak. The response of various sections for appeal to the Viceroy and the Privy Council was spontaneous. Although nothing was achieved from all these efforts, Bhagat Singh's popularity increased in the hearts of the common people. Indeed, the marvellous achievement of Bhagat Singh for the cause of the country and for his cherished aim of achieving independence for India, was realized by sacrifice of life at a tender age of twenty-four.

His own personality and heroism were well-depicted at the dock. His refusal to oblige his father's plea in the form of a petition depicted his righteousness for the cause he always kept very dear to his heart.

Indeed, these youths by their singular sacrifices imbibed patriotic and nationalistic values amongst the people. Thus these martyrs became pioneers in the revolutionary movement as far as the supreme sacrifice of youthful lives were concerned.

By refusing to refute the charges against themselves the revolutionaries disregarded and ridiculed the British justice. Their refusal to attend the court was tantamount to contempt of the court. Bhagat Singh's criticism of his father's plea for life had immense effect on the minds of the youths of India. It was they who laid the foundation for India's freedom and thus rendered the edifice possible. They are the immortals who have served and suffered and shall live enshrined in the hearts of future generations. Their radiating self-confidence was spontaneous in their thinking. And with the passage of time, this strengthening self-confidence and pride in them became a message of manliness, strength, unity, service and sacrifice.

In his short career which lasted hardly for twenty-four years, Bhagat Singh was undoubtedly sincerely devoted to the sacred cause of winning independence for the country. His ideal and tactics were preduently followed by his comrades. His ideal was to see the end of the British rule in India and to establish a kind of socialist state. Their organised struggle was opposed to the slow-moving constitutional and non-violent practices adopted by the leaders functioning in Indian National Congress or Swaraj Party.

In fact, they wanted to infuse ... '... revolutionary ideals and tactics in the public' and the expression of such ideas, actions and practices looked more glorified from the minds of those who stood as comrades-in arms on the gallows for the cause they upheld most dear and sacred.[17] It was in fact a most saddening aspect of the revolutionary movement when the bomb factory of the Hindustan Socialist Republican Army in Lahore was found out by the Criminal Investigation Department , the revolutionaries were arrested enmasse ; Bhagat Singh's Bomb Assembly Case was linked with the murder of Saunders and last but not the least, some of the revolutionaries had given in on account of the severe pressure and torture by police to save their skin from the onslaughts of the gallows.

Until the case was not finally decided by the judicial tribunal, there was excitement, tension, propaganda, demonstrations, meetings, by students and others ; dissatisfaction and resentment among the people. People had started questioning the kind of law under which the British administration functioned. Later on ex-parte justice involving Bhagat Singh and his comrades was severely criticised and condemned by numerous well-wishers and sympathisers.

Irwin felt concerned about the political developments in India in 1930s. These developments were mainly the result of the political activities and mass participation of the people of India in the Civil Disobedience Movement launched soon after the Dandi March under the leadership of Gandhi and both secret and open activities of the revolutionaries whose one of the prominent leaders was Sardar Bhagat Singh. The nightmare of these happenings on the mind of the Viceroy was incessant and consistent and he tried his best to resolve it by a solution which should have a wide support in various circles of India as well as the Home Government.

Refusal to Commute

The refusal to commute Bhagat Singh's death has been interpreted in some ways. It was in fact a dimensional decision, which was at last taken much to the distaste, anger and dissatisfaction of Indians. It was evident in the opening months of 1931 that Bhagat Singh's execution could lead to tumultous, noisy and rowdy scenes mainly against Gandhi and the Pact which he signed on 5 March 1931. Irwin has recorded in Fullness of Days, thus :[18] 'After we had made our so-called Irwin-Gandhi Pact he visited the next morning and said that he wished to talk about another matter.

He was just proceeding to the meeting of the Congress at Karachi, which he thought would ratify our agreement, and he wished to appeal for the life of a young man called Bhagat Singh who had been recently a death sentence punished by for various terrorist crimes. He himself opposed capital punishment, but that was not now in debate. If the young man was hanged, said Mr. Gandhi, there was a high chances that he would become a national martyr, and the general atmosphere would be seriously biased. I told him that, while I quite appreciated his feeling in the matter, I also was not concerned with the merits or demerits of capital punishment, since my only duty was to work the law as I comprehended it. On that basis, I could not think of anyone who had more thoroughly deserved capital punishment than Bhagat Singh.

Moreover, Mr. Gandhi's plea for him was made at a particularly unfortunate moment, for it so happened that on the previous evening I had received his appeal for a reprieve, which I had felt bound to reject and he was accordingly due to be hanged on Saturday (the day of our conversation being if I remember rightly, Thursday) Mr. Gandhi would be going to Karachi for the meeting of Congress in the afternoon or evening of Saturday after the news would have come through, and the coincidence of date from his point of view could therefore hardly be more difficult.

'Mr. Gandhi said that he greatly feared unless I could do something about it, the effect would be to destroy our pact. I said I should regret that no less than he, but it would be clear to him there were only three possible courses. The first was to do nothing and let the execution proceed, the second was to change the order and grant Bhagat Singh a reprieve, the third was to hold up any decision till after the Congress meeting was well over. I told him that I thought he would agree that it was impossible for me from my point of view to grant him his reprieve, and that merely to postpone decision and encourage people to think that there was such a chance of remission was not straightforward or honest. The first course alone, therefore, was possible in spite of all its attendant difficulties. Mr. Gandhi thought for a moment, and then said, 'Would Excellency see any objection to my saying that pleaded for the young man's life? I said that I saw none, if he would also add that from my point of view he did not see what other course I could have taken. He thought for a moment, then finally agreed, and on that basis went off to Karachi. There it happened much as anticipated ; the news had come through, many of the crowd were in a highly emotional state, and I was told afterwards that he was quite roughly received. But when he had opportunity he spoke in the sense agreed between us.'

It was indeed a unique class of devoted, disciplined and sincere workers whose political activities had spread like wild fire in many regions of India.

They provided a matchless kind of leadership to the movement of socio-political and economic transformation. It was thus a completely different class which provided zeal and new dimensions of dynamism to the people of India. And at that juncture of time, it looked slightly small in number if the number is considered to judge the real momentum of the movement. Its protests were strong and its slogans and cries were unsubdued. Besides, the main objective of the application of this kind of technique was to fight inequality and misrule that had become in many ways and at various stages during the first three decades of the twentieth century, unbearable. The padlock of indecision was aborted without any kind of extraneous consideration and the new class consolidated its position in a manner that it rose and showed results into a unique political phalanx and ultimately a serious challenge for the *Raj.*

Gandhi's object was always to convert his opponent by love. He did not set much store by political freedom on the crest of a passing wave of emotion ; he believed that India would be independent when she came of age and then no power would be able to suppress her in bondage. With this kind of feelings, Gandhi firmly believed that the popular 'Bhagat Singh cult' had been overdone and he did not hesitate in advising the young revolutionaries to abstain from violent actions—If you must kill English officials,why not kill me instead?

Lord Irwins Speaks

Three days after the executions, Lord Irwin gave vent to his feelings in a speech at a dinner in the Chelmsford Club, New Delhi, when he spoke about Gandhi, Bhagat Singh and the action of his government which he tried to justify as far as the law of the country was concerned.[19] The first necessity of progress in this or indeed in any such matters, is that everybody should do what they can to assist the bring back of a calmer atmosphere, and it is in this respect that I have been told that Government of India and I myself have made Mr. Gandhi's task far mighty by failure to commute the sentences recently passed upon Bhagat Singh and his companions. I can well believe that our action has at this juncture been a real difficulty for Mr. Gandhi and those associated with him, and I owe it to Indian opinion generally that I should use this opportunity, in a few words, of placing them in clear possession of my own thought. I take full responsibility for the decision at which Government arrived. I realise no heavier responsibility that rests upon the shoulders of a Viceroy than the decision of whether he should or should not make use of his special power conferring him with commutation or remission of sentences. As I listened the other day to Mr. Gandhi laying the case for commutation forcibly before me I reflected, first, of what significance it was that the apostle of non-violence should so earnestly be pleading the cause of devotees of a creed so fundamentally opposite to his own. I pondered also upon the quality of the responsibility that falls on those in whose hands it lies and whose duty it is to decide finally whether their fellow men should live or die. And I am free to confess that I would frankly regard that responsibility as an intolerable one to any man to support, unless he guided his conduct by adherence to certain very clear and definite principles. What should those be? First of all, he must satisfy himself that no facts have been put before him which were not placed before the sentencing tribunals and which might suggest a possible miscarriage of justice. There was nothing of this sort in this case, and it is significant that none of the petitions in any form, directly or indirectly, suggested that the prisoners were not guilty of the crimes alleged against them. For the rest, I comprehend it right that I should have regard, in the exercise of clemency, to the actual merits, as I can judge them, of the case pending before me. Of these principles, I, from time to time, on the advice of my council, concur in or remit death sentences that have been imposed. But I should regard it as wholly wrong to allow my judgment on these matters to be influenced or deflected by purely political considerations. I am well aware of the interest taken by large numbers of people in the fate of Bhagat Singh. But I could discover no argument by which commutation of that sentence could have been justified that would not have involved, if justice was to be equal, the commutation of all other sentences involving the death penalty. For I could imagine no case in which, under the law, the penalty had been more directly deserved. I have seen it suggested in the press that, even supposing commutation was impossible, it was highly undesirable that executions should take place on the eve of the Congress meeting at Karachi. I was fully alive to these considerations, and I will state with complete frankness the principal reason which led me to think the suggestion of postponement was not one that my Government could possibly accept.

'To suggest to Congress that there was after all a chance that the sentence would be remitted, whereas I should have in my own mind been clear that the sentence must be carried out as soon as the Congress had concluded, seemed to me—as it would have to you—a wholly indefensible proceeding. I am quite prepared to think that it would have made the immediate atmosphere at Karachi easier, but only at the cost of enabling Congress to say which justice that it had been treated by the Viceroy and by the Government with complete lack of candour. For those reasons I felt that the action suggested to me was impossible.'

In the tragic episode of the highest punishment of death by hanging awarded to Bhagat Singh, Rajguru and Sukhdev, a sense of anger, unhappiness and dissatisfaction have been expressed in connection with the efforts to save them were made by Mahatma Gandhi or any other Congress leader at the time.

The question is indeed not without complexity and it needs a thorough analysis of the events, efforts if any, ideologies professed and practised by Congressmen and the revolutionaries and last but not the least, the attitude and the working of the minds of British bureaucracy in early thirtees. It is a historic fact that Gandhi started the movement in a non-violent way ; the methods he preached and professed were against the cult of the bomb ; his technique of *satyagraha* maintained no secrecy and the whole movement, an anti-Raj indeed, was an open-type revolutionary anguish in a peaceful way.

Comparing Gandhi and Bhagat Singh

Gandhi always was against violent methods and was often critical of these kinds of devices practised by any Congressman in any nook or corner of India or by any youth professing the revolutionary cult. Under this kind of thinking a few questions knocks one's mind and the most important question is why at all Gandhi should save Bhagat Singh. Both had differences in their political ideologies and adopted policies and methods which were undoubtedly poles apart ; both never met each other at any point of time ; the former was a matured and seasoned leader of sixty-one years of age with a huge following of political workers of a well organised body and the latter was hardly twenty-three representing some youths of northern and eastern regions of India ; one was moving cautiously and slowly towards the goal of *swaraj,* the other was in a haste to achieve the desired resolution by adopting all methods beyond the perview of Gandhi's horizons the one believed in negotiations with the highest official representing the Crown in India, the other moved in the opposite direction by using violent means ; the one was highly-educated flanked by well-known lawyers, doctors, professors, business magnates and others, the other had come out of the college while he was not yet a fullfledged graduate with a following of the type of youths who had left their educational institutions not to return there again ; the task for one was straight, open and devoid of any kind of secret element in it ; the other had a zigzag way to travel in which maintenance of secrecy and hiding the exact identity was the predominant principle and lastly the one had tremendous experience of continuing the satyagraha movements for more than two decades ; feeling the pulse of the masses and seeking support of the numerous followers—men and women ; the other had little experience for launching a revolutionary movement at an all-India level.

One fails to understand the reason as to why Sardar Kishan Singh went to Karachi to attend the Congress session held a few days after the executions. If there had been anything much adverse against Gandhi and the Congress leadership, this kind of action on the part of the father of the martyrs is not understandable. Not only that. He eulogised the services of some Congress leaders for saving Bhagat Singh and his comrades and advocated the youths to work peacefully for winning freedom.

He further stated, 'You must support your general. You must support all the Congress leaders. Only then, you would be able to win independence for the country'. This kind of approach on the part of Sardar Kishan Singh clearly indicates a sense of reconciliation with the party and its leadership which had successfully maintained a deep contact and linkage with the masses living in far flung villages. Probably, he realized that the remaining youths would be able to deliver efficiently if they give up violent approach and reestablish their identity with much vigour and vitality by remaining united with the Congress leadership. After the executions, a deep void was felt in many quarters of the revolutionaries and they required a cementing force at an all-India level which could be vocal in giving vent to their feelings in a meaningful way. It seems Gandhi felt concerned about the order of the executions of Bhagat Singh and his comrades.

In his meeting with the Viceroy on 18 February 1931, he discussed about Bhagat Singh. He told the Viceroy '. . . if you want to make the present atmosphere more favourable, you should suspend Bhagat Singh's execution.' The Viceroy indeed was adamant and replied, 'I am very grateful to you that you have put this thing before me in this manner. Commutation of sentence is a difficult thing, but suspension is certainly worth considering.'

In between the first and the last meeting with the Viceroy to solicit the case of Bhagat Singh and his comrades, Gandhi greatly praised their bravery in a well-attended public meeting on 7 March 1931 in Delhi.

He also reasoned why Bhagat Singh and the rest of the youths had not been released. '...if you have been negotiating you might have secured better terms from the Viceroy, but we the Working Committee would secure no more than what we have. I may tell you that throughout the negotiations, I was not acting on my own...we brought all the pressure we could to bear on our negotiations and satisfied ourselves with what in justice we could have under the provisional settlement... . I cannot in all conscience agree to anyone being sent to gallows, much less a brave man like Bhagat Singh.'

Another meeting between Gandhi and Viceroy took place on

19th March 1931. 'As he was leaving, he asked (the Viceroy) if he might mention the case of Bhagat Singh saying that he had seen in the press the intimation of his execution by March 24th. This was an unfortunate day, as it coincided with the arrival of the new President of the Congress at Karachi and there would be much popular excitement.' The Viceroy at this brink of time would not agree to any viewpoint and was determined to carry out the execution.

We have already discussed in the last chapter that on the last day, Gandhi pleaded to the Viceroy about the commutation of the sentence. 'In the present case the chances are that, if commutation is granted, internal peace is most likely to be promoted. In the event of execution, peace is undoubtedly in danger.' But the Viceroy did not agree to commute the sentence. '. . . I am afraid' he wrote, 'for the reasons I sought to explain fully to you in conversation, I cannot see my way to feel that it would be right to take the action you respect.'

It appears from the meetings of Gandhi and Irwin as well the sum and substance of their statements that some efforts were made by Gandhi to save the life of Bhagat Singh. But it was not raised as an important political issue during the negotiations. There was no political pressure on the Viceroy. But even after political pressure, such a complex problem could never have been resolved in favour of the revolutionary youths.

Undoubtedly Bhagat Singh was an extremely brave and fearless revolutionary. For him death was immaterial. He was not to plead for mercy of file any kind of appeal for commutation of death-sentence. He discouraged his parents, near relatives and sympathisers to support his cause because he felt the British Government might attribute this kind of approach to cowardice or timidity. He was very angy with his father when he wrote a letter to the Government proving the fact that Bhagat Singh was not at Lahore at the time of the murder of Saunders.

Bhagat Singh wished to die for the cause of the country and he went to gallows without any kind of sadness or tinge of repentance on his face. During his jail life, he kept his morale very high and also greatly inspired his comrades. He always advised them about the great mission they were fulfilling by sacrificing their lives. This kind of model was indeed symbolic. It is quite evident that Bhagat Singh willingly surrendered to the police soon after throwing the bomb in the Central Assembly. This kind of gesture was not advisable as it ultimately proved fatal for him, his comrades and the organization.

He should not have courted arrest. Earlier he was an absconder after murdering Saunders, and even if now he had escaped, it would have proved fruitful for him and the party. Since then the police did not leave him even for a day.

Numerous cases were hatched up against him and his comrades. Unfortunatley, some of the youths became witnesses and as a result thereof, the police got full knowledge of their whereabouts. It became a serious problem for them to escape. The jail life and the arbitrary judicial proceedings adversely affected them and their organisation. They were condemned as murderers along with other anti-Raj activities for which they were hanged. A leader must live free if he is to fulfil the programme which he cherishes as sacred.

In case of these revolutionaries, the tragedy was serious and horrible. Most of them were cut off at the prime of their youth. Before their ideology could be shaped in a proper perspective, they were no more on the scene. Weighed in the balance, Bhagat Singh was a remarkable brave young man who always dreamt of a free India. And for the attainment of his objective, he was prepared to sacrifice anything dear to him, viz. his life. His sacrifice was indeed ultimate and therefore he became a symbol for the nation.

References

1. Ajoy Kumar Ghosh, p. 15.
2. Jawaharlal Nehru, *An Autobiography,* Delhi, 1962, pp. 175–76.
3. Manmathnath Gupta, *Bhagat Singh and His Times.* Delhi, 1977.
4. Transcript of interview with Jai Dev Gupta.
5. Transcript of interview with Manmathnath Gupta, N.M.M.L.
6. Transcript of interview with Durga Das Khanna, N.M.M.L.
7. Bhagat Singh knew about the availability of books in various libraries at Lahore.
8. Quoted in Gurdev Singh Deol, pp. 128–29.
9. Jai Dev Gupta.
10. A shirt without collar.
11. Trousers.
12. Turban.
13. A typical Indian exercise of continuous sitting and standing postures.
14. Ajoy Kumar Ghosh, p. 3.
15. Transcript of interview with Manmathnath Gupta, N.M.M.L
16. A K Gupta, 'The Executions of March 1931, Gandhi and Irwin', *Bengal: Past and Present,* 1971, pp. 99 ff.

17. Home Poll. File 139, 1931.
18. Earl of Halifax, *Fullness of Days,* London 1957, pp. 149–50.
19. Speech by Lord Irwin, Vol. II, Simla, 1931, pp. 362 ff.

12

Bhagat Singh and his Comrades

Chandrashekhar Azad

Bhagat Singh enjoyed the company of great personalities and learnt a lot from them and conceded a lot to them in return as he himself was no less. The revolutionaries who were accused in the Kakori Conspiracy Case, but who were evading the police namely Ashfaqulla and Bakshi were arrested after a few months and were implicated together in a supplementary case. Chandrashekhar Azad could not be arrested till the very end. He hailed from Bhabhra, Madhya Pradesh and had come to Benares to learn Sanskrit. Sanskrit students are generally conservative, but when the call for non-cooperation was given in 1921, it was the Sanskrit students of Benares who led the trail. Chandrashekhar Azad was one of them. In the 1921 movement he was punished 15 stripes. At every stroke of the stripe he said, "Mahatma Gandhi Ki Jai". This made him overnight the idol of the nation. His photo was published in the prestigious *Maryada* (Hindi monthly) edited by Sampurnanand. He was subsequently disillusioned with Gandhi and joined hands with the revolutionaries. He worked assiduously and turned to be a prominent figure in every sphere of revolutionary work. His was a restless soul. He was so devoted to his work and so vagarant that he was nicknamed 'quicksilver' by Ramprasad Bismil

When he saw that after the train hold-up at Kakori, police vigilance had beefed up, he quietly disappeared from the scene. When after the Kakori round up, the revolutionaries again began to reorganise, Azad came forward.

He had an open mind and although he had worked under

Shachindranath Sanyal and Ramprasad Bismil, conservatives among revolutionaries, he could foresee the storm that was brewing. Although a fighter all his life, there was an inner tranquility about the man and he did not turn about from new ideas. When he met people like Bhagat Singh, Sukhdev, Bejoykumar Sinha who had become Marxists, he had no difficulty in complying with them. There was no communication gap. For him learning was a process of growth. From a recalcitrant Gandhite, he had become an ardent revolutionary.

He was a man of courage, character and penetrating mental powers. His bone-deep honesty overshadowed his rugged, pock marked face. The party intellectuals felt that here was a psyche that was at peace with itself despite the fact that there was a price on his head. The relationship between Bhagat Singh and him became fervent and trusting one. With the modesty of truly great men Bhagat Singh and the intellectuals of the party gave credence to Azad's superiority.

Thus Bhagat Singh and Azad, this incomparable twin were like one personality. Neither of them felt that the other was working under the wing or shadow of the other. Their minds were so similar that there was hardly any need for them to talk a great deal.

Dr. Mahore writes : "The secret of Azad's success did not lie so much in his heroism as in his capacity to establish soulful rapport immediately with all and sundry he met. He did not confine himself to touching political cords, he touched the more delicate human cords. Hefty, rather short, of brownish colour with a pock marked rugged face, this exterior was amply compensated by nature by a bestowal on him of a beauty reflecting inner tranquillity. To know him was to adore him."

As long as the Kakori conspiracy case was raging on, Azad was kept in leash for if he did anything, the judge would spew his vengeance on the accused. Manindranath Banerjee was forbidden by the leadership from becoming a live wire on the same ground. But when by December 1927 Bismil and 3 others were hanged, that excuse no longer held and Azad came out of his long hibernation.

Bhagat Singh was already active. A band of bold youths now inseparable from him had gathered round him. When Azad and Bhagat Singh were girding up their loins to take a huge leap into history, Manindranath Banerjee, a youth from Benares lugged two bullets into Jatin Banerjee, D.S.P. , police saying—'Here are your thirty pieces of silver for getting Lahiri hanged.'

The weapon used by Manindra could not be recovered although Manindra was arrested on the spot. This weakened the court case and he could only be sentenced to 10 years R.I. Later on Manindra Banerjee died under very tragic circumstance on the 20th of June, 1934, in Fatehgarh Central Prison.

The union of Bhagat Singh and Azad was a great event in the revolutionary movement. Thus burgeoned a relationship, which executed wonders. There had never been a time when both did not achieve rapport stimulating and enjoying each other's heroism.

Up to this time Bhagat Singh had been more or less a bookish type of revolutionary. Azad contrastingly was a seasoned and hardened revolutionary. He had seen action, was an expert in hold-ups. He had participated in at least a dozen of them.

He had not wasted his period of hibernation. He had become a crack shot and a good driver. He had become an expert in giving the police spies the slip. He had many narrow escapes.

Again we shall quote Dr. Mahore : "Once while living on the bank of the Satar in Jhansi he was returning to Jhansi along with another *sadhu*. Two constables interrupted him and asked him to accompany them to the police station. Probably the story of the price on Azad's head had reached them and they were suspecting and apprehending everybody. They shot the question—'Tell us if you be Azad'.

Immediately he came out with a story punning on the word *Azad* (independent). Baring his teeth like a fool, in a drawl that was natural to *sadhus* he said, 'Er . . . of course I am Azad, independence being our very nature. We pray to the monkey god Hanuman and lead a life without worries er . . .' But the policemen were adamant. Azad gently threatened, 'If we are late, the god Hanuman er . . would also be late, and you know er . . . .' The constables were not impressed, they still insisted. At this, as became a holy man, he lost his temper and admonished, 'For you, may be, the inspector be important, but I will only obey the monkey god'."

Saying this he walked away. Dr. Mahore writes : "It was fortunate for the constables that this stance convinced them that he was really a holy man, otherwise it would have been their last day."

"A murder occurred in the vicinity of the hideout. The police suspecting that burglars were hiding in the nearby jungle were very active in that area. Azad was quite safe as Harishanker, the brother of the village chief. But now the police asked him about his antecedents, to which Azad said, 'Er . . . . the *Sadhu* is homeless. You shouln't ask a *sadhu* about his antecedents, because this militates against his vow'."

For a while, everything cooled down, but he anticipated that another wave, and he would be washed away. His drawl and his quaint mannerisms would not save him. He realised it was time to change his jungle hide-out. Master Rudranarayan, a photographer of Jhansi lodged him with one Ramanand, a motor driver. Here he lived as the younger brother of the driver and started working in a motor company.

Both Azad and Bhagat Singh needed each other, fulfilled each other. Without Azad, Bhagat Singh could not become what he was nor could Azad attain the eminence that he achieved.

Yashpal in a couple of paragraphs brings out the essence of Azad's leadership—

"Azad is reputed to be a dare devil. As an individual he was certainly a dare devil, but when he was leading some action , he was very calculative and cautious. Every step that he took was measured. He did not lose sight of the objective. No risk-no game, this he knew full well, but the question was would he win after the risk? On such occasions he was not emotional, he was all mathematics . On the day we went to rescue Bhagat Singh from the gate of the Borstal prison, I was spoiling for a fight, my hands were itching. Azad understood my condition and growled—'Stop.' After ten minutes I understood that he was right. Had I been allowed to follow my inveterate itch, some six or seven casualties would have occurred which would have included Bhagat Singh and Dutt. It was owing to this sterling quality that he became the unquestioned commander-in-chief of the party."

Bhagavaticharan Vohra

Among Bhagat Singh's eminent companions Vohra should be rated only second to Azad. It occurred to an important outsider like Muzaffar Ahmed that Bhagat Singh was working under Vohra. Ahmed was not very much off the mark. Bhagat Singh is known as the leader of *Naujawan Bharat Sabha,* but Yashpal disclosed that it was under their twin leadership that the Sabha marched from victory to victory. Vohra had held the key post of publicity secretary.

This proves that in the eyes of the comrades, Vohra was effective in doing the work of mass contact. Vohra's predecessors had come from Gujarat. His father was a railway official, whose work was rated so high to honour him with the title *Rai Sahib.* Bhagavaticharan's grandfather used to do *kitabet* (copying for lithography). It is said he used to do that much to earn one rupee each day. After that, he would stop all work. In 1925 'The Revolutionary' was distributed secretly through the length and breadth of India. A copy of the leaflet came to Prof. Jaychandra, but they were stacked in Bhagavaticharan's home, because he till then was considered a safe layman in the eyes of the police.

Bhagavaticharan Vohra was married very early. Durga, his wife, was devoted to him and, became a revolutionary knowing fully well that the path was one that bristled with thorns. When she first married, she had no pretensions to learning, but gradually she qualified all the examinations, working at the same time in the party. Bhagavaticharan's life culminated with an accident.

Rajguru

Rajguru and Sukhdev were hanged along with Bhagat Singh. Born in Poona in 1909, Rajguru lost his father at the age of 6. He was looked after by his elder brother.

Rajguru was an asset to the revolutionary party. He was always the leader in taking risks. When the blue-print for forcibly rescuing Jogesh Chatterjee from jail was prepared, Rajguru was not included in the plans. When he was apprised of it he almost forced the leaders to include him. Again when a decision was reached to avenge the death of Lala Lajpat Rai, Rajguru insisted that he should do the shooting. He offered to step inside the police headquarters, Lahore, and shoot the British police chief. Azad had reconnoitred the terrain thoroughly, so he thought Rajguru's offer too reckless.

He had formed a plan and stuck to it. It was an integrated plan and nothing was left to chance. When it was decided that Bhagat Singh should go alongwith another revolutionary and drop bombs in the Central Assembly and Bhagat Singh went for B.K. Dutta as his companion, Rajguru protested. Rajguru wanted to take the place of Bhagat Singh and when he was told that the latter was chosen because, if apprehended, he could utter the right statement regarding socialism being the goal of the party, Rajguru insisted on replacing Dutt.

According to Dr. Mahore : "Rajguru remarked to Azad—'Was it necessary to give the statement in English? If so, I shall learn the whole damned thing by throat and deliver it, I assure you, without a single mistake. I learned the whole of Sanskrit grammar by rote, so a few pages of the statement is nothing to me.' When he pleaded his case very hard, Azad gave him a chit and sent him to Bhagat Singh to take him along in place of Dutt. But Bhagat Singh was adamant. Then Rajguru returned saying, 'By myself I can work wonders'." May be one could say that this was not a very healthy streak in him, as apparent in all this, but his was a dedicated and a very restless soul.

He had the reputation of sleeping very soundly and also falling asleep at awkward times. Once he and Bhagat Singh were travelling together. The train was to arrive at the station at 2 a.m. Bhagat Singh had not slept some nights, so he asked Rajguru keep awake and wake him up at one-thirty. Bhagat Singh woke up at the stroke of three and found Rajguru missing. This intrigued him. Ultimately he found the latter happily coiled and sleeping in a corner.

Once Azad, Rajguru and Dr. Mahore were travelling from Kanpur to Jhansi. They were cleverly dressed in dirty clothes to pass off as working class people. When the train entered the hilly area of Bundelkhand, Rajguru burst out—'This terrain is good for Shivaji type of guerilla warfare . . .' This outburst chilled Azad to his bones. This could expose their identity to the other passengers. Azad immediately snapped—'Sonny, forget that nonsense about Shivaji or whoever he is and you my wife's brother, better sing that *Jab qua fas se lash nikli bulbule nashad ki*', and gave him a kick. Rajguru realised his mistake.

In the case of the murder of Saunders, it was his first bullet that did the job. People praised him but he remorsefully answered—'I had put my sight on his chest and the bullet hit him on the head.' Later on Dr. Mahore discovered that Rajguru's marks-manship was not to be blamed but the bullet was a bit different. It had been forcibly fitted into the pistol.

Once Bhagat Singh, Rajguru and Shiv Verma were sleeping in a room. Shiv Verma woke up with an awkward feeling at a hissing sound. He pulled out his torch and found that a snake with its hood spread out was hissing some 2 feet from Rajguru. Verma woke Bhagat Singh up and dragged Rajguru by his feet warning him about the snake. Rajguru turned on his side and said, 'Don't disturb me', and napped again. By that time the snake, disturbed by the torch had left.

Shiv Verma has related another story about him. Verma and Rajguru were to board a train at Gorakhpur, but there was still a lot of time. So Verma went to meet a revolutionary friend Haldhar Bajpai and asked Rajguru to wait for him. Verma returned from his meeting on time for the train, but Rajguru was missing. So he boarded the train. Next day Rajguru reached the place and complained : 'How is it, you travelled without me?' He revealed that to spend time and to ward the police off he had gone to enjoy a nap among the beggars at the railway station.

Rajguru had somewhere come across a beautiful calendar which he liked. He hung it on the wall inside the hide-out. When Azad came in he noticed the calendar with the picture of a beautiful nymphet. This seemed to Azad a breach of the revolutionary vow. He tore the calendar to pieces and threw them in the corner saying, 'If this is what the fellow is after, he should leave his pistols and go home. No room for double think here. When Rajguru came back, he noticed that his calendar was gone. People directed him to the torn pieces. Rajguru picked up the pieces and growled—'Who has done this?'

At this Azad snarled, ' It is I . . . .'

'—Why did you tear this thing of beauty.'

'—Because it was beautiful.'

'—Would you then tear to pieces and break everything that is beautiful?'

'—Yes, I would . . .'

'—Would you break the Tajmahal?'

'—Yes I would if I could.'

All this was said in anger.

One hour after this Rajguru was still complaining, 'We set out to make this world more beautiful, and here we are out to destroy all beauty. This is nonsense.' This monologue of a tried comrade cooled Azad. He felt that he had overshot the mark and had been misunderstood. He said, 'Look , I didn't mean that I would break the Tajmahal. What I meant was that we have taken a vow and we should have all our sights on the target. I do not want that beauty should lead us astray . . . just now.'

Sukhdev

Sukhdev was born at Lyallpur in 1907. His father passed away 3 months before he was born and he was brought up by his father's brother, a grain merchant. His uncle was a freedom fighter. Sukhdev esteemed him for this. Sukhdev was a weak child. In reality all the members of his family were like that. He used to make mockery of this weakness—'My father had 8 brothers and sisters. One of them was gobbled by mice'.

By nature Sukhdev was outspoken and independent. His dress and living style verged on the border of eccentricity. He was nicknamed *ganwar* (rugged, rustic). For a long time he and Bhagat Singh were at par and comrades could not decide which one of them would take the leadership.

Even Shiv Verma says, 'It seemed to me that Sukhdev was a greater organiser.' Sukhdev was a man who gave thought to detail, whereas Bhagat Singh was a man of vision ignoring small things. Shiv Verma disliked Bhagat Singh's 'self-centredness'. "Bhagat Singh," he says, "cared for his own likes and dislikes, his won food and clothes so much that he ignored the needs of others. Sukhdev was just the opposite. He thought more for others and less of himself."

Sukhdev showed a great affinity of flowers specially the jasmine. Once Shiv Verma and Sukhdev were strolling in front of a temple, where garlands were on sale. Sukhdev was attracted by the jasmine garlands. He immediately bought two, one he wore round his own neck, the other he offered Verma, who twined it round his hand. Sukhdev insisted that Verma should wear it round his neck properly. But Verma refused. He snatched the garland from Verma's hand, twined it round his own and playing with it, barked out—'If you don't love the fragrance of flowers, go and smell something else . . . .' In reality, all revolutionaries adored beauty but they forcibly restrained themselves to focus more on their objective.

The importance of Sukhdev as a revolutionary is evident from the fact that although he was not actually involved in the murder of Saunders, he was sentenced to death. He, however, behaved sometimes very quizzically.

Once during a long hunger-strike he broke it and later again rejoined it. After arrest he made a confession, then denied. He confessed, not out of fear or a weakness of the mind, but out of eccentricity and pride that without him the country would not be emancipated, and that the earth would fail to rotate on her axis. Ideologically he was very clear as is evident from the letter which he wrote to Gandhi :

"The goal of revolutionaries is to establish a socialist republic. In this there is no room for compromise. You have been labouring under the idea that we believe in outright destruction. Nothing can be further from the truth. The truth is that we weigh every step that we take, alone with the environment, and we are fully alive to our responsibilities. In spite of understanding the importance of our constructive responsibilities, the present circumstances have forced us to concentrate on the destructive side. . . However the day is not far when the masses under the leadership of revolutionaries would march towards the lofty goal of socialist republic."

Giving a personal opinion, he wrote in the course of this letter : "The three revolutionaries condemned to death, have accidentally become very famous, but they do not constitute the revolutionary movement. Indeed the country would gain more, if they are hanged."

Jatindranath Das

Jatin Das was in no sense a junior partner of Bhagat Singh. Das is the representative of another glorious tradition of the revolutionaries in which death lays his icy hand very slowly, though all the time keeping an option of life open to the victim.

Revolutionaries are in general associated with violence, but death by hunger-strike is the noblest form of non-violence. It is not necessary to esteem hunger-strike spiritually as Gandhi did, although every time Gandhi went on fast, he did it with great show keeping his gun-powder of propaganda obscure. Bukharin interpreted hunger-strikes as an intense appeal to public opinion in which the man using this weapon stakes his own life. The first ever Indian freedom-fighter to sacrifice his life in this way was Ramrakha, revolutionary who was imprisoned far away in the Andamans. He is completely forgotten. When he went to the Andamans, prisoners were not allowed to put on the sacred thread. To him it appeared to be a great humiliation he went on hunger-strike and starved to death. That was in the second decade of gone century.

Revolutionaries, who appeared after Ramrakha, thought the sacred thread a cause not worth fighting for, indeed they would themselves burn the so-called sacred thread, as it is only a caste-mark, but all this does not mitigate the importance of Ramrakha as a pioneer freedom fighter.

Jatin Das was born in Calcutta in 1904 in a well-to-do family. The call of the non-cooperation movement was hot when he had just left school. He plunged into the movement, was arrested and released after 4 days. He was re-arrested and this time he was sentenced to one month.

After release he was again found to be on the culpable side by the British law and was sentenced to 3 months R.I. He returned with his health broken. He joined a college later on, then came in contact with Shachindranath Sanyal and joined the revolutionary party. He rose to be one of its leaders when the Kakori group was inside jail and died on the 63rd day of his hunger-strike (details later on).

He was hailed as a national hero. In spite of this Gandhi kept quiet, and when he did speak, he said that Das could die in such a manner because he was a supporter of non-violence. This was a completely false and a misleading statement. Das had been a leader of the party and had come to Benares and taken part in a hold-up. I do not believe in hierarchy among freedom fighters, but it is a fact of history that only revolutionary prisoners gave their lives in hunger-strikes. It is another important fact of history, that the present classification of prisoners, still in vogue in free-India, was the result of the supreme sacrifice of Jatin Das.

The Lahore case partially owes its phenomenal fame to the fact that it presented the various ways in which revolutionaries offered their lives. Bhagat Singh, Rajguru and Sukhdev were hanged ; Jatin Das starved to death and Chandrashekhar Azad was killed in a gunfight.

B.K. Dutt

Batukeshwar Dutt sentenced to a life term became as famous as Bhagat Singh, Sukhdev and Rajguru, who were hanged. Yet it is true of history that none of his associates, who have written about Bhagat Singh in detail, gave him much importance beyond this that he was chosen to be his associate in the Assembly Bomb affair. Dutt proved quite competent for the job he was selected for. He made an indepth study of Marxism in the Andamans, but it appears that later on he was swirled back into the vortex of some form of religion like many other Marxists.

At least he was better than those, who wear their Marxism like an overcoat while on the platform, and discard it on entering their house, and inside they behave like good Hindus or devoted Muslims.

Bejoykumar Sinha

Studious Rajkumar Sinha was convicted in the Kakori revolutionary conspiracy case. After his incarceration his younger brother, who was a successful journalist became more active. Suresh Bhattacharya was the lynchpin round whom a galaxy of important revolutionaries gathered. The Sinha brothers and B.K. Dutt were the most unparalled of them. Bejoy rose to be one of the party intellectuals. He wrote *In Andamans—the Indian Bastille* and other books.

Yashpal

Yashpal wrote his revolutionary memoirs *Simhavalokan* in 3 volumes. He, however, had no connection with either the Saunders murder or the Assembly bomb case. He rose to be a top Hindi novelist. His life is itself a novel with plenty of ups and downs.

Kamalnath Tiwari

Tiwari was not connected with any action, he was active in the organisation. In free India he remained a member of parliament for many years and was an important Congress leader. Apart from him, there were some other ex-revolutionaries, who became members of parliament, for instance, Vishnusharan Dublish, Jogesh Chatterjee, Damodar Swarup Seth and Premkishen Khanna of the Kakori case and a few others from Bengal, UP and MP, such as Bishwanath Roy, Tarakeshwar Pande, Rajdeo Singh, Arunchandra Guha.

It would be interesting to analyse how far they served the revolutionary cause inside the parliament and outside during their membership.

Shiv Verma

Among Bhagat Singh's companions there were many lesser luminaries like Shiv Verma. Verma wrote his memoirs in Hindi entitled *Sansmritiyan.* From a human and literary point of view this is one of the best memoirs written by a revolutionary on Bhagat Singh.

Women Revolutionaries

Some women also played a prominent part during this period. Durga, the wife of Bhagavaticharan, Sushila Prakashvati (later Mrs. Yashpal) are quoted as important. One of the interesting episodes of the revolutionary movement was that Yasphal was more inclined towards Prakashvati (not yet married) than the rules of the revolutionary party would allow.

Chandrashekhar Azad, the Supremo sentenced Yashpal to death for this breach of rules and Virbhadra Tiwari was entrusted with carrying out of the sentence. But Tiwari apprised Yashpal, who took to his heels. It was good that the sentence could not be carried out, because Hindi literature would have lost a giant. At the same time Azad was right, because he acted according to the established traditions of revolutionary movement, with firmness and with malice towards none.

These above, were some of the men and women who shone as gems in Bhagat Singh's sky.

13

Left Wing Opposition and Role of Subhas Chandra Bose

I

The Calcutta Congress

The Left Wing opposition at the Calcutta Congress had indeed been formidable and if his leadership was to be retained, he would have to deal with the opposition in a diplomatic manner. The tactics employed by the Mahatma during the next twelve months were indeed superb. He took the wind out of the sails of the Extremists,[1] by himself advocating independence at the next Congress and divided the ranks of the opposition by winning over some of the Left Wing leaders. The Left Wing opposition had become a menace to all sections among the older leaders, to the Swarajists as much as to the 'No-changers', and the Calcutta Congress had found the Swarajist Pandit Motilal Nehru standing side by side with the 'No-Changer' Mahatma Gandhi, in order to fight the common danger. This temporary alliance was further strengthened during the ensuing months and with the help of a section of the Left Wing leaders, it became possible for the Mahatma to regain his hold on the Congress machinery and his prestige in the country, which had been badly shaken by the proceedings of the Calcutta Congress.

Therefore, one would be entitled to hold that at the Calcutta Congress the Mahatma was merely playing for time, because he was personally unprepared to launch a fight in the immediate future. In fact, even at the Lahore Congress in December 1929, the Mahatma had no plans for launching an anti-Government campaign of any sort—though he moved the resolution on independence, which was unanimously adopted by the

Congress. Not till February 1930, after much searching of heart, did he make up his mind to start a civil-disobedience movement in the country, beginning with the campaign for the manufacture of salt. But though the Congress did not give a bold and intelligent lead to the country during the whole of 1929, the unrest did not abate in any way. On the contrary, the forces making for revolution began to grow stronger and stronger, while owing to lack of co-ordination much dissipation of energy resulted. Besides the main current of the Congress movement, three other lines of activity were clearly visible at this time. There was an undercurrent of revolutionary activity with a certain amount of following in northern India, an unrest in the labour world which extended to every part of the country, and an awakening among the middle-class youths which was manifest everywhere.

The visible expression of the revolutionary movement was afforded by two incidents which occurred at Lahore and at Delhi. At Lahore an Asstt. Supdt. of Police, Mr. Saunders, a Britisher, was assassinated. It was reported that the revolutionaries believed that Mr. Saunders was responsible for the attack on Lala Lajpat Rai at the time of the anti-Simon demonstration in Lahore in 1928, which ultimately resulted in his death and that his assassination was an act of reprisal. The other incident was the throwing of a bomb in the Assembly at Delhi during a sitting and two young men, Sardar Bhagat Singh and Mr. Batukeshwar Dutt, were arrested in connection therewith. After these overt acts, there was a round-up of a large number of young men from all over the country and an All-India conspiracy case was started at Lahore about the middle of 1929. For some reason or other, the Lahore conspiracy case excited not only public interest but public sympathy as well. The reasons probably were that prior to his arrest, Sardar Bhagat Singh was known to be the leader of the youth movement (called the *Naujawan Bharat Sabha*) in the Punjab, and the fearless and defiant attitude adopted by him and his comrades, after their arrest and during their trial, made a deep impression on the public. Moreover, Sardar Bhagat Singh came from a wellknown patriotic family—being a nephew of Sardar Ajit Singh, who had been deported to Burma in 1909 along with Lala Lajpat Rai. The *Naujawan Bharat Sabha* was first started as a thorough-going nationalist movement, in order to fight communalism and religious fanaticism in the Punjab. If the official allegations are to believed, the Sabha developed into a revolutionary organisation and some members of the Sabha also went in for terrorist activities. Whatever the truth or otherwise of the allegations may be, there is no doubt that the Sabha developed a frankly Socialistic tendency. And incidentally it may be remarked that all youth organisations in the Punjab have a strong Socialist bent. In March 1931, when a session of the All-India Naujawan Bharat Sabha was held at Karachi, members of the *Punjab Naujawan Bharat Sabha* openly declared that they were against terrorism and that they believed in mass action on Socialist lines.

Demands for Better Treatment

Soon after their arrest, the Lahore Conspiracy Case prisoners, headed by Sardar Bhagat Singh, made a demand that they should be accorded better treatment than ordinary criminals on the ground that they were political prisoners and under trial, who should be deemed to be innocent until they were actually convicted. After trying usual constitutional methods, when they found that no remedy was forth-coming, they resorted to hunger-strike. Among the prisoners was a young man from Calcutta, Mr. Jatindranath Das, who was at first rather averse to hunger-strike because he regarded it as a dangerous game to play. The enthusiasm of the rest forced him to join the strike but before doing so, he warned them that come what may, he would not turn back until their demands were fully conceded. There was an intense agitation throughout the country over the hunger-strike and there was a public demand that the Government should redress their just grievances and thereby save their lives. When the condition of the prisoners grew serious, the Government made half-hearted attempts at compromise. For instance, they offered better treatment to the hunger-strikers on medical grounds. But their demand was not merely for better treatment for themselves, but for all prisoners similarly circumstanced and on the ground that they were political prisoners.

Jatin Das

As the days rolled by, one by one the hunger-strikers dropped off but young Jatin was invincible. He never hesitated, never faltered for one small second—but marched straight on towards death and freedom. Every heart in the country melted but the heart of the bureaucracy did not. So Jatin died on September 13th. But he died the death of a martyr. After his death the whole country gave him an ovation which few men in the recent history of India have received. As his dead body was removed from Lahore to Calcutta for cremation, people assembled in their thousands and tens of thousands at every station to pay their homage. His martyrdom acted as a profound inspiration to the youths of India and everywhere youth and student organisations began to grow up. Among the many messages that were received on the occasion was one which touched the heart of every Indian. It was a message from the family of Terence McSwiney, the Lord Mayor of Cork, who had died a martyr under similar conditions in Ireland. The message ran thus: 'Family of Terence McSwiney have heard with grief and pride of the death of Jatin Das. Freedom will come.'

The Agreement

The Pact—called the Delhi Pact or the Gandhi-Irwin Pact—was published the next morning in all papers. It was a lengthy document and from the Congress point of view the drafting was faulty, because it did not give the impression that the Congress had scored a victory. The perusal of the terms of the Pact had a damping effect on all 'Congressite' readers. Bose was in the Alipore Central Jail in Calcutta at the time. For days the papers had published substantially correct forecasts of the terms of the coming Pact. Even the blind followers of the Mahatma, when they read the forecasts, invariably remarked that it was unthinkable that their leader—meaning the Mahatma—would agree to those terms. Nevertheless, what was unthinkable came to be actual. The Mahatma was not blind to the realities of the situation, and in a Press statement issued simultaneously with the Pact, he stressed the point that the settlement did not imply a victory for either party and that he would strain every nerve to make final what was provisional, so that the Pact would prove to be a precursor of the goal, to attain which the Congress had been striving. The terms of the Pact were briefly as follows: Mahatma Gandhi on behalf of the Congress agreed:

1. To suspend the Civil-Disobedience Movement.
2. To participate in the deliberations of the forthcoming Round Table Conference for drafting a Constitution for India on the basis of (a) Federation; (b) Responsibility and (c) adjustments and safeguards that may be necessary in the interests of India.
3. To forge the demand for an investigation into the allegations of police atrocities in different parts of India.

The Viceroy on behalf of the Government agreed:

1. To release simultaneously all political prisoners incarcerated in connection with the non-violent movement.
2. To restore confiscated property and land to the owners where it had not been already sold or auctioned by the Government.
3. To withdraw the emergency ordinances.

4. To permit people who live within a certain distance of the seashore to collect or manufacture salt free of duty.
5. To permit peaceful picketing of liquor, opium and foreign-cloth shops, the last item designed not as a discrimination against British goods but as an encouragement to the Swadesi movement (i.e., indigenous industries).

With the announcement of the armistice, the official machinery of the Congress began to work expeditiously and with great efficiency. The Working Committee decided to hold the annual session of the Congress at Karachi and suspending the constitutional procedure for the election of the President, it elected Sardar Vallabhbhai Patel, than whom a stauncher follower of the Mahatma it was difficult to find, as the President. Every member of the Working Committee felt that his prestige was at stake and strained every nerve to get the largest number of supporters from his province to attend the Karachi Congress. Besides the members of the Working Committee, all the leaders of the Right Wing felt called upon to exert themselves in order to secure the ratification of the Pact at the Karachi Congress. All the monied interests also desired to see the armistice followed up by a permanent peace, so that they could settle down to business peacefully. Consequently, there was no dearth of funds for those who wanted to go to Karachi to support the Mahatma. On the other hand, the oppositionists were at great disadvantage. Many of their adherents were still in prison and did not get the benefit of the amnesty which the Pact had promised. Defections among their leaders had weakened their position in the country and even those who were in a position to attend the Karachi Congress, were handicapped by want of necessary funds. After the Lahore Congress, Mr. Srinivasa Iyengar had retired from public activity. Along with other Left Wing leaders, he had been treated shabbily by the President of the Lahore Congress and by the Mahatma, who was instrumental in excluding him from the Working Committee, though he was the most outstanding leader from Madras and was an ex-President of the Congress. This insult he had taken to heart so much that he had vowed he would have nothing to do with the Congress so long as Mahatma Gandhi remained the leader. Besides Srinivasa Iyengar, there was another defection in the person of Dr. Mohammed Alam of Lahore who had played a prominent part at the Lahore Congress, but who became a supporter of the Mahatma after the Gandhi-Irwin Pact. Of all the Provinces, Bengal was most hostile to the Pact but even then, there was a party led by the late Mr. Sengupta pledged to support the Mahatma.

In these circumstances, what could the Left Wingers do? Before my release from prison on March 8th, Bose ascertained that the political prisoneres, as a rule, were hostile to the Pact, and he naturally shared their feelings. But after coming out, he realised that the Pact was a settled fact and there was no possibility of preventing its ratification at the Karachi Congress. The only question that we had to decide was whether we should put up an insignificant opposition at Karachi, or whether we should refrain from dividing the House while disapproving of the Pact. Before coming to a decision, he considered it advisable to meet the Mahatma personally. Bose therefore undertook a journey to Bombay which also enabled me to gauge public feeling in the provinces through which he passed. At Bombay he had long conversations with the Mahatma. After criticising the Pact, the point that he urged was that we would be prepared to support him as long as he stood for independence—but the moment he gave up that stand, we would consider it our duty to fight him. At the end, the Mahatma gave the following assurances:[2]

1. He would ask the Karachi Congress for a mandate to bind the hands of the Congress Deputation of the Round Table Conference.
2. That mandate would contain nothing that was not consistent with the status of independence for which the Lahore Congress had declared.
3. He would use all his influence and strain every nerve to secure amnesty for those who had been left out in the Pact.

From Bombay the Mahatma left for Delhi and Bose travelled in the same train with him. This gave Bose a further opportunity not only of supplementing our talks at Bombay but also of observing how the public were reacting to the Pact. From the ovation he received everywhere, it was quite apparent that his popularity had reached the high watermark. It had surpassed even the record of 1921. At Delhi, no sooner did we arrive than we received a bombshell in the shape of news, to the effect that the Government had decided to execute Sardar Bhagat Singh and two of his comrades in the Lahore Conspiracy Case. Pressure was brought to bear upon the Mahatma to try to save the lives of these young men and it must be admitted that he did try his very best. On this occasion, Bose ventured the suggestion that he should, if necessary, break with the Viceroy on the question, because the execution was against the spirit, if not the letter, of the Delhi Pact. Bose was reminded of a similar incident during the armistice between the Sinn Fein Party and the British Government, when the strong attitude adopted by the former, had secured the release of an

Irish political prisoner sentenced to the gallows. But the Mahatma who did not want to identify himself with the revolutionary prisoners, would not go so far and it naturally made a great difference when the Viceroy realised that the Mahatma would not break on that question. However, at that time, Lord Irwin told the Mahatma that he had received a largely-signed petition asking for the commutation of the death-sentence passed on the three Lahore prisoners. He would postpone their execution for the time being and give serious consideration to the matter, but beyond that he did not want to be pressed at the moment. The conclusion which the Mahatma and everybody else drew from this attitude of the Viceroy, was that the execution would be finally cancelled and there was a jubilation all over the country and especially in Bengal, where some revolutionary prisoners were also going to be executed.

The Karachi Congress

About ten days after this incident the Congress was to meet at Karachi. The general expectation being that the execution would be cancelled, it was a most painful and unexpected surprise when on March 24th, while we were on our ways to Karachi from Calcutta, the news was received that Sardar Bhagat Singh and his comrades had been hanged the night before. Gruesome reports were also afloat in the Punjab about the manner in which their dead bodies had been disposed of. Somehow or other, Bhagat Singh had become the symbol of the new awakening among the youths. People did not stop to inquire if he was really guilty of the murder charge brought against him. It was enough for them to know that he was the father of the *Naujawan Bharat Sabha* (the Youth Movement) in the Pubjab. Every one felt that the Congress was meeting under the shadow of a bereavement. The President-elect, Sardar Vallabhbhai Patel, gave orders that the usual festivities on the first day of the Congress would be suspended. Nevertheless, when the Mahatma alighted near Karachi, there was a hostile demostration, and several young men received him with black flowers and black garlands. The feeling among a considerable section of the youths was that the Mahatma had betrayed the cause of Bhagat Singh and his comrades.

The All-India Congress Committee was to meet on March 26th and the plenary session of the Congress on the 29th. The execution having taken place on March 23rd, caused a great deal of nervousness among the supporters of the Pact and they apprehended an open split in the Congress. But the official party machinery had worked with great thoroughness and from all the provinces supporters of the Pact had been elected as delegates in large numbers. The Left Wing, to which Bose belonged, had resolved previously to come to Karachi, survey the situation there, consider carefully what the Mahatma had communicated to me in Bombay as to his future attitude and then make their final decision. At Karachi it was quite clear that they would not have much support from the elected delegates who alone could vote at the Congress—though among the general public and particularly the youths—they had larger support. There was another factor which had to be considered. If we were consistent and honest, it would not do to merely oppose the Pact and then go back home. We would have to give notice to the Government and start the movement again. What support would we get if we did so? There was no doubt that the response in men and money would be disappointing. There was therefore no possibility that if we continued the fight, we would achieve better results than the Mahatma had done. In the circumstances, what would we gain by dividing the House? If we were defeated, as we were sure to be, our opposition would be futile. If we succeeded in throwing out the Pact—which was unlikely in the circumstances—but failed to carry on a more vigorous campaign, the country would not gain by our opposition. Moreover, the execution of Bhagat Singh and his comrades had to be considered. The Government had sufficient cognizance of the situation in the country to realise that the execution on the eve of the Congress was likely to create a split in the Congress and would considerably strengthen the position of anti-Pact Party. If the Government were so anxious to create a split, there was something to be said in favour of avoiding it. In times of crises, a party has sometimes to stand by its leaders even when it is known that they are committing a blunder. This was the first occasion for an agreement between the Nationalist leaders and the Government.

Patel as President

Sardar Vallabhbhai Patel presided over the Congress. In his opening speech he gave the go-by to the Lahore resolution on Independence and advocated Dominion Status for India. Much of his speech was devoted to agrarian grievances and to social and economic reforms, necessary for the uplift of the country. Among the resolutions adopted at the Congress was one appreciating the courage and self-sacrifice of Sardar Bhagat Singh and his comrades, while condemning all acts of violence. This resolution was on the same lines as the 'Gopinath Saha resolution' adopted by the Bengal Provincial Conference in 1924, of which the Mahatma had strongly disapproved. The circumstances at Karachi were such that this resolution had to be swallowed by people who, under ordinary circumstances, would not have come within miles of it. So far as the Mahatma was concerned, he had to make his conscience somewhat elastic. But that was not enough. To perfect the stage-management, Sardar Kishan Singh, the father of the late Sardar Bhagat Singh, was brought to the rostrum and made to speak in support of the Congress leaders. The tactics of the official party were superb. The other resolutions passed at the Congress referred to:

1. The ratification of the Gandhi-Irwin Pact;
2. The mandate given to the Congress delegation to the Round Table Conference; and
3. The fundamental rights of the Indian people for which the Congress would strive.

The mandate given to the Congress delegation was in keeping with the assurance given by the Mahatma to the writer in Bombay. The 'fundamental rights resolution' was meant to placate the Socialist elements in the Congress. As for the personnel of the Congress delegation, the Working Committee was empowered to make the selection. Towards the end of the session, the Working Committee for the next year was chosen and, as at the Lahore Congress, only such men were selected as would be inclined to follow the Mahatma blindly. During the Congress session, the Mahatma used to hold a public prayer in the morning and unprecedented crowds attended it. No propaganda could be more effective in drawing public support.

Simultaneously with the Congress, a session of the All-India Naujawan Bharat Sabha (All-India Youth Congress) was held in Karachi over which Bose was called upon to preside. At that time there was a distinct tendency among the youths in Punjab and Sindh to break away from the Indian National Congress and run a separate organisation. Bose pleaded strongly against this viewpoint and urged the capture of the official Congress machinery in place of boycott. With regard to the Gandhi-Irwin Pact Bose made the following criticism:

Bose's Assessment

"1. The Pact had gone into many petty and unnecessary details but had avoided the main issue of *Swaraj*

2. The Conference was really no Round Table Conference because there was no finality about the decisions of the Conference and the whole matter would be considered *de novo* by the British Parliament. In a real Round Table Conference, as the South Africans and the Irish had, the

decisions are always final and binding on both parties. The name Round Table Conference had been used only to hoodwink foolish Indian politicians.

3. The Indian delegates to the Round Table Conference would be selected not by the Indian people but by the British Government.
4. The Conference would not be confined to the representatives of the two belligerent parties. Non-descripts of all kinds who had nothing to do with the fight for Swaraj, would be there to throw obstacles in the path of the real nationalists.
5. The proposal of a Federation between nationalist British India and the autocratic Indian Princes was an absurd one. The Princes or their nominees would act as a dead weight aganist the national forces.
6. 'Safeguards' take away what 'responsibility' gives. It was a gross error on the part of the Mahatma to talk of 'Safeguards' in the interests of India. The only safeguard that the Indians want is liberty. The actual 'safeguards' are demanded by Britishers and are against the interests of Indians. It is wrong to induce the Indian people to accept such safeguards by saying that they are in the interests of India.
7. The amnesty provided under the Pact was inadequate because the following classes of political prisoners were excluded"

   (a) The state prisoners and 'detenus' imprisoned without trial, of whom there were about one thousand in Bengal alone.
   (b) Prisoners convicted of revolutionary offences.
   (c) Prisoners under trail for alleged revolutionary offences.
   (d) The under-trail prisoners in the Meerut Conspiracy Case.
   (e) Prisoners incarcerated in connection with labour strikes and other labour disputes.
   (f) The Garhwali soldiers who had been court-martialled and given heavy sentences for refusing to fire on unarmed citizens.
   (g) Prisoners sentenced in connection with the civil-disobedience movement, the charges against whom referred to violence of some sort.

8. The demand originally made by Mahatma Gandhi for an

inquiry into police atrocities during the period of the civil-disobedience movement was excluded from the Pact.

The above criticism met with general approval at the Youth Congress and a resolution was adopted condemning the Delhi Pact. The Delhi Pact, proved to be not a blessing but a curse. The time was not opportune for an understanding of the sort attempted. The struggle should have been continued for some time longer. The Pact, as drafted, contained nothing of value. Ever since the negotiations started in 1929, the Congress leaders had always insisted on an assurance from the Government, regarding the grant of Dominion Status. Because that assurance was not forthcoming, the fight had to be launched in 1930. For the same reason, the peace-negotiations prior to the First Round Table Conference in 1930, had proved abortive. How the fight could be suspended without such an assurance, passes one's comprehension. The only reason one can suggest is that there was no one in the Working Committee to point out the correct thing to the Mahatma and with the lamented death of Pandit Motilal Nehru, the last intellectual stalwart of the Congress had disappeared. He towered head and shoulders above this contemporaries and in 1931, he was the one man in the Congress Working Committee who could have influenced the Mahatma for good. It was therefore a misfortune that at the time of the Delhi negotiations he was on his deathbed and it was nothing short of a national calamity that he passed away early in March 1931.

Police Atrocities

On the demand for an inquiry into the police atrocities, Mahatma had been informed that if he stuck to it till the breaking-point, the Government would yield. Nevertheless, he voluntarily gave up the demand on an appeal from the Viceroy. With better bargaining, even in March 1931, one could have extracted more from the Government, because they were really anxious for a settlement. But men with fixed ideas are not well-qualified for political bargaining. So far as the Mahatma is concerned, he alternates between obstinacy and leniency and moreover, he is too susceptible to personal appeals—and with such habits of mind, it is difficult to get the better of one's opponent in political bargaining. The Delhi truce was a great help to the Government. It gave them time to inquire more deeply into the tactics of the Congress and thereafter to perfect their machinery for dealing with that body in future. In the case of the Congress, the Pact had a soporific effect. The enthusiasm of the people began to evaporate and it is out of public enthusiasm that one gets men and money for a non-violent mass movement. While the Government could resume their activity at any time because they had no dearth of men or money, the Congress would have to wait till public enthusiasm could be worked up once again. During the period of the Delhi truce while the Round Table Conference was sitting in London, the Government were perfecting their plans for striking at the Congress. For instance, by October 1931, the emergency ordinances for the next year had been already prepared. Dr. M.A. Ansari, the Nationalist Moslim leader of Delhi, had unquestionable proofs of this and he duly passed them on to the Congress President, Sardar Vallabhbhai Patel. It was easy for the Government to prophesy future developments because they knew that nothing substantial would be offered to the Congress. But the Congress guided by the honest and straightforward policy of Mahatma made no preparations for the coming fight. In fact, before he left for London, Mahatma assured Lord Irwin that he would try his level best for a settlement there and when he left London, he assured the Premier, Ramsay Macdonald, that he would endeavour till the last to avoid a resumption of hostilities and if that was impossible, he would at least strive to avoid bitterness as far as possible.[3] Further, the day before Mahatma Gandhi landed in Bombay, he sent by radio an exceedingly conciliatory message which was immediately published in all the papers. But that had no effect on the new Viceroy, Lord Willingdon, who had already perfected his arrangements and was spoiling for a fight in order to avenge himself for the slight humiliation which the Government had to face in agreeing to an armistice with the Congress.

In spite of the inadequate provisions of the Pact, if it had provided for an inquiry into the alleged atrocities, it would have had a very healthy check on such misdeeds in future. During the preceding of twelve months there had been excesses committed by the police and the military in Peshawar, Gujrat, the United Provinces and the Midnapore district in Bengal, in connection with which the public had demanded redress. We have already referred to the shooting in Peshawar. In Gujrat, the United Provinces and Midnapore, excesses had been committed by the forces of the Crown in trying to suppress the no-tax campaign and in the United Provinces there had been allegations of assault on women of a revolting description. In addition to these, a recent incident which was still fresh in the public mind was the assault by the police on a peaceful procession in Calcutta on Independence Day (January 26th, 1931). This procession which was being led by Bose who was then the Mayor of Calcutta, was suddenly attacked without warning by British mounted police armed with *lathis* (powerful sticks covered with leather) and mercilessly belaboured.

The next day Bose was sentenced to six months' imprisonment for rioting,[4] by the Chief Presidency Magistrate of Calcutta. That the Mayor of the first city in India could be treated by the police in this fashion was something which even the Indian public could not stand. The police, on the other hand, felt that they could do just as they liked because they would never be called upon to appear before the bar of public opinion.

Views on Amnesty

The restricted scope of the amnesty promised under the Pact, caused considerable disappointment among certain sections of the people and alienated the Mahatma still more from the revolutionaries and from trade-union circles, including the friends and followers of the Meerut prisoners. If the Mahatma could have secured amnesty for all these classes of prisoners, he would have stood out not only as the representative of the Nationalists but also of the trade-unionists and the revolutionaries, and he could have exerted his influence on them for good. The Government, too, if they had taken courage in both hands and opened wide the gates of the prison-house, would have made a magnanimous gesture which would have lost nothing thereby—because if anyone happened to abuse his liberty, he could again be put back in prison through the help of the Regulation and the Ordinances. Since Mahatma confined himself to the cause of the Satyagrahis, the revolutionaries in prison addressed a letter to Lord Irwin stating that a settlement with Mahatma Gandhi would not necessarily be binding on them and that if His Excellency desired a real settlement of the Indian question, the Government should come to a separate understanding with the Revolutionary Party. This letter reached the Viceroy's hands through a prominent Indian politician.[5]

This representation was not altogether useless, because a few months later, the Governor of Bengal, Sir Stanley Jackson, made an effort to come to an understanding with the revolutionaries. At his instance the late Mr. J.M. Sengupta went to Buxa Detention Camp in North Bengal and interviewed some of the leaders. The result was not unsatisfactory. The interviewed prisoners said that they were prepared to discuss terms, but they insisted that the negotiations should be carried on direct with the Government and not through any police-officer. They also gave a preliminary outline of the terms which the late Mr. Sengupta duly conveyed to the Governor. Thereafter, a reference was made by the Government to the prisoners through the Superintendent of the Camp, who was a police-officer. But they refused to move further in the matter, if the negotiations were not carried on direct with them. As the Government were not agreeable to that, the negotiations fell through.

In spite of all that has been written above, to the unsophisticated masses, the Delhi Pact appeared to be a victory for Mahatma. Only with the lapse of time were they to be gradually disillusioned. Many intelligent people seriously believed that besides the written, there were other unwritten terms which would be disclosed later on and many of those who were against the Pact maintained that Gandhi should be given a free hand till the end of the Second Round Table Conference. The Karachi Congress undoubtedly represented the pinnacle of Gandhi popularity and prestige. Bose travelled with him for some days and was able to observe the unprecedented crowds that greeted him everywhere. Bose wonder if such a spontaneous ovation was ever given to a leader anywhere else. He stood out before the people not merely as a Mahatma but as the hero of a political fight. The question that stirred Bose at the time was as to how he would utilise the unique position he had been able to attain.

Critical of Gandhi

While the first move of Mahatma after the Karachi Congress was not a wise one, the second move was a positive blunder. In private and in public, he began to say that his going to the Round Table Conference depended on his ability to solve the Hindu-Moslem question beforehand. Along with this statement he also began to say that if the Muslims made a united demand on the question of representation, electorate, etc., in the new Constitution, he would accept the demand. The effect of these statements was a most tragic one. After the Delhi Pact, the reactionary Muslims had been somewhat overawed by the strength and power of the Congress and they were in a mood to come to terms with that body on a reasonable basis. The first statement of Mahatma immediately changed that mood and made them feel that they held the key position, since if they refused to come to an understanding with him, they could prevent his attending the Round Table Conference. The second statement of Gandhi made the reactionary Muslims feel that if only they would remain firm and secure the support of the Nationalist Moslems, the Mahatama could be forced to accept all their extreme demands. After the above statements had been made, the Mahatma had a conference with some reactionary Muslim leaders in Delhi in April. I was in Delhi at the time and I went to see him the same evening, after the conference. He seemed to be in a depressed mood, because they had presented him with the fourteen demands made by Mr. Jinnah (known in India as Jinnah's fourteen points) and he felt that an agreement would not be possible on that basis. Thereupon I remarked that the Congress should only care for an agreement between Nationalist Hindus and Nationalist Muslims and that the agreed solution should be placed before the Round Table Conference as the Nationalist demand and that the Congress need not bother what other anti-Nationalist elements thought or said. Gandhi then asked me if I had any objection to separate electorates since it could be argued that in the absence of the third party the different communities would live and work in concord. To this I replied that separate electorates were against the fundamental principles of Nationalism and that Bose felt so strongly on the subject that even *Swaraj* on the basis of separate electorates was, in my opinion, not worth having. While we were engaged in this discussion, Dr. Ansari and some of the Nationalist Muslim leaders including Mr. Sherwani, arrived on the scene and joined in the discussion. They said that if for any reason the Mahatma gave up the demand for a common electorate for both Hindus and Muslims and accepted the demand of the reactionaries for a separate electorate for each community, they would oppose the reactionary Moslems and also Gandhi because they were convinced that separate electorates were bad not only for the country as a whole, but also for the different communities. The strong attitude of the Nationalist Muslims on this occasion was largely responsible for preventing the Mahatma from agreeing to separate electorates, and forced him to wriggle out of the uncomfortable situation in which he had placed himslef.[6] Soon after this, the Mahatma issued a public statement saying that he could not accept the demands made by the communalist Moslem leaders, since the Nationalist Muslims were opposed to them.

Atmosphere in Delhi

At this point of time the atmosphere in Delhi was then (i.e., in April 1931) full of intrigue. Though Lord Irwin was inspired by a sincere desire for a settlement, there were many officials who were against it. These diehard elements were encouraged by the impending departure of Lord Irwin from India and the advent of Lord Willingdon, who had the reputation of being a strong man. While we were in Delhi, information reached from a reliable source as to the tactics that the British Government would follow at the Round Table Conference and every effort would be made to drag Mahatma Gandhi at the very outset into minor issues with a view to getting the Indians to fight among themselves, so that they would not be able to combine against the British Government over the major issues. Bose duly conveyed to the Mahatma this information for what it was worth. He said in reply that his plan was to meet the authorities concerned soon after his arrival in London and try to obtain satisfaction from them on the major issues. If he felt satisfied, he would go into the minor issues—otherwise his work in England would end there and then. Unfotrunately, when Mahatma Gandhi was in England, the minorities problem assumed the greatest importance and all the major problems were put aside. Events took place exactly as it had been prophesied in April at Delhi.

On April 18th, Lord Irwin's tenure of office came to an end. Before leaving Delhi he made an exceedingly conciliatory speech at the Chelmsford Club. Though a prominent member of the Conservative Party, he had proved himself to be a well-wisher of India. After Lord Ripon, no Viceroy had adopted such a friendly attitude towards the Indian people as he had. That he could not do more for India was due to the reactionary forces that were working against him both in India and in England. With the arrival of Lord Willingdon, the official attitude began to stiffen. Effect was not given to the Pact by officials in different provinces. In Gujrat the peasantry had great difficulty in getting back their confiscated lands and Mahatma had to spend practically the whole of his time between the Karachi Congress and his departure for London in attending to their grievances. In the United Provinces, though the civil-disobedience movement was suspended, the peasants said that they were made unable to pay the rent. Even Mahatma's advice that they should pay 50 per cent of their dues—they could not give effect to. The situation was, however, worst in Bengal. In spite of the Pact, imprisonment without trial continued from day to day.

II

Speech at All-India Naujawan Bharat Sabha in Karachi, 5 April 1931

"My Dear Friends,

You have called upon me to preside over the deliberations of the second session of All-India Naujawan Bharat Sabha at Karachi. I am grateful to you not only for the honour you have done me by your selection but also for the affection that has undoubtedly inspired your choice. You are holding this conference at a momentous period in our history and I only hope that I shall be able to throw some light on the problems that are ahead of us and the path that we shall have to travel.

Since the earliest ages humanity has been in search of a better order of things. This search has gone on alike in the East and in the West and not only sages and dreamers, but politicians and statesmen as well, have been after it. The vision of an ideal society or state has appeared in different forms in different climes, but the impulse behind them all has been the same. In the East people dreamt of an ideal republic. People have sometimes endeavoured to go back to the state of nature from whence they think they came—at other times, they have tried to demolish the agelong social, economic and political structure in order to rear up something great and noble on the ruin of the past.

The psychological impulse behind this universal human effort is a feeling of acute discontent with the present order and environment and a desire for a radical change. Urged by this impulse people have in utter helplessness looked beyond this earth and beyond this human existence to a kingdom of heaven where the human soul could live an ideal life amidst ideal surroundings. Others have followed a different course of action and believing that the kingdom of heaven is within us, have sought, through asceticism and worship, or through song and prayer, to attain the maximum peace and happiness here on earth.

We are not concerned with these two schools of thought and we need neither accept nor reject either of them. We are concerned more with the consideration of that socio-economic structure and body-politic which will bring us the maximum happiness, will help us to foster manhood and develop character and will translate into reality the highest ideals of collective humanity. We are also interested in investigating the methods that will bring about the earliest attainment of the above goal.

Search for Better Order

In the search for a better order humanity has throughout the ages been groping in the twilight of darkness and light. Religion, philosophy and literature have all tried to throw some light on that elusive will-o'-the-wisp—the Ideal. It would be interesting to trace and study these efforts made in almost every civilised country from age to age but that would take too much time and may divert us from the immediate problem before us. It will suffice to say that mankind has now accepted the theory of progress and has rejected the opposite theory viz., the theory of man's fall and his subsequent degradation. This theory of progress may be made the starting point of our discussion.

If we undertake a comparative analysis of the different socio-political ideals that have inspired human endeavour and activity we shall arrive at certain common principles. The same result may be attained by searching our heart and asking ourselves as to what principles and ideals would make our life worth living. By following either course I am led to the conclusion that the principles that should form the basis of our collective life are—justice, equality, freedom, discipline and love. There is hardly any necessity of arguing that all our affairs and relations should be guided by a sense of justice. In order to be just and impartial, we shall have to treat all men as equal. In order to make men equal we shall have to make them free. Bondage within the socio-economic or political system—robs men of their freedom and gives rise to inequalities of various kinds. Therefore, order to ensure Equality, we must get rid of bondage of every kind—social, economic and political—and we must become fully and wholly free. But freedom does not mean indiscipline or license. Freedom does not imply the absence of law. It only means the substitution of our own law and our own discipline in a place of an externally imposed law and discipline. Discipline imposed on us by ourselves is necessary not only when we have attained freedom but is more necessary when we are struggling to achieve freedom. Therefore discipline, whether for the individual of for society, is necessary as a basis of life. Lastly, all these fundamental principles, viz., Justice, Equality. Freedom and Discipline—presuppose or imply another higher principle, viz., Love. Unless we are inspired by a feeling of love for humanity we can neither be just towards all, nor treat men as Equal, nor feel called upon to suffer and sacrifice in the cause of freedom nor enforce discipline of the right sort. These five principles therefore, should in my opinion be the basis of our collective life. I shall go further and say that these principles constitute the essence of Socialism as I understand it, and the Socialism that I would like to see established in India.

Bose believed that in the future that is before us India will be able to evolve a socio-economic and political structure which will be in many respects an object lesson to the world just as Bolshevism today has many useful lessons for humanity. But I do not believe that abstract principles can be applied in the same manner, form and degree to different nations or countries. Marxian principles when applied to Russia and Russian conditions gave birth to Bolshevism. Similarly, socialism when applied to India and Indian conditions will develop a new form or type of socialism which we may hail as Indian Socialism. Environment, racial temperament, socio-economic conditions all these cannot be ruled out by a stroke of the pen. They are therefore bound to influence or modify and principle that is sought to be translated into reality.

While seeking light and inspiration from abroad, we cannot afford to forget that we should not blindly imitate any other people and that we should assimilate what we learn elsewhere with a view to finding out what will suit our national requirements as well as our national genius. There is a great deal of truth in the proverb—'What is one man's meat is another's poison.' Bose therefore liked to strike a note of warning to those who may feel tempted to follow blindly the tenets and methods of Bolshevism. With regard to the tenets of Bolshevism Bose opined that Bolshevik theory is at present going through an experimental stage. There has been a departure not only from the original theory of Marx but also from the principle enunciated by Lenin and other Bolsheviks before they captured political power. This departure has been caused by the peculiar conditions or circumstances prevailing in Russia which have compelled a modification of original Marxian or Bolshevik theory. With regards to the methods and tactics employed by the Bolsheviks in Russia. He further stated that they will not necessarily suit Indian conditions. As a proof of this I may say that in spite of universal and human appeal of communism, communism has not been able to make much headway in India—chiefly because the methods and tactics generally employed by them are such as tend to alienate rather than win over possible friends and allies.

Socialist Republic

To summarise what I have said I want a Socialist republic in India. The exact from the Socialist State will take—it is not possible to detail at this stage. We now only outline the main principles and features of the socialist state.

The message which Bose had to give is one of complete, all-round undiluted freedom. We want political freedom, whereby is meant the constitution of an independent Indian State, free from the control of British Imperialism. It should be quite clear to everybody that independence means severance from the British Empire and on this point there should be no vagueness or mental reservation. Secondly, we want complete economic emancipation. Every human being must have the right to work and the right to a living wage. There shall be no drones in our society. There must be equal opportunities for all. Above all there should be a fair, just and equitable distribution of wealth. For this purpose it may be necessary for the state to take over the control of the means of production and distribution of wealth. Thirdly, we want complete social equality. There shall be no caste, no depressed classes. Every man will have the same rights—the same status—in the society. Further there shall be no inequality between the sexes either in social status or in law—and woman will be in every way an equal partner with man.

We therefore have a new message for every group or class or

individual in society who may be exploited or oppressed in any way. We have a message for the political workers, for the wage earner, for the landless and propertyless proletariat, for the so-called depressed classes in society and for the weaker sex. These exploited or oppressed classes represent the radical—or if I may say so—revolutionary elements in our society. If we can go out to greet them with a new message—the message of complete all-around freedom—Bose had no doubt that they can be inspired in no time. Until these radical or revolutionary elements are stirred up—we cannot get freedom and we cannot stir up the revolutionary elements among us except by inspiring them with a new message which comes from the heart and goes straight to the heart.

The fundamental weakness in the Congress policy and programme is that there is a great deal of vagueness and mental reservation in the mind of the leaders. Further the programme is based not on radicalism but on adjustment. Adjustment between the landlord and the tenant, between the capitalist and the wage earner, between the so-called upper classes and the so-called depressed classes, between man and woman—may be an ideal state of thing for one who would like to maintain the present equilibrium—but I am doubtful whether this adjustment can stir up the revolutionary elements in society which alone can win freedom. I doubt if the Indian National Congress with its present attitude of the adjustment in all controversial matters—can win independence for India; it will be a cheap price to pay for freedom. But whether this small price can bring us freedom—I seriously doubt.

We do not want to tinker with the gigantic problem we have to solve—therefore, we want a radical militant programme. I shall not in this introductory address go into details on this question, but shall content myself with outlining the main features of the programme. In consonance with 5 principles I have enunciated at the outset, and keeping in view the different aspects of freedom—we should direct our activities along the following lines:

(1) Organisation of peasants and workers on a socialist programme.
(2) Organisation of the youths into volunteer corps under strict discipline.
(3) Abolition of caste and the eradication of social and religious superstitions of all kinds.
(4) Organisation of women's associations for getting our women folk to accept the new gospel and work out the new programme.
(5) Intensive campaign for the boycott of British goods.
(6) Countrywide propaganda for explaining the new cult and for organising a new party.

(7) Creation of a new Literature for propagating the new cult and programme.

Appeal to Workers

Workers and comrades to whom the new cult and programme appeal should seriously consider whether or not they should organise themselves as the Left-Wing of the Indian National Congress. There is much to be said in favour of doing so. The Indian National Congress in the first place has a tradition as well as an international reputation. Further, it is built on the gigantic sacrifices made by successive generations. And if the Left-Wing is properly organised, I have no doubt that the time will soon come when they will be called upon by the sheer logic of events to take charge of the Congress. Once this party comes into existence with its own programme it will be the only alternative to the present order and the present programme.

Friends, before I wind up, you will no doubt like me to express my views on the truce that has been arrived at, between the Government and the Working Committee of the Congress. But before I do so, I should like to unburden myself on a matter which has profoundly moved the whole of India. I mean the recent execution of Sardar Bhagat Singh and his comrades. This event is an historic one and is pregnant with lessons for the future and I shall crave your indulgence for dwelling on it at length.

Praise for Bhagat Singh

Bhagat Singh is dead! Long live Bhagat Singh! For months and months have the people of India watched and waited with tense anxiety for the end of the tragic drama that was being enacted at Lahore. The end has at last come. The curtain has ultimately been rung down on a scene indescribable for its deep pathos and memorable for its selflessness. From start to finish the drama has been so rich in variety and so alive in its colouring that we have had to hold our breath in awe and anxious expectation. It ended with the self-sacrifice of Bhagat Singh and Jatin Das. With rapture and reverent admiration do we gaze at these two rare types of martyrdom which recent history has produced. Just as the funeral procession of Jatin Das was one long triumphal march so also the execution of Bhagat Singh is an act of consecration which will inspire the whole nation. No wonder that the Lahore Conspiracy here have stirred the heart of India to its very depth. But do the Government realise it? Again I say 'Bhagat Singh is dead! Long Live Bhagat Singh! Bhagat Singh is not a person. He symbolises the spirit of revolt which has taken possession of the country from one end to the other. The spirit is unconquerable, the flame that spirit has lit up will not die. Therefore we do not grieve that Bhagat Singh, Rajguru and Sukhdev are no more. India may have to lose many more sons before she can hope to be free. But if we grieve it is because they have had to die at a time when the premier nationalist organisation in the country—the Indian National Congress—has declared a truce with the British Government. What fate is in store for the other sons of India, like Harkishinalal, Dinesh Gupta and Ramkrishna Biswas cannot be easily visualised. The question may therefore be pertinently asked what is the value of this truce if these acts of hostility are to go on and if we cannot save the lives of our best heroes?

It may be argued logically that there was nothing in the truce terms to say that the capital sentences would not be given effect to. I admit this point. But may we not ask what the object of the truce is? It will be admitted on all hands that the object of the truce is to bring about an atmosphere of peace and goodwill, prior to the negotiations at the Round Table Conference, so that the discussions take place in a cool and dispassionate manner, and without bitterness or prejudice. Will that atmosphere be created if capital sentences are passed and executed and if a large number of political prisoners are still in imprisonment? If the Government today are so exacting about the letter of the truce terms—if they are so keen about having their pound of flesh—what hope is here that they will part with power when the time for negotiation or discussion arrives? It is not for nothing that Mahatma Gandhi has always insisted on a change of heart prior to a settlement or negotiations for a settlement. The Government that continues to have the same bureaucratic, and if I may say so vindictive, mentally is not the Government that will voluntarily hand over India to the people's representatives. It may be urged that we shall negotiate for transference of power not with the Indian Civil Service or the Government of India, but with the British Cabinet or with the British people altogether. But if in the matter of holding an enquiry into police excess or commuting death sentence the British Government has to surrender to the will of men on the spot, is it not to be expected that in much larger questions involving transference of power, the same Government will be guided to a very large extent by the will of the steel frame?

Critical of Executions

The recent executions are to me, therefore, a sure indication that there has been no change of heart on the side of the Government. The time for an honourable settlement is not yet ripe. We have yet to travel a long way along the path of suffering and sacrifice before we can hail the advent of Swaraj. A page from recent Irish history will substantiate my point. Alderman MacSweeney Lord Mayor of Cork went on hunger strike as a protest against his imprisonment. When he was on the point of death, passionate appeals were made to His Majesty the King on behalf of Britishers and Irishmen alike asking him to exercise his royal prerogative and save MacSweeney's life. The King was deeply moved but announced through his Secretary's that he was unable to do anything because his ministers were opposed to clemency. The King therefore had to capitulate. The effect of this in Ireland was that the fight with Britain went on with increasing bitterness. After some time both parties felt it desirable to call a truce and settlement. The question of amnesty to political prisoners was then broached and the Sinn Fein leaders demanded the release of all prisoners, including those who had been sentenced to death. The British Cabinet agreed to release everybody except Seon McKeon who had been condemned to death. The Sinn-Fein leaders thereupon threatened to break off the truce if Seon McKeon was not released within twenty-four hours. In reply to ultimatum, the same Cabinet which had declined to spare the life of Terence MacSweeny in spite of country-wide agitation released Seon McKeon within twenty-four hours. MacSweeny had to die because the time for settlement had not arrived. Seon McKeon was saved because there was going to be a lasting peace and a change of heart had taken place on the side of the British people. May we not apply the same moral to Indian history?

Brave as Bhagat Singh and his comrades were, they did not ask for clemency. They had resolved to give their all, so that India could be free. But the whole country desired their lives to be spared. If truce had been declared, if peace was within sight then the lives of these brave and selfless men could be transformed and could be utilised in the task of national reconstruction. The whole country, including all parties and shades of opinion, had given unmistakable expression to the desire and demand for commutation. But if every possible effort had been made on the side of the people, there was one more effort which could have been made. When the negotiations for a truce were going on, the Congress as the one representative nationalist organisation in the country could have espoused the cause of the revolutionaries and of the Labour Party of India. The Congress need not thereby have identified itself with the methods or tactics of the revolutionaries and of the Labour party. It could have simply pointed out that since these two parties existed and since they were also working for the salvation of India according to their own light, abiding peace could not possibly be established until they were somehow made parties to it.

A generous gesture on the part of Government at this juncture would have had a most wholesome effect on these two parties and on the country at large. If after a generous gesture coming from the official side—any group, party or individual did not reciprocate it, then that group of individual would stand condemned in the eyes of the whole world. The Government with all its strength and resources would in either case have lost nothing if by conciliation they could placate all the militant parties in the country, it would be a moral triumph for them. If conciliation failed, they could once again resort to repression and could then do so with greater justification.

Blunder of Congress

If the Government have blundered, so also has the Congress. During the truce-talks the Congress could have spoken for the whole country, just as Sinn Fein had spoken for the whole of Ireland. Without identifying itself with the methods of the revolutionary and Labour parties, the Congress could very well have identified itself with their demands. But the Congress failed to do so and in failing it had only lowered itself in the estimation of the country and of the world. A similar attitude could have been adopted by the Congress after the petition for the commutation of the death sentences passed on Bhagat Singh and others was rejected by the Government.

If the Congress had officially demanded the commutation of the death sentences it would not have lost anything but have risen in the estimation of the whole country and might possibly have saved the life of Bhagat Singh. Even if the demand had been rejected by the Government, the Congress would have had this satisfaction that it had done its duty and no one could then have nursed any complaint or grievance against the Congress for not doing its best to save Bhagat Singh and his comrades.

Views on Gandhi-Irwin Pact

With regard to the truce embodied in what is known as the Gandhi-Irwin Pact I may say that it is exceedingly unsatisfactory and highly disappointing. What pains me most is the consideration that at the time this pact was drawn up, we actually had more strength than would appear from the contents of the document. I shall here summarise some of the unsatisfactory features of the truce terms:

(1) Ordinances like the Bengal Ordinance (Bengal Criminal

Amendment Act) and the Burma Ordinance whereby people are incarcerated without trial on mere suspicion have not been repealed.

(2) Provisions for the return of fines and of confiscated property are not satisfactory.

(3) The demand for the enquiry into the police excesses should not have been given up, particularly after it was made on behalf of the Congress. Further the Congress should have stood by Garhwalis who refused to fire on unarmed people and the policemen who were dismissed on political grounds. The Government refused to let down their own men in spite of the many excesses committed by them whereas the Congress did not stand by their own men.

(4) The Congress should not have given up the boycott of British goods—particularly when this does not form part of the Civil Disobedience Movement. In normal times before the Civil Disobedience was started last year we could carry on the Boycott of British Goods, but unfortunately now we cannot. Therefore we are now in a worse position after the Civil Disobedience Movement than we were before it.

(5) The provisions for the manufacture of salt are not adequate—since salt could be manufactured only within a limited area.

(6) The restrictions that have been agreed to in connection with picketing places us in a more difficult position than before the Civil Disobedience Movement was started last year. If these restrictions are strictly adhered to it will be difficult, if not impossible, to have picketing at all.

(7) Above all, the provisions regarding amnesty are exceedingly unsatisfactory. In the first place all Civil Disobedience prisoners have not so far been released. Further we cannot, under the truce terms claim amnesty for revolutionary and Labour party prisoners. The hanging orders will not be stopped—the different conspiracy cases like Chittagong Armoury Raid Case and Meerut Conspiracy Case are to go on. Political prisoners who had been in prison for 10 or 12 years like the Martial Law prisoners in the Punjab are to remain in jail. Last but not the least, the Bengal detenus imprisoned as detained without trial are not to be released. What then is the value of this amnesty. I should further point out that the distinction between violent and non-violent prisoners now made by the Congress is a new stunt. It was not made in the Delhi Manifesto in 1929 nor was it made in the celebrated eleven points of Mahatma Gandhi.

It does not require any further argument to expose the unsatisfactory character of the truce terms. On perusing the document one cannot help feeling that it was agreed to with a defeatist mentality on the side of the

Congress and the language at several places militates against our sense of self-respect and honour. If we really had been in a weak position when the truce was arrived at—I would not have made much protest—but were we really so weak at that time? I doubt it.

But the truce is now an accomplished fact and the question is that we should ponder very carefully before we take any aggressive step. Instead of wasting our energy in negative criticism, let us do something positive and beneficial. I do not for one moment question the patriotism of those who are responsible for the true terms. Far from it. Consequently the best course for us would be to do some positive work which will further strengthen the nation and the nation's demands. For this purpose at the very outset I have indicated the outlines of a new programmes which the more radical section among our country would do well to adopt and carry out. This will avoid unnecessary conflict with the Congress leaders at a time when such conflict may tend to weaken the people and strengthen the Government. Above all let us have restraint and self-control even when we have to criticise others. We shall lose nothing by being courteous and restrained and we may gain much. If we believe in our programme let us carry it out to the best of our ability. If our programme is based on truth it is bound to be accepted by our country men in the long run for truth will ultimately prevail in this world. Friends, I have taken up a lot of your valuable time but I have done. Let us address ourselves to our task in all seriousness, with unflinching courage but in all humility. The vision of free India, a completely free and emancipated India is what has captivated my soul. It is the dream of my life and the goal of all my activities. India has much to contribute to the culture and civilisation of the world. The whole world is anxiously awaiting that gift. And the last gift which India will make to the world is a new socio-economic order and a body politic which will have lessons for the whole of humanity. India is the keystone of the world edifice and free India spells the destruction of Imperialism throughout the world. Let us therefore rise to the occasion and make India free so that humanity may be saved.

References

1. He began this propaganda soon after the Calcutta Congress by stating publicly that if by December 31st, 1929, the Government did not concede Dominion Status to India, he would become on 'Independence-wallah' on January 1st, 1930. This time-limit of one year was reminiscent of his promise of *Swaraj* within one year in 1921.

2. Bose also learnt from Mahatma that he had voluntarily withdrawn the demand for an inquiry into the police atrocities.
3. True to his assurance, on the eve of his arrest under Regulation 25 of 1827 on January 4th, 1932, the Mahatma issued an appeal in which he said, 'Discard every trace of violence from your heart; give absolute protection to every English man, woman and child.'
4. On this occasion the Bose had to spend 24 hours in the Lalbazar Central Police Station without food and drink and without change. There was only a small quantity of Tincture of Iodine available at the station for application to his injuries. This was soon exhausted and when he asked for more, he did not get any. The next day he had to appear in Court with his clothes covered with blood and his arm in a sling. He made a statement before the Magistrate regarding his treatment in the Police Station which was duly recorded. After his removal to prison he was X-rayed and it was then found that two of the fingers in his right hand had been fractured.
5. Bose came to know of these facts after my release from prison in March 1931.
6. In the light of these facts, the attitude of the Nationalist Muslims in 1934 to the Prime Minister's Communal Award is inexplicable.

APPENDIX I

The Government Advocate's Speech

Below is given the full text of Govt. Advocate Carden Noad's opening speech.

"There are 32 persons involved in the case of whom 7 are approvers, 9 are absconding and are still at large and 16 are place on their trial present in Court. They will be tried under the ordinary criminal law of the land for offences alleged to have been committed by them while evidence will be recorded under Section 512 of the Criminal Procedure Code against the absconding accused.

I desire to emphasise the fact that this is an ordinary trial under ordinary law (though of singular importance) and that these individuals alone are upon their trial. No political action or system is in any way involved. No social, religious or educational body or institution is or can be affected by the outcome of this prosecution except so far as it is in their interest of all citizens of a civilised community that offences against the law of the land shall, if proved according to law, be suitably punished.

I wish also to say on behalf of myself and my colleagues, Khan Sahib Kalandar Ali Khan and Mr. Gopal Lal, that we shall do our best to assist the Special Magistrate in giving the accused fair, patient and impartial enquiry and I confidently ask for the cooperation of the learned counsel appearance on behalf of the defence in attaining this object. It may not be out of place at this stage to recall the occurrence of the murder of Mr. Saunders, ASP and Channan Singh, Head Constable. Two unarmed men were shot down in broad daylight in the streets of Lahore on the17th December, 1928 and the police were unable at that time to apprehend the culprits. Coupled with universal condemnation of this dastardly murder severe criticism was levelled against the police in Council and in the newspapers because of the delay which took place in the detection of the culprits. The Special CID with K.B. Abdul Aziz and his staff all working under the direct instructions and orders of Mr. Stead, Inspector General of Police, have now discovered the facts and are prepared to prove that these murders were committed in pursuance of a widespread conspiracy as a part of a series of criminal acts and designs of the most serious nature. I am confident that every member of the public will now be interested in seeing that justice is done. I may not be misunderstood. We desire the Court as well as the public to hold the scales evenly between the case of the Crown and the case of the accused now before the Court.

Constitution of Revolutionary Party

I should like to give a short summary of the various intentions, designs and acts which form part of the subject matter of the case to be placed before the Court.

The accused above-mentioned were members of a revolutionary party which became active throughout Northern India. At a meeting held at Delhi in August 1928, a Central Committee was constituted representing different provinces. In that meeting the following plans and resolutions were adopted and passed.

1. Phonindra Nath, approver was elected officer-in-charge of Behar and Orissa. Sukh Dev and Bhagat Singh accused were to be in charge of the Punjab. Shiv Varma, Bijoy Kumar Sinha and Chandra Shekhar Azad, the last two are absconding, were to be in charge of the United Provinces. Kundan Lal alias Partab absconding was elected for Rajputana and the Central Office. Chandra Shekhar Azad was also to be in charge of the Military Department.
2. It was decided that officers in charge should be held responsible for any work or action to be accomplished in the Province under their orders and that if any outside assistance were required in any provincial action the case should be submitted to the Central Committee which would issue final orders.
3. That all matters relating to finance, income and expenditure were to be dealt with by the central body.
4. That all arms and munitions should be placed with the central body to be issued for use by members of any province wherever and whenever required.

Aims and Objects

The main aims and objects of this revolutionary party as will be proved by the evidence of witnesses and of documents were as follows :

1. To establish a Republican Government by means of an organisation known as the Hindustan Republican Association and Indian Republican Army. For this purpose the policy of non-violence was to be discarded and armed forces organised with a view to overthrow the present Government and to overawe all officials and persons interested in the Administration.
2. To establish a reign of terror by the murder of officials who took a prominent part in such cases as the Kakori Conspiracy Case and other persons who were for various reasons obnoxious to the conspiracy. By such murders it was hoped to obtain the approval and financial support of persons in foreign countries interested in the propagation of revolution in India and such murders were definitely advocated as a means for obtaining funds abroad.
3. To organise the escape of convicts undergoing sentences in the jails for complicity in the Kakori conspiracy and similar cases.
4. To raise funds by every possible means by voluntary subscription, by dacoity or by contributions from abroad. Money thus collected was to be utilised for purchasing arms, manufacturing bombs and helping the members in spreading their republican propaganda and obtaining recruits throughout India.
5. The seduction of educated youths with a view to enlist them in the Indian Republican Army.

Fictitious Names

Evidence will be led to show that in prosecution of the objects of the conspiracy secret meetings were held by the members at different places for the constitution of Committees and for the arrangement of various crimes. The accused were moving about from place to place and from province to province under fictitious names some of which were as follows :

Sukh Dev	Dayal, Swami, Villager.
Kishori Lal Rattan	Dev Dutt, Mast Ram Shastri
Agya Ram	Masterji
Prem Dutt	Master, Amrit Lal
Surindra Nath Pandey	Stone
Jai Dev	Harish Chandar
Shiv Varma	Parbhat, Har Narain, Ram Narain
Gaya Prashad	Dr B.S. Nigam, Ram Lal, Ram Nath, Desh Bhagat
Mahabir Singh	Partab
Bhagat Singh	Ranjit
Batukeshwar Dutt	Battu Mohan
Ajoy Kumar Ghosh	Negro-General
Shachindra Nath Sanyal	Sachin Sanyal

Absconders

Chandra Shekhar Azad	Panditji
Bijoy Kumar Sinha	Bachu
Kailash Patti	Kali Charan
Raghunath	'M', Ram Guru
Bhagwati Charan	B.C. Vohra
Kundan Lal	Partap, No. 1 of Benares
Kailash	Gunthala of Jhansi

Approvers

Jai Gopal	Harbans Lal, Gopal, Krishen Chand
Hansraj Vohra	Tarlok Chand
Phonindra Nath Ghosh	Dada
Brahm Dutt	Manmohan
Manmohan Bannerji	Manohar Bannerji

Overt Acts

The overt acts committed in furtherance of the conspiracy included the following :

1. *Saunders and Channan Singh Murder.* The Committee of the revolutionary party deputed Jai Gopal, approver, Bhagat Singh, Chandra Shekhar Azad, and Raghu Nath, the last two are still absconding, with arms to murder Mr. Scott. The said party of four culprits used to frequent the neighbourhood of the police office with a view to watch Mr. Scott's movements and to know the locality better. It so happened that Mr. Scott

did not attend the office for a few days before the occurrence while Mr. Saunders attended the office daily. On 17th December, 1928, when Mr. Saunders came out of the office and was about to get on his motorcycle he was shot by the culprits in mistake for Mr. Scott. Hearing the report of the shots, Channan Singh, Head Constable, rushed towards the spot, ran and followed the accused when he too was fired at. Mr. Saunders died instantaneously and Channan Singh died shortly after. The culprits after shooting these men ran away.

2. *Assembly Bomb Outrage.* With a view to create terrorism Bhagat Singh and Batukeshwar Dutt were deputed to throw bombs in the Assembly Chamber, Delhi. Consequently, these two accused threw bombs and fired shots in the Assembly Chamber on 8th April, 1929 causing severe injuries to Sir Bomanji Dalal and others. Both the culprits were arrested at the spot and placed on trial with the result that both of them were sentenced to transportation for life.

3. *Dacoity at Punjab National Bank, Lahore.* When the course of activities in Lahore was a house in Mozang, a meeting was held at which several of the accused were present. One of the members, namely, Panditji proposed a raid on the Punjab National Bank in order to secure funds. The members who formed a party for this raid were fully equipped with arms and specific duties were assigned to each of them. Bhagat Singh and Partap had to bring a taxi there in order to take away the body. Consequently all the members detailed for the dacoity arrived on the appointed day, i.e., 4th December, 1928 at the premises of the Punjab National Bank and waited for the arrival of Bhagat Singh and Partap. At about 4 p.m. only Partap turned up in a tonga and informed the conspirators that a taxi could not be obtained. The project was then for the time being dropped.

4. *Dacoity at Maulina in Behar and Orissa.* In order to raise funds the members of the revolutionary party resolved to commit dacoity at Maulina. With the object in view a dacoity was conducted on 7th June, 1928 in the house of a rich man named Dank Mahton Koori, a Hindu gentleman. The owner of the house was shot and died later on and a quantity of jewellery was taken by the culprits.

5. *Attack on Mr. Bannerji, DSP, CID of UP.* Mr. Bannerji was an officer in the CID of UP who took a leading part in connection with the Kakori Conspiracy Case. The revolutionary party decided to do away with him and for this purpose two of them, namely, Mani Bannerji and Tarak Nath, were deputed. Mani Bannerji happened to meet Mr. Bannerji, DSP in Benares on 13th January, 1928 who shot at him with a revolver.

Mr. Bannerji got injuries but luckily survived them. Mani Bannerji was arrested, tried and convicted.

6. *An Embezzlement of Rs. 3,199.* Kailash Patti alias Kali Charan, an absconder, who was an employee in the Post Office, Burhal Ganj, District Gorakhpur, was one of the members of this revolutionary party. He embezzled Rs. 3,199 from that post office on 26th June, 1928 to be utilised by the party in furtherance of their common object.

7. *Manufacture of Bombs.* The revolutionary party learned how to manufacture bombs and during the course of their activities they were manufacturing bombs for the purpose of using them when occasion arose. Members of the conspiracy manufactured bombs at Lahore, Saharanpur, Calcutta and Agra. The factories at Lahore and Saharanpur have since been captured. On search, bombs, revolvers, ammunitions, implements for manufacturing bombs, books on bomb making and various prescribed literature were found. The Saharanpur and Agra cases have also been transferred to this province by order of the Government of India as they form an integral portion of the conspiracy under trail.

Crimes Not Carried Out

Certain crimes were discussed and planned by the conspirators but for various reasons not carried out. Among them were the following :

1. Proposal to blow up the train carrying the members of the Simon Commission by means of dynamite. For want of funds this plan could not be carried out.

2. Proposal to make arrangements for the escape of Jogesh Chandra Chatterji , a convict in connection with the Kakori Conspiracy, and Sachin Sanyal, another convict. These also could not be carried out for want of funds and also because the convicts were well guarded. The conspirators were apparently not prepared to face the personal risk involved.

Having briefly discussed the activities of the accused the next point I will deal with is how the case has been discovered.

How the Police Got Information

On the occasion of Dussehra festival in 1928 a bomb was thrown on a crowd near the Roshanai Gate in Lahore which resulted in numerous deaths and severe injuries. As a similar outrage on the occasion of the Dusehra festival in 1926 had taken place and the case had remained untraced, the Punjab Government deputed Khan Bahadur Abdul Aziz, Superintendent of Police, Montgomery to investigate this outrage. During the course of investigation of these bomb outrages, it transpired that two ex-students of the Oriental College had been frequenting the Boarding House situated on the 2nd floor of Roshanai Gate, the place where the latter bomb explosion had taken place. Enquiries further showed that these two persons belonged to the Revolutionary Party.

As a result of a statement made by one of them, the police for the first time came to know that Bhagat Singh accused was one of the murders of Mr. Saunders and that Bhagwati Charan an absconder, a member of Naujawan Bharat Sabha, was his Chief Lieutenant in the Punjab. Bhagat Singh accused could not be found in spite of the fact that strenuous efforts for his arrests were made in the Punjab, UP and Bengal. He suddenly appeared in the Assembly as one of the perpetrators of the Assembly Bomb outrage.

Lahore Bomb Factory

Shortly before these certain persons had engaged some iron moulders of Lahore to make certain oblong implements which on enquiry they stated were intended to be parts of a gas machine. The curiosity of a local workman was aroused and he happened to mention these facts to a constable of his acquaintance. The information was passed on to the police who instructed their informant to watch the individuals who had given the orders and to follow them to their house. Sukh Dev accused happening to pass by was duly followed to No. 69, Kashmir Buildings and this house was pointed to the police. The enquiry showed that the tenant of the premises was Bhagwati Charan who has been named as the Chief Lieutenant of Bhagat Singh and of the conspiracy in the Punjab. The house appeared to be locked and empty and a strict watch was kept to ascertain when it was visited. In the meantime, information from Delhi showed that the bomb thrown in the Assembly corresponded closely with the description of the alleged oblong gas machine parts. The careful watch kept on the house eventually resulted in information which led to a raid on 15th April, 1929. Sukh Dev, Jai Gopal and Kishori Lal, accused, were captured in the house. From the facts disclosed by these accused, the whole history of the revolutionary organisation came to light. The lengthy statement of Sukh Dev cannot be referred to by me in this statement except so far as it led to discoveries which render it admissible under the Evidence Act. But it is sufficient to say that from the moment when these accused were captured, information in the possession of the police led them steadily and by regular steps to the unravelling of the whole conspiracy and to the detailed knowledge of its activities which will be placed before the Court in evidence in this case.

The Charges

The charges against the accused will include murder, abetment of murder and conspiracy to murder, conspiracy to revolution and other offences against the State and also offences under the Explosive Substance Act. With regard to offences against the State a complaint has been that in accordance with the requirements of law by the Senior Superintendent of Police, Lahore. The facts which I have very briefly mentioned will be fully proved by the evidence which will be laid before the Court."

—*The Tribune*, July 11, 1929, pp. 4 and 13

APPENDIX II

Jinnah's Speech in the Central Legislative Assembly on September 12 and 14, 1929

"Sir, one is placed somewhat in a difficult position when one has got to deal with a speaker like the last one. It was his maiden speech, and it is the tradition of this House, that when a Member makes his maiden speech, he is in a privileged position and is not to be attacked. Whatever reasons or grounds, therefore, he may have given me for criticising him, I will not wish to depart from that tradition which, I think, ought to be maintained in the House. But I would say this, that in his concluding portion he remarked that the Hon'ble Members may have admiration and sympathy for the accused in the Lahore case. I think I am speaking on behalf of a very large body of people when I say that, if there is sympathy and admiration for the accused, it is only to this extent, that they are the victim of the system of government. It is not that we approve or applaud their actions if they are guilty, which still remains to be proved. If they are guilty of the offences of which they are charged, then I am sure it is not that we admire them or approve of their actions, but, on the contrary, I am sure a large body of thinking people feel that these young men, whatever be the provocations, are misguided in resorting to actions for which they now stand charged.

Now, Sir, the Hon'ble Home Member asked the House that we must approach this question without prejudice, and impartially. Sir, I am sure the Hon'ble Home Member himself tried his best to follow the same principle, but has he been able to apply the same principle when he brings this before the House? Do the facts justify that? The last speaker, whom

I am not going to attack, almost gave away the case in his concluding remarks when he said that the only way to break the hunger-strike is to pass this Bill.

Well, I am not concerned at present so much with the account that was given by the Hon'ble Member with regard to the treatment in jails of various classes of prisoners, but one thing is clear, and it is this. From the statement that was issued by Bhagat Singh and Dutt, what is an admitted fact now, even from the speech of the Hon'ble Member who spoke last, is that they were not given the treatment—not on racial grounds—but according to the standard and the scale which is laid down for Europeans in the matter of diet and bare necessities of life. It is not a mere question that they want to be treated as Europeans. As a matter of fact, according to the admission and the definition given by the Hon'ble Member who spoke last on behalf of the Treasury Benches, so far as I know, Bhagat Singh and Dutt wear topees, and their figures appeared in shorts. Therefore, they ought to have been treated as Europeans. The Hon'ble Member in reply to a question said that whether the man is a European or an Indian—and he accepted the definition of my honourable friend Mr. Neogy—if one wears a topee, then one is a European for the purpose of jail rules. Then why should you not treat Bhagat Singh and Dutt, who wear topees and European clothes, as such for the purpose of treatment in jails? Why do not the Punjab Government give them the treatment that they are entitled to, at once, and be done with? They wear topees and they are entitled to that treatment.

What do they say in their statement which was read out? This is what they say :

> "We, Bhagat Singh and Dutt, were sentenced to life transportation in the Assembly bomb case, Delhi, on 19th May, 1929. As long as we were undertrial prisoners in Delhi jail we were accorded very good treatment and we were given good diet. But since our transfer from the Delhi Jail to Mianwali Jail and Lahore Central Jail,—

Which is represented by the Hon'ble Member, who spoke last—the Punjab seems to be a terrible place . . .

Mian Muhammad Shah Nawaz (West Central Punjab) : Don't go there.

M.A. Jinnah: I won't. To continue what they say :

"We are being treated as ordinary criminals".

So, in Delhi they received very good treatment and in the Punjab they are treated as ordinary criminals. Surely, Sir, if the Government of the Punjab was not wanting in statesmanship, if the Government of the Punjab had any brains, they would have found a solution to this question very easily and long ago. But, Sir, it is a question—the more I examine it and the more I analyse it, I find—it is a question of declaration of war. As far as the Punjab Government are concerned, the Government do not merely wish to bring these men to trial and get them convicted by a judicial tribunal, but Government go to war against these men. They seem to me in this frame of mind : "We will pursue every possible course, every possible method, but we will see that you are sent either to the gallows or transported for life, and in the meantime we will not treat you as decent men."

Sir, the whole spirit behind this is that and nothing else. I do not for a moment wish to say that the Government are not bound—in fact, it is their bounden duty—to prosecute those people that commit offences. I do not wish to say that the Government should not do every thing in their power to see that their convictions are secured. But may I ask, with whom are you at war? What are the resources of these few young men who, according to you, have committed certain offences? You want to prosecute them, and after duc trial, you want to secure their convictions. But before they are convicted, surely this is not a matter on which there should be this struggle, that you should not at once yield to their demands for bare necessities of life. After all, so far as the Lahore case prisoners are concerned, surely they are political prisoners and undertrial. You ask me, what is a political prisoner? It is very difficult to define a political prisoner. It is very difficult to lay down any particular definition. But if you use your common sense, if you use your intelligence, surely you can come to the conclusion with regard to the particular case and say, here are these men who are political prisoners, and we do not wish to give them proper treatment. We want to give them treatment as undertrial prisoners. If you had said that, the question would have been solved long ago. Do you wish to prosecute them or persecute them?

Sir, I do not wish to base my opposition to this Bill on this issue of bad treatment, because this is only one aspect of the issue, or rather one aspect of the Bill before us. This Bill has got to be looked at, as far as I can see, from three points of view. The *first,* form the point of view of criminal jurisprudence ; *second*, political point of view or the policy of the Bill ; and *third*, treatment to the accused when they are undertrial. I think it will be admitted, I think even the Hon'ble Home Member conceded, that by the Bill which he has brought before the House, he is introducing a principle, in the criminal jurisprudence, of a very unprecedented character. I do not think, Sir, there is any system of jurisprudence in any civilised country where you will find such a principle in existence as is involved in this Bill. Some of the Hon'ble Members who are not lawyers might not have appreciated fully the implications of this Bill. This Bill not only dispenses with the presence of the accused at the trial, but I will give you a picture as to what will happen under this Bill. Under this Bill the Government will apply to the Magistrate before whom the inquiry is going on and say : "Here is a law which we have secured from the Legislature. Now the accused have voluntarily made themselves incapable of attending the Courts and, therefore, you have to dispense with their presence". The inquiry will then proceed *ex parte* before the Magistrate. Evidence will be led, oral and documentary, which will go without being tested by cross-examination. The documentary evidence will go without being even seen by the accused, against whom it is produced, and how will you identify the accused in their absence? Then we know, and particularly those who are lawyers would know, that when the Magistrate has concluded the recording of the evidence for the prosecution, under Section 209 of the Criminal Procedure Code, he must ask the accused whether he has any explanation to offer with regard to the evidence which is recorded by him against the accused. It is after that statement is made that the Magistrate has got the power either to commit or discharge the accused. That statement of the accused under Section 209 is absolutely obligatory. It is not the choice of the Magistrate. The Privy Council has laid down that an omission in that regard would vitiate the whole trial. Under this Bill the accused will not be there to give any explanation to the Magistrate with regard to the evidence that has been already recorded *ex parte*.

Then, Sir, we come to important Sections. Under Section 287 that statement again will have to be made before the Sessions Court. There also, the accused will not be present. The evidence before the Sessions Court will be recorded *ex parte* and if it is a jury, the jury will be asked to return their verdict. If it is a case of assessors, they will be asked to express their opinion, and the Judge will pass his judgement or sentence, as the case may be. I ask the Hon'ble Home Member, and I ask the Hon'ble Law Member of the Government of India whether that will be a trial or a farce?

Sir Brojendra Mitter (Law Member): Not a farce. The accused can always go before the Court if she chooses to.

Gaya Prasad Singh: But what about the evidence that has already been recorded in his absence?

M.A. Jinnah: I am very glad that the Hon'ble Law Member has given me a reply. Then you want by this Bill really to break the hunger-strikers. You want this House to give you a Statute laying down a principle generally in the criminal jurisprudence for this particular case, so that you may use it for breaking the hunger-strike in the Lahore case. Remember, you have no other case that you can cite. One swallow does not make a summer. It is the Lahore case. Well, you know perfectly well that these men are determined to die. It is not a joke. I ask the Hon'ble Law Member to realise that it is not everybody who can go on starving himself to death. Try if for a little while and you will see. Sir, have you heard anywhere in the world, except the American case, which may honourable friend Mr. Jamnadas Mehta pointed out, of an accused person going on hunger-strike? The man who goes on hunger-strike has a soul. He is moved by the soul and he believes in the justice of his cause ; he is not an ordinary criminal who is guilty of cold-blooded, sordid, wicked crime.

Mind you, Sir, I do not approve of the action of Bhagat Singh, and I say this on the floor of this House. I regret that, rightly or wrongly, youth today in India is stirred up, and you cannot, when you have three hundred and odd millions of people, you cannot prevent such crimes being committed, however much you may deplore them and however much you may say that they are misguided. It is the system, this damnable system of Government, which is resented by the people. You may be a cold-blooded logician : I am a patient cool-headed man and can calmly go on making speeches here, persuading and influencing the Treasury Bench. But, remember, there are thousands of young men outside. This is not the only country where these actions are resorted to. It has happened in other countries, not youths, but greybearded men have committed serious offences, moved by patriotic impulses. What happened to Mr. Congrave, the Prime Minister of Ireland? He was under sentence of death a fortnight before he got an invitation from His Majesty's Government to go and settle terms? Was he a youth? Was he a young man? What about Collins? So what is the good of your putting forward this argument? You have got a situation which you have got to meet, not by introducing and enacting measures which go to the root of the fundamental principles of criminal jurisprudence, and lightly, saying, "Oh! but it is common sense!" Law is common sense ; it is not common sense of one individual.

Mr. President: I hope the Hon'ble Member is not inconvenienced when I ask him to resume his speech at the next meeting.

Pandit Madan Mohan Malaviya: Sir, cannot we go on for another 15 minutes?

Mr. President: What is the idea of going on for another 15 minutes? I can understand the House asking me to sit till 6 o'clock, but there is no idea in sitting for another 15 minutes only.

> The House was then adjourned. Mr. Jinnah concluded his speech at the next sitting, after the adjournment motion had been admitted for discussion.

"Sir, when the House last adjourned I was dealing with this Bill from the point of view of criminal jurisprudence—and I brought to the notice of the House what would be the position if this Bill was passed, so far as the trial and proceedings of this particular case, or any other case under it, were concerned. It is quite clear, as I said, that the trial will be a travesty of justice. Let us consider the point further. The trial would proceed in the absence of the accused. I ask the Home Member, is there a Judge or jury who would feel that they were administering law or justice in that case? The moment this Bill is passed, the prosecution can go before the Court and say : "Here is a voluntary act of the accused person ; he has or they have incapacitated himself or themselves, and we ask you now to proceed *ex parte*". Remember, Sir, that in a particular case that procedure may be adopted from the very start. Even the plea of the accused may not be recorded, guilty or not guilty. Then the Judge will be asked to proceed to empanel a jury and the jury will be empanelled : You will have a Judge on the Bench and the jury by his side. What will they do? They hear the *ex parte* evidence, oral and documentary. I ask the Home Member, I ask this House, what would you consider of that Judge, what would you think of that Judge or jury, sitting there solemnly, seriously, proceeding with a charge of murder, going through this farce as His Majesty's Court—what conclusion do you think any jury can come to under those circumstance? That prisoner stands already condemned. What is the good of this farce? I say that no Judge who has got an iota of a judicial mind or a sense of justice can ever be a party to a trial of that character and pass sentence of death without a shudder and a pang of conscience. This is the farce which you propose to enact under this procedure ! I say this, that if ever there was a conscientious Judge and he was strong enough, if he had a judicial mind, and if he had any independence, let me tell you, that, in spite of this provision of yours, he would say, "True, the law has to be administered; I am obliged to make the order that the trial shall proceed *ex parte* ; but

I realise and I feel that it will be a travesty of justice and I cannot be a party to it ; and I shall, therefore, adjourn this case until further orders". Have you considered that? I suppose you have not. It seems to me, Sir, that the great and fundamental doctrine of British jurisprudence, which is incorporated and codified in the Penal Code and the Criminal Procedure Code, has very wisely not made such an absurd provision in the criminal law of this country and I am not satisfied that there is a lacuna in our system of criminal law.

The Home Member said that it is a well-known doctrine and a fundamental doctrine of criminal jurisprudence that the man is taken to be innocent until he is proved to be guilty. May I remind him of another doctrine which goes to the very root of the criminal jurisprudence, or for the matter of that of even civil law, that no man is to be condemned until he is given a hearing? Sir, I think there cannot be the slightest doubt that we are now engaged in considering a cardinal principle, a principle of very vital and paramount character, to be introduced into the criminal jurisprudence of this country. It must be admitted that this is a most revolutionary, unheard of, unprecedented change that is proposed in our criminal jurisprudence. I know the Home Member will tell me, "Yes, the doctrine is that no man shall be condemned unless he is heard and until he is given a hearing ; but here it is the voluntary act of the accused, and if he chooses not to go there and insist upon his being heard, it is his fault." Sir, this is not a new question ; it has been considered in England and there is a long history about it and behind it and you will find that in old days there was the strictest formality observed as to the recording of the plea of the prisoner. And if the prisoner was mute of malice, that is to say, if he refused deliberately to open his mouth when he was arraigned in a Court of law and when the question was put to him as to whether he pleaded guilty or not—he had to make his plea, and there are cases where he refused to speak, and the old law was—even England has advanced—in that case he was condemned and executed or must be committed to imprisonment . . .

E.L. Price (Bombay : European): Torture.

M.A. Jinnah: I am glad that you are up to date. I know that. I am only dealing with this one point, that he used to be executed or committed to prison. Further, when it was thought that it was rather a serious thing that, because a man was mute of malice, he should be condemned to death or imprisonment—then comes the point of my learned friend over there, who I undestand is a member of the Bar—that they resorted to torture. Torture for what? That he should make his plea, not that an *ex parte* trial should proceed. That is what you want to do here by this Bill, that *ex parte* trial should proceed. The old law was then altered, because the result of the torture was that some of them died and the form of torture was the most cruel form of tortune, and I will read to you a passage from the Stephen's *History of Criminal Law* :

> *If he was accused of felony, he was condemned, after much exhortation to the peine forte et dure, that is to be stretched, naked on his back, and to have 'iron laid upon him as much as he could bear and more', and so to continue, fed upon bad bread and stagnant water on alternate days, till he either pleaded or died.*

But they did not proceed *ex parte*. Then the old form of trial was trial by ordeal. That was done away with because the plea that a prisoner had to put forward was in a particular form. When he was asked he had to say that he wanted to be tried "By God and by my country". That was the trial by ordeal. That was done away with and in 1827 by a Statute it was enacted that in such cases a plea of not guilty should be entered. Now, Sir, before that Statue was passed there is one case which I will bring to the notice of this House and which will illustrate how much importance was attached to the form and the procedure even in olden days. Of course, my honourable friend Sir Darcy Lindsay will say that matters of this kind can be decided by the common sense of a single individual such as himself. Sir, I must remind him—for he is a man of peace, and especially when we get old we love peace, and common sense is sometimes regulated by that state of mind—, I will remind him, and I think the House will agree with me, that law is nothing but the essence of common sense, that law is the concentrated essence of experience, of knowledge, of practice of centuries and generations, and even Sir James Stephen will point out to you that, when these rules, when these forms have been laid down as the essence of common sense and experience of generations, they are not lightly to be departed from.

What do we find in this House now? Have we not got forms and are we not slavishly following them? Some of them would appear to the strangers in the gallery or any outsider to be most absurd and against common sense, at first sight. If any one passes across between you and the speaker he will be guilty of a gross breach of the forms of this House and you would call him to order at once. Why is that? Without meaning? Without reason? Without experience? What common sense is there? Why should the man not pass across? It is, therefore, no use treating these matters lightly and saying that we have got to decide everything by the common sense of an individual. The instance that I was going to refer to is this. In one case :

> Mr. Pike produces some evidence to show that in the early part of Edward I's reign, people who refused to put themselves on their trial were executed . . .

Better, people who refuse to put themselves to trial, execute them, rather than go through the force of an *ex parte* trial ; much better.

> " . . . but this practice was opposed to the statute which provided that 'notorious felons' and which openly be of evil name and will not put themselves in inquests of felonies that men shall charge them with before the justices at the King's suit, shall have strong and hard imprisonment, as they which refuse to stand to the common law of the land."

Then he cites a case which I think will interest the House. He says this :

> 'But this is not to be understood of such prisoners as be taken of light suspicion.' According to Barrington this meant that the prisoner who refused to plead was to be starved till he died, but not tortured—(so they improved later on)—and he quotes in proof of it a pardon granted in the reign of Edward III to a woman who *pro eo quod se tenuit mutam* was put in *areta prisona* and there lived without eating or drinking for forty days, which was regarded as a miracle."

Well, Sir, I know that there is a passage which is likely to be quoted in this House in Stephen's *Digest of Criminal Procedure.* It is a curious thing that the Government of India, who have hardly given this House evern seven days' notice and call upon this House to endorse a vital, cardinal principle of a novel or unheard of character, do not possess in their library even an edition of the *Law of Criminal Procedure* by Stephen of a later date then 1883. And they seriously ask this House, "The Government case is that they find that a deadlock is created. The law is paralysed, and in fact, even the Government of India might tumble down altogether, and we, therefore, call upon the Legislature to come to our rescue we admit it is unprecedented, we admit it is unheard of, we admit it is unknown to any system of jurisprudence ; but you as a responsible body—would you not endorse this Bill straightaway within these few days' notice?" You do not possess in your library an edition of a textbook which is the standard book except of the year 1883 ! And it is a tall order to ask the House to pass the Bill now and here. I will read the passage now, which is likely to be quoted, and I want the House not to be misled by it. But before I do so, I will request the Law Member, to consider what I am going to submit. That is a branch of the law which comes under the category of contempt of Court, and we know that the King's Bench in England and Superior Courts in India, who have inherited the jurisdiction under the Charter, have got unfettered power to deal with cases of contempt. That is the one branch of the law which is neither codified nor restricted by any law. It is entirely left to the Supreme Court or the High Courts in India to deal with cases of contempt as they think proper. That is a branch which comes under that doctrine of law of contempt of Court and even there, while the Courts have asserted that they have the power to refuse to hear the party who is guilty of contempt of Court, the footnote says that it has never been done in a criminal case. I will read to you what it says :

> "The Prisoner has a right to be present at the trial so long as he conducts himself properly, but the Court may, in its discretion, permit his absence in cases of misdemeanour, and may proceed with the trial in his absence in cases in which he has pleaded to an indictment or information in the High Court (Queen's Bench Division).
>
> "If a prisoner so misconducts himself as to make it impossible to try him with decency, the Court, it seems, may order him to be removed and proceed in his absence."
>
> The footnote says this :
>
> "I have never known or heard of this being done, but Lord Cranworth (then Rolfe, B.) threatened to have Rush removed from Court, at his trial for murder at Norwich in 1849, if he persisted in a singularly indecent and outrageous course of cross-examination. I have heard from eye-witness an account of a trial before Shee, J. (then acting as Commissioner) at Dorchester, where the prisoner (a convict at Portland, tried for the murder of a warder) behaved with such

desperate violence that it was necessary to fasten him down with chains and straps. He was not, however, removed from the Court, and it is obvious that in capital cases, or indeed in any trial involving severe punishment, almost any measures, short of removing the prisoner, should be resorted to."

The *raison d'etre* of this principle is very different and requires no more words to understand it. Now, Sir, I shall not weary the House with any further legal quotations. I am driven to think the object of Government in bringing in this Bill is political, but if their real object is to supply a lacuna, not for the purpose of this particular case, but in the general interest of the country and the administration of justice, if that is their object, let them remove this case from their mind, for Heaven's sake. Come to us dispassionately and without prejudice. Let them tell us that they find a lacuna, and that it is necessary to make some provision. If that is their object, then their honest and straightforward course is to come before the House and place all the facts before us. Now, I do not admit for a moment that there is a lacuna, and I do not admit that such a principle should be introduced in the criminal jurisprudence of our country, especially and admittedly when it does not exist anywhere else. I am prepared to assume that you honestly and sincerely believe that it is necessary, in the interest of the people and the administration of justice, that some such measure of the kind should be introduced. Then your honest course is to go slowly. Pause and consider. Let those outside this House who are competent to speak, express their opinion. What are you going to lose? What is the harm that will be done? Remove from your mind this Lahore conspiracy case. But if you say that this course will cause you inconvenience and that you want this instrument now and at once, then I say that I am not satisfied with your plea and I can't support it, nor am I satisfied with the version that you have placed before the House about your difficulties. I am not going to give you this power standing on the floor of this House, today, now and here.

Sir, can you imagine a more horrible form of torture than hunger-srike? If, rightly or wrongly, these men are inflicting this punishment upon themselves and thereby you are inconvenienced, is that any reason why you should ask us to abandon one of the cardinal principles of criminal jurisprudence? If these young men pursue this course, and I am sorry to hear that one of them has died, what will happen? Is this a matter which can continue indefinitely? Certainly not. As I say, I am not satisfied with the version that you have placed before this House. I understand that some of the prisoners are not on strike. If you are solicitous and anxious that their trial should proceed and should not be delayed, then split up the trial. Proceed against them and bring home the guilt to them if you can. I am told that it means expense. I am told that 400 witnesses are going to be produced and 200 more may be added. Now, I appeal to the common sense of the House and not only of Sir Darcy Lindsay. Can you imagine that 600 witnesses are necessary to prove the case against each one of the accused? And, Sir, I ask, is it not an amazing fact that, in order to prove this case, 600 persons should have been cited as witnesses? Well, Sir, it may seem a joke and it may seem that I am making fun of the statement made to this effect, but the first impression that one gets is that, when a case cannot be proved without the testimony of 600 witnesses, that case is a very bad case. Therefore, I say that it is open to Government to split up the case. You think of expense? But are we here to abandon this cardinal principle because it is going to cost some money to Government? Is that the reason? Is that a plea which can be accepted by any responsible Legislature?

Well, Sir, I was told that some of them go on a hunger-strike for a short time and then they get better for a little while and again they start, and so it goes on. Sir, I cannot understand the anxiety of the Government to proceed with this trial when these men are inflicting the greatest possible punishment upon themselves by prolonged fasting? Is it your fault? Does it mean that you are not treating them properly and, therefore you are compelling them to resort to these extreme methods? Well, then I appeal to you with all the emphasis I can command, do not be vindictive. Show that you are fair, generous, that you are willing to treat these men decently. At any rate, before they are released or sentenced, give them proper treatment. What treatment do they want? What is it that bothers them? Do they want spring mattresses? Do they want dressing tables? Do they want a set of toilet requisites? No, Sir, they ask for nothing but bare necessities and a little better treatment. I ask you in all decency, why cannot you concede this small thing? Well, Sir, if this Bill is passed, perhaps I might ask the Hon'ble Member when he goes to Court how would he base his application? Will he base his application on the point that the period of a hunger-strike which has already taken place for a short period is not to be counted? Or is it to be counted? Supposing I tried to put myself in the position of a Judge when the application is made that the presence of the accused in this case should be dispensed with, because by their own voluntary act they have rendered themselves incapable. Now, from what period shall I take the disability? From the period after this Statute is passed? Shall I disregard the disability which has already taken place before the passing of the Act? Supposing something else happens to these men on hunger-strike and they do not get well for two or three months. Will the trial not be delayed? Do you think you can avoid considerable delay even if the Bill is passed? Further, can you give a guarantee that all the prisoners will be well enough in the course of these two of three months from now to stand their trial. Even if they abandon hunger-strike? When you say that this Bill will not have retrospective effect, how is it going to work? Then will you give them notice that in view of the fact that this measure is passed, if you do not cease your hunger-strike from today and if you are not better within two or three months, as you ought to be, then we shall apply to the Court that your presence will be dispensed with and we shall proceed *ex parte*? Does it not come to this, that you want to carry this Bill, you want to have this Bill placed on the Statue-book, and then you want to give notice to the prisoners that, unless they cease their hunger-strike within a certain period, you are going to proceed *ex parte*? Under that threat you think these prisoners will cease their hunger-strike? Can you give the House that assurance, and if they do not cease their hunger-strike, what will you do? You will proceed *ex parte*? Just imagine the absurdity of the whole position.

Sir, now I have finished from the point of view of the jurisprudence. I do not wish to go into details so far as their treatment is concerned. I have, in the course of my speech, already indicated their grievances and how they can be met. But there is a political aspect of this Bill and the policy underlying this measure. I think the Hon'ble the Home Member must admit that this is not a measure which is only brought here for the purpose of putting the law in order. Sir, it reminds me of a story, an old Persian story. A man got stomach-ache because he had eaten some very rotten bread. So he went to the doctor and told him that he had stomach-ache. The doctor said, yes, and he promptly started treating his eyes. Then he said, "What have my eyes got to do with my complaint?" Then the doctor said, "Well, if you had eyes, you would never have got stomach-ache because you would not have eaten rotten bread". Similarly I would say to the Hon'ble the Home Member, "Have you got eyes? Well, if you had, you would never gave go, this stomach-ache". Now, will you open your eyes? Will you have a little more imagination? Have you got any statesmanship left? Have you got any political wisdom? This is not the way you are going to solve the root cause of the trouble. You may temporarily, provisionally, get over this particular trial. But now let us see what is the real cause of the trouble.

I ask this House to consider this. Is there today in any part of the globe a civilised government that is engaged, day in and day out, week in and week out month in and month out, in prosecuting their people? You have read the daily papers for the last six, eight months. You will find prosecutions in Bengal, prosecutions in Madras, prosecutions in the Punjab, prosecutions all over the country. In fact I am afraid you will soon have to open a new department and to have an additional Member to manage these prosecutions if you go on at this rate and in this way. Do you think that any man wants to go to jail? Is it an easy thing? Do you think any man wants to exceed the bounds of law for the purpose of making a speech which your law characterises as a seditious speech, knowing full well the consequences, that he may have to go to jail for six months or a year? Do you think that this springs out of a mere joke or fun or amusement? Do you not realise yourself, if you open your eyes, that there is resentment, universal resentment, against your policy, against your programme?

Then, Sir, what has happened so far as this House is concerned? What have you done since 1924 with regard to the protests that we have made session after session? Have you accepted the proposal or suggestion of any reasonable section of this House? I do not wish to go into the details, Sir, but what has been the attitude of the Government towards this House and the country outside over the constitutional reforms since 1924, leave alone the past prior history? The reply is : "We have appointed the Simon Commission and we must must await its Report." Well, the Simon Commission was not accepted by this House—but that does not matter. What is the answer in regard to the Indianisation of the Army? You appointed a Committee to go into that very important question : I attach more importance to it than to any other question. What have you done with the unanimous Report of the Skeen Committee which was endorsed by this House, without a division, the responsible House as you call it today and to which you appeal today in the name of "responsibility"? This House endorsed that Report without a division. What have you done with it? The attitude of Government has been an amazing one. The Army Secretary stood there on the floor of this House last session and said : "We cannot get even 20 suitable candidates". Sir, the apparent untruth of that statement is enough to condemn the Government. You cannot get 20 young men out of 300 odd millions of people, who are suitable candidates for the King's Commission?

Then, there are many other matters. What has been your attitude always? Don't you think that, instead of trying to proceed with an iron hand and pursuing a policy of repression against your own subjects, it would be better if you realised the root causes of the resentment and of the struggle that the people are carrying on? Don't you think that it is high time that you made your position more clear? I understand that there is something in the atmosphere—I hope it is true—that some satisfactory announcement is going to be made in Parliament very soon, when it meets next, which I trust will satisfy this House and the people. Do you want to prepare an atmosphere for it, or you do not? Do you want reconciliation between the Government and the people or you do not? Don't you think that these difficulties and troubles of yours are of a temporary character? They are an obstruction in the trial of this particular case which can be managed by other methods, but that is a very small matter when you compare it with the bigger issues which are awaiting the decision of the Government, this House and the country.

Sir, the Hon'ble Member asked, what are the Government to do? I think I understood the Hon'ble Member aright when he said that the Government have no other course. What are the Government to do? They are, therefore, compelled to bring this Bill. Now, let me tell you that your course is to open your eyes, have more imagination, do not be guilty of bankruptcy of statesmanship, do not merely sit there as if the wheels of the Secretariat must not be clogged at any cost, but try and understand the root cause and deal with the situation as politicians, as statesmen and not as bureaucrats, who can see no other way but to come forward before this House and ask for more statutory powers the moment any difficulty arises. You have got several courses open to you. The first and the foremost course open to you is this. Give these men decent treatment, and I think you will get over your difficulty. At least I hope so. If you do not, you will, at any rate, be exonerated in the eyes of the public and at the Bar of public opinion. Behave as a humane and decent Government, and that is enough for you. I am not going to urge upon the Government to withdraw prosecution cases against men if they have evidence enough to bring home to them their guilt. So try that better treatment first. Secondly, if you do not succeed, split up the trials. Try those with whose trial you can proceed, and leave the rest. After you have made it clear to them that you stand for a decent treatment being given to them and they still wish to torture themselves and follow that course, then you cannot help it ; and I venture to say that it will not last very long or indefinitely. And the last words I wish to address the

Government are, try and concentrate your mind on the root cause and the more you concentrate on the root cause the less difficulties and inconveniences there will be for you to face, and thank Heaven that the money of the taxpayer will not be wasted in prosecuting men, nay citizens, who are fighting and struggling for the freedom of their country."

Legislative Assembly Debates, Vol. IV, Part I, pp. 752-55 and 757-65.

APPENDIX III

Text of Statement of Bhagat Singh and B.K. Dutt in the Assembly Bomb Case

(Read in the Court on 6th June, 1929, by Mr. Asaf Ali on behalf of Bhagat Singh and B.K. Dutt)

"We stand charged with certain serious offences, and at this stage it is but right that we must explain our conduct.

In this connection, the following questions arise.

1. Were the bombs thrown into Chamber, and, if so, why?
2. Is the charge, as framed by the Lower Court, correct or otherwise?

To the first half of first question, our reply is in the affirmative, but since some of the so-called 'eye witnesses' have perjured themselves and since we are not denying our liability to that extent, let our statement about them be judged for what it is worth. By way of an illustration, we may point out that the evidence of Sergeant Terry regarding the seizure of the pistol from one of us is a deliberate falsehood, for neither of us had the pistol at the time we gave ourselves up. Other witnesses, too, who have deposed to having seen bombs being thrown by us have not scrupled to tell lies. This fact had its own moral for those who aim at judicial purity and fairplay.

At the same time, we acknowledge the fairness of the Public Prosecuter and the judicial attitude of the Court so far.

Viceroy's Views Endorsed

In our reply to the next half of the first question, we are constrained to go into some detail to offer a full and frank explanation of our motive and the circumstances leading upto what has now become a historic event.

When we were told by some of the police officers, who visited us in jail that Lord Irwin in his address to the joint session of the two Houses described the event as an attack directed against no individual but against an institution itself, we readily recognized that the true significance of the incident had been correctly appreciated.

We are next to none in our love for humanity. Far from having any malice against any individual, we hold human life sacred beyond words.

We are neither perpetrators of dastardly outrages, and therefore, a disgrace to the country, as the pseudo-socialist Dewan Chaman Lal is reported to have described us, nor are we 'Lunatics' as the *Tribune* of Lahore and some other would have it believed.

Practical Protest

We humbly claim to be no more than serious students of the history and conditions of our country and her aspirations. We despise hypocrisy. Our practical protest was against the institution, which since its brith, has eminently helped to display not only its worthlessness but its far-reaching power for mischief. The more we have pondered, the more deeply we have been convinced that it exists only to demonstrate to world India's humiliation and helplessness, and it symbolizes the over-riding domination of an irresponsible and autocratic rule. Time and again the national demand has been pressed by the people's representatives only to find the waste paper basket as its final destination.

Attack on Institution

Solemn resolutions passed by the House have been contemptuously trampled under foot on the floor of the so-called Indian Parliament. Resolution regarding the repeal of the repressive and arbitrary measures have been treated with sublime contempt, and the government measures and proposals, rejected as unacceptable by the elected members of the legistatures, have been restored by a mere stroke of the pen. In short, we have utterly failed to find any justification for the existence of an institution which, despite all its pomp and splendour, organized with the hard earned money of the sweating millions of India, is only a hallow show and a mischievous make-believe. Alike, have we failed to comprehend the mentality of the public leaders who help the Government to squander public time and money on such a manifestly stage-managed exhibition of India's helpless subjection.

No Hope For Labour

We have been ruminating upon all these matters, as also upon the wholesale arrests of the leaders of the labour movement. When the introduction of the Trade Disputes Bill brought us into the Assembly to watch its progress, the course of the debate only served to confirm our conviction that the labouring millions of India had nothing to expect from an institution that stood as a menacing monument to the strangling of the exploiters and the serfdom of the helpless labourers.

Finally, the insult of what we consider, an inhuman and barbarous measure was hurled on the devoted heads of the representatives of the entire country, and the starving and struggling millions were deprived of their primary right and the sole means of improving their economic welfare. None who has felt like us for the dumb driven drudges of labourers could possibly witness this spectacle with equanimity. None whose heart bleeds for them, who have given their life-blood in silence to the building up of the economic structure could repress the cry which this ruthless blow had wrung out of our hearts.

Bomb Needed

Consequently, bearing in mind the words of the late Mr. S.R. Das, once Law Member of the Governor-General's Executive Council, which appeared in the famous letter he had addressed to his son, to the effect that the 'Bomb was necessary to awaken England from her dreams', we dropped the bomb on the floor of the Assembly Chamber to register our protest on behalf of those who had no other means left to give expression to their heart-rending agony. Our sole purpose was 'to make the deaf hear' and to give the headless a timely warning. Others have as keenly felt as we have done, and from under the seeming stillness of the sea on Indian humanity, a veritable storm is about to break out We have only hoisted the 'danger-signal' to warn those who are speeding along without heading the grave dangers ahead. We have only marked the end of an era of Utopian non-violence, of whose futility the rising generation has been convinced beyond the shadow of doubt.

Ideal Explained

We have used the expression Utopian non-violence, in the foregoing paragraph which requires some explanation. Force when aggressively applied is 'voilence' and is, therefore, morally unjustifiable, but when it is used in the furtherance of a legitimate cause, it has its moral justification.

The elimination of force at all costs is Utopian, and the new movement which has arisen in the country, and of that dawn we have given a warning, is inspired by the ideals which guided Guru Gobind Singh and Shivaji , Kamal Pasha and Riza Khan, Washington and Garibaldi , Lafayette and Lenin.

As both the alien Government and the Indian public leaders appeared to have shut their eyes to the existence of this movement, we felt it as our duty to sound a warning where it could not go unheard.

We have so far dealt with the motive behind the incident in question, and now we must define the extent of our intention.

No Personal Grudge

We bore no personal grudge or malice against anyone of those who received slight injuries or against any other person in the Assembly. On the contrary, we repeat that we hold human life sacred beyond words, and would sooner lay down our own lives in the service of humanity than injure anyone else. Unlike the mercenary soldiers of the imperialist armies who are disciplined to kill without compunction, we respect, and, in so far as it lies in our power, we attempt to save human life. And still we admit having deliberately thrown the bombs into the Assembly Chamber. Facts, however, speak for themselves and our intention would be judged from the result of the action without bringing in Utopian hypothetical circumstances and presumptions.

No Miracle

Despite the evidence of the Government Expert, the bombs that were thrown in the Assembly Chamber resulted in slight abrasions to an empty bench and some slight damage to less than half a dozen cases, while Government scientist and experts have ascribed this result to a miracle, we see nothing but a precisely scientific process in all this incident. Firstly, the two bombs exploded in vacant spaces within the wooden barriers of the desks and benches, secondly, even those who were within 2 feet of the explosion, for instance, Mr. P. Rau, Mr. Shanker Rao and Sir George Schuster were either not hurt or only slightly scratched. Bombs of the capacity deposed to by the Government Expert (though his estimate, being imaginary is exaggerated), loaded with an effective charge of potassium chlorate and sensitive (explosive) picarate would have smashed the barriers and laid many low within some yards of the explosion.

Again, had they been loaded with some other high explosive, with a charge of destructive pellets or darts, they would have sufficed to wipe out a majority of the Members of the Legislative Assembly. Still again we could have flung them into the official box which was occupied by some notable persons. And finally we could have ambushed Sir John Simon whose luckless Commission was loathed by all responsible people and who was sitting in the President's gallery at the time. All these things, however, were beyond our intention and bombs did no more than the deliberate aim which landed them in safe places.

We then deliberately offered ourselves to bear the penalty for what we had done and to let the imperialist exploiters know that by crushing individuals, they cannot kill ideas. By crushing two insignificant units, a nation cannot be crushed. We wanted to emphasize the historical lesson that letters de cachets and Bastilles could not crush the revolutionary movement in France. Gallows and the Siberian mines could not extinguish the Russian Revolution. Bloody Sunday, and Black and Tans failed to strangle the movement of Irish freedom.

Can ordinances and Safety Bills snuff out the flames of freedom in India? Conspiracy cases, trumped up or discovered and the incarceration of all young men who cherish the vision of a great ideal, cannot check the march of revolution. But a timely warning, if not unheeded, can help to prevent loss of life and general sufferings.

We took it upon ourselves to provide this warning and our duty is done.

Bhagat Singh was asked in the lower court what he meant by word "Revolution". In answer to that question, he said "Revolution" does not necessarily involve sanguinary strife nor is there any place in it for individual vendetta. It is not the cult of the bomb and the pistol. By "Revolution" we mean that the present order of things, which is based on manifest injustice, must change. Producers or labourers in spite of being the most necessary element of society, are robbed by their exploiters of the fruits of their labour and deprived of their elementary rights. The peasant who grows corn for all, starves with his family, the weaver who supplies the world market with textile fabrics, has not enough to cover his own and his children's bodies, masons, smiths and carpenters who raise magnificent palaces, live like pariahs in the slums. The capitalist and exploiters, the parasites of society, squander millions on their whims. These terrible inequalities and forced disparity of chances are bound to lead to chaos. This state of affairs cannot last long, and it is obvious, that the present order of society in merry-making is on the brink of a volcano.

The whole edifice of this civilization, if not saved in time, shall crumble. A radical change, therefore is necessary and it is the duty of those who realize it to reorganize society on the socialistic basis. Unless this thing is done and the exploitation of man by man and of nations by nations is brought to an end, sufferings and carnage with which humanity is threatened today cannot be prevented. All talk of ending war and ushering in an era of universal peace is undisguised hypocrisy.

By "Revolution", we mean the ultimate establishment of an order of society which may not be threatened by such breakdown, and in which the sovereignty of the proletariat should be recognized and a world federation should redeem humanity from the bondage of capitalism and misery of imperial wars.

This is our ideal, and with this ideology as our inspiration, we have given a fair and loud enough warning.

If, however, it goes unheeded and the present system of Government continues to be an impediment in the way of the natural forces that are swelling up, a grim struggle will ensure involving the overthrow of all obstacles, and the establishment of the dictatorship of the proletariat to pave the way for the consummation of the ideal of revolution. Revolution is an inalienable right of mankind. Freedom is an imperishable birth right of all. Labour is the real sustainer of society. The sovereignty of the people is the ultimate destiny of the workers.

For these ideals, and for this faith, we shall welcome any suffering to which we may be condemned. At the altar of this revolution we have brought our youth as an incense, for no sacrifice is too great for so magnificent a cause. We are content, we await the advent of Revolution. "Long Live Revolution".

APPENDIX IV

Government Order on the Classification of Prisoners and Undertrials

Text of the Press Communique

Important decisions of the Government of India regarding the Jail Rules are announced in a Press Communique which runs :

"The Government of India have for some time had under consideration the amendment of jail rules in certain respects. The matter had been referred to Local Governments who have formulated their views after extensive consultation of unofficial opinion. A conference of the provincial representatives was thereupon held and the Government of India have also had discussions with some prominent members of the Legislative Assembly. The problems under examination have been found difficult and complex and have led to the expression of widely divergent opinions. The Government of India have endeavoured to give due weight to these even when they have not been able to accept in full the representations made. The conclusions at which they have arrived on the more important points and which are designed to secure on matters or principle substantial uniformity throughout India, are now announced.

Classification of Prisoners

Convicted prisoners will be divided into three divisions or classes, A, B and C. Prisoners will be eligible for Class 'A' if (1) they are non-habitual prisoners of good character (2) they, by social status, education and habit of life, have been accustomed to a superior mode of living and (3) they have not been convicted of (a) offences involving elements of cruelty, moral degradation or personal greed, (b) seditious or premeditated violence, (c) seditious offences against property, (d) offences relating to possession of explosives, fire-arms and other dangerous weapons with the object of committing an offence or of enabling an offence to be committed, (e) abetment or incitement of offences falling within these sub-clauses.

Prisoners will be eligible for class 'B' who, by social status, education or habit of life have been accustomed to a superior mode of living. Habitual prisoners will not be excluded automatically. The classifying authority will be allowed discretion to suggest their inclusion in this class, having regard to their character and antecedents, subject to confirmation of revision by the Local Government.

Class 'C' will consist of prisoners who are not classified in classes 'A' and 'B'.

The classifying authorities are High Courts, Sessions Judges, District Magistrates, Stipendary Presidency Magistrates, Subdivisional Magistrates and Magistrates of the first class (the two latter through the District Magistrate) in cases tried by them originally or in any other case. The District Magistrate should make an initial recommendation for classification in classes A or B to the Local Government, by whom these recommendations will be confirmed or reviewed.

Privileges of Prisoners

Certain forecasts of their decisions which have been brought to the notice of the Government of India indicate considerable misapprehension in regard to this tripartite division and its effect upon the existing classes of prisoners. It should be clearly understood that all prisoners within the 'A' Class are eligible for the privileges of that class. No class of prisoners will be eligible for any additional privileges on grounds of race. All privileges now given to special class prisoners will be continued to 'A' class prisoners, such as separate accommodation necessary articles of furniture, reasonable facilities for association and exercises, and suitable sanitary and bathing arrangements.

In other matters, the following decisions have been arrived at :

The diet of classes 'A' and 'B' will be superior to the ordinary prison diet given to prisoners in class C and will be based on a flat rate of cost per prisoner, within the limits of which the actual food may vary. The cost of the superior diet provided in the classes A and B should be borne by the Government as special class prisoners are under the existing rules permitted to supplement prison diet at their own expense. This privilege will be retained as at present as regards 'A' class prisoners.

The existing rules regarding privileges of special class prisoners to wear their own clothes will continue. As regards 'A' class prisoners, if they desire to have clothing at Government expense, they will be provided with that prescribed for 'B' class prisoners. 'B' class prisoners will wear prison clothing modified in certain respects and of a better type than that worn by C class prisoners.

Accommodation

A separate jail in each Province for classes A and B is desirable, and its provision though it must depend on the available financial resources of the Local Governments, should be regarded as the goal to be aimed at. Meanwhile, the Government of India hope that Local Governments will carefully review the resources of the jails now existing in the Provinces and endeavour, by such measures as are within their power, to secure the end in view.

In addition to separate accommodation, the Government of India desire to emphasise the necessity of a special staff to deal with 'A' and 'B' class prisoners and are of opinion that this matter should receive the earliest possible attention.

In accordance with the principle already applied, the importance of which is reaffirmed, the tasks allotted to prisoners in 'A' and 'B' classes should be assiged after due consideration on medical grounds, and with careful regard to the capacity, character, previous modes of life and antecedents of the prisoners.

Prisoners' Intellectual Requirements

The Government of India accept the principle that reasonable facilities, subject to safeguards, should be provided by the Government for the intellectual requirements of the educated and literate prisoners. Local Governments will be requested to examine the condition of jail libraries in the Provinces and in cases where those are non-existent or defective, to take early steps to establish or improve them. Literate prisoners may be allowed to read books and magazines from outside subject to the approval of the Jail Superintendent.

Newspapers will be allowed to 'A' class prisoners on the same conditions as under the existing rules, they are allowed to special class prisoners, that is, in special circumstances and with the approval of Local Government. As regards literate prisoners generally, where the Local Governments publish a jail newspaper or where they intend to publish it, this publication will be available once a week for literate prisoners. Where the Local Governments are unable to publish a weekly newspaper, the Government of India have decided that a few copies of a weekly paper approved by the Local Government should be provided at Government expenses for 'A' and 'B' classes of prisoners.

'A' class prisoners will be allowed to write and receive one letter and have one interview a fortnight, instead of once a month as at present. 'B' class prisoners will be allowed to write and receive one letter and have an interview once a month instead of at the considerably longer intervals now permitted under the various jail manuals. Publication of matters discussed at interviews or of the substance of the letters received from prisoners may entail the withdrawl or curtailment of the privilege.

Treatment of Undertrial Prisoners

The Government of India accept the principle that some differentiation of treatment is desirable in the case of undertrial prisoners who, by social status, education or habit of life, have been accustomed to a superior mode of living. There will, therefore, be two classes of under-trial prisoners based on the previous, standard of living only. The classifying authority will be one trying court, subject to the approval of the District Magistrate. The diet provided for 'A' and 'B' class convicted prisoners will be given to the former and the diet of 'C' class prisoners to the latter. Undertrial prisoners in either class, will be allowed to supplement this diet by private purchase through the jail authorities. Under the existing rules, they are allowed to wear their own clothing. The suggestion has been made that in cases where undertrial prisoners are inadequately clad or are unable to obtain clothing from outside, suitable clothing, which should not be prison clothing, should be provided by jail authorities. The Government of India commend this suggestion for adoption to the Local Governments.

The Government of India are of opinion that the interpretation of the existing rules in a liberal spirit, together with the modifications now proposed and the provision of better cellular accommodation, will effect improvements in the directions which enquiry has indicated as desirable. They, therefore, hope that Local Governments will make every effort to improve the existing accommodation and will at once utilize and adapt their existing resources to the best possible advantage. In many of the opinions received by the Government of India, stress had been laid on the desirability of separating under-trial prisoners, who are habituals or charged with grave offences, from those who have not been previously convicted. On this subject, the Government of India consider that no further orders are necessary as they understand that this is the existing practice.

The local Governments are now being invited to amend their jail manuals in the light of these principles, and to frame rules where necessary under Section 60 of the Prisoners Act. Pending such revision they are being requested as far as possible to give immediate practical effect to these changes."

APPENDIX V

Petition dated 20th September, 1930 by Sardar Kishan Singh to the Special Tribunal

---

Petition of Sardar Kishan Singh, father of Bhagat Singh, accused :

"In this case, the accused persons wanted to produce defence evidence after the perusal of the prosecution evidence. They wanted time to find out the material from the prosecution evidence because they could not produce the defence evidence without fully knowing what they had to meet. The time asked for was about a week, but the Hon'ble Members of the Tribunal, for the reasons best known to them, refused to allow the time. I, therefore, beg to submit the following points for the consideration of the Hon'ble Judges :

1. No reliance should be placed on the evidence of the alleged eye-witnesses, for when Bhagat Singh was brought from Delhi to Lahore during the course of the investigation of this murder case of Mr. Saunders, he was not taken to the Central Jail or the Borstal Institution where the prosecution witnesses could have an opportunity to see him before the formal identification parade held by the Magistrate at the Lahore Cantonment police station. The distance between the Lahore Cantonment Police Station and the Central Jail is only 2 miles. Bhagat Singh could very easily have been brought to the Central Jail, and the identification parade could have been held there. At the Cantonment Police Station, the witnesses were procured by the investigating staff, and the Magistrate, who had to hold the identification parade was also sent by the investigating staff. There could be no other object of the police to go out of the way, and to arrange the identification parade at the Cantonment Police Station

than to give an opportunity to the witnesses to see Bhagat Singh before the farce of an identification parade. I at once made an application to the District Magistrate, Lahore that identification parade was of no value and referred 21 P.W.R. 19, 1917 (Cr. Ruling) in that application drawing the attention of the learned District Magistrate to this abnormal conduct of the investigating officer. It has been clearly laid down by the Punjab High Court that the evidence of identification is considerably decreased, if the witnesses get an opportunity to see the accused person before holding the identification parade. That application of mine was published in the local newspapers *Milap* and very probably in *The Tribune*. No weight, therefore, should be attached to the evidence of those withnesses, who identified Bhagat Singh at the identification parade. You, yourselves, are great Judges and presumably read the newspapers. Photos of Bhagat Singh were published in almost all the newspapers of India after the 'Assembly Bomb Case', and the witnesses should be presumed to have seen these photographs of Bhagat Singh before the present identification parade took place.

2. There is no manner of doubt that Mr. Pearne, European gentleman and Traffic Inspector of Police, who had plenty of opportunity to see the real criminals, could not identify the culprits. This man being a Traffic Inspector had developed his sense of identifying the natives by virtue of his profession and calling in life. He could not pick out Bhagat but it is curious that Ganda Singh, Head Constable, and a Naib Court Police Constable and other witnesses, who were accidently present on the spot, could spot Bhagat Singh. It means that accused was shown to those witnesses before the identification parade.

3. No reliance be placed on the evidence of the approvers in this case, because the provisions of Sec. 167, Clause (iii) of the Cr. P. Code have been abused by the Magistrate in remanding the accused persons to police custody. Bhagat Singh and other persons, who have been admitted or likely to be admitted as approvers were kept in the police custody in the Lahore Fort and other different police lock-ups for about 3 months continuously. They were not shown the air of the world. Magistrates extraordinarily went over to the lock-ups and remanded the accused persons for fortnights. Instead of being the governors of the police, they were at the beck and call of the police. The object of taking remands in this extraordinary way was that the public might not come to know what grievances the accused persons, who were confined in the strange lock-ups, made before the Magistrate at the time of the remands. Presumably, the police did not want any legal practitioner to contend before the

Magistrate at the time of the remands that there are no sufficient reasons for further remanding the accused persons to police custody. The accused persons had no opportunity to know the reasons for which the British subjects were being detained by the police. In 90 days, any amount of evidence can be prepared, the accused persons confined can be made to talk by the notorious methods of the police well known to courts. In Z.C.W.N. page 457, the Hon'ble Judges of the Calcutta High Court have held that the evidence of the accused person, who has confessed and has been admitted or is likely to be admitted as approver, and who has been detained in the police custody up to the time of the trial, is open to the greatest suspicion that the police have arranged his statements so as to fit in with any evidence that they may have obtained elsewhere.

About 100 persons, including the Superintendent Police, Deputy Superintendent, Inspectors, were on the investigating staff in this case. They were the officers of the C.I.D. and the local Police Board vying with one another to contribute some material evidence in this case. It is for the protection of the accused persons and to prevent the fabrication of false evidence in this case that Sec. 167 Cr. P.C. and other similar sections were enacted. In 90 days, even stones can be pulverized into smooth powder. In this case, the accused persons were boys of easy living habits and delicate nature. They could be very easily rehearsed and drilled for a theatrical representation. The C.I.D. keeps record of suspicious persons and their activities, they are in possession of the seditious literature, and have got inter-provincial communications in the country. They could very easily get the seditious literature and the prescriptions (formulae) for bomb-making and fit them in the statements of the approvers purchasing their immunity at the sacrifice of the lives of others. And the fiction appears to be more real than the truth. The officers investigating the case, like the experienced craftsmen and engineers, have built up a structure by violations of the remand law. I, therefore, pray that the orders of the remands may kindly be perused at the time of weighing the evidence of the approvers. These persons were certainly kept and detained by the police without any sufficient reasons against the Punjab Chief Court Ruling No. 24 of 1902 Cr. No person can be detained in police custody without the commencement of the trial for more than 15 days. The law protects the accused persons.

4. The witnesses for the prosecution appeared at a very late stage of the investigation and in this country witnesses can be procured and they come forward to give evidence in order to achieve their own private ends, and the police officer investigating big cases did get witnesses from

their friends and hangers-on to corroborate the approvers. Sec. 179 Cr. P. Code has been made to take the assistance of the Police diaries to find out the dates on which their statements were recorded by the police. It is also essential for the prosecution to reveal before the Tribunal, how all the witnesses were traced out. I, therefore, pray to the court to see whether it had been done or not.

It is, therefore, in this case that the accused persons have not cross-examined the prosecution witnesses, but the Bench is composed of judges of experience. They themselves should apply the tests for testing the veracity of the witnesses. Bhagat Singh was in Calcutta on the day of the occurrence and he actually wrote and despatched a letter to one, Ram Lal, Manager of the *Khaddar Bhandar*, Pari Mahal, Lahore, which was duly received by him. There are respectable gentlemen to swear that Bhagat Singh was in Calcutta on the day of the occurrence. I can produce them if I am given an opportunity, according to justice, or they may be called as court witnesses in the interest of justice, equity and good conscience. The question in this case is of life and death. The right of defence is to be jealously preserved for the accused. If an opportunity of defence would have been given, I would have exposed, according to the Evidence Act Sec. 155, who the witnesses for the prosecution are, and what is their position in life, and what are their objects in giving the evidence, when and how they were made witnesses. I still humbly pray that Bhagat Singh may be given an opportunity to produce his defence.

KISHAN SINGH,
Father of Bhagat Singh,
Bradlaugh Hall, Lahore

Dated :
Accused 20th September, 1930

APPENDIX VI

Gandhi-Irwin Pact S. 481/31-Political Home Department

New Delhi, the 5th March, 1931

"Notification

The following statement by the Governor General-in-Council is published for general information :

(1) Consequent on the conversations that have taken place between His Excellency the Viceroy and Mr. Gandhi, it has been arranged that the Civil Disobedience movement be discontinued, and that, with the approval of His Majesty's Government, certain action be taken by the Government of India and Local Governments.

(2) As regards constitutional question, the scope of future discussions is stated, with the assent of His Majesty's Government, to be with the object of considering further the scheme for the constitutional Government of India discussed at the Round Table Conference. Of the scheme there outlined, Federation is an essential part. So also are Indian responsibility and reservations or safeguards in the interests of India, for such matters as, for instance, Defence, External Affairs, the position of Minorities, the financial credit of India, and the discharge of obligations.

(3) In pursuance of the statement made by the Prime Minister in his announcement of the 19th January, 1931, steps will be taken for the participation of the representatives of the Congress in the further discussions that are to take place on the scheme of constitutional reform.

(4) The settlement relates to activities directly connected with the Civil Disobedience Movement.

(5) Civil Disobedience will be effectively discontinued and

reciprocal action will be taken by Government. The effective discontinuance of the Civil Disobedience movement means the effective discontinuance of all activities in furtherance thereof, by whatever methods pursued, and in particular the following :

(1) The organised defiance of the provisions of any law.

(2) The movement for the non-payment of Land Revenue and other legal dues.

(3) The publication of news-sheets in support of the Civil Disobedience movement.

(4) Attempts to influence Civil and Military servants or village officials against Government or to persuade them to resign their posts.

(6) As regards the boycott of foreign goods, there are two issues involved ; firstly, the character of the boycott, and secondly, the methods employed in giving effect to it. The position of Government is as follows. They approve of the encouragement of Indian industries as part of the economic and industrial movement designed to improve the material condition of India, and they have no desire to discourage methods of propaganda, persuasion or advertisement pursued with this object in view, which do not interfere with the freedom of action of individuals, or are not prejudicial to the maintenance of law and order. But the boycott of non-Indian goods, (except of cloth, which has been applied to all foreign cloth) has been directed during the Civil Disobedience movement chiefly, if not exclusively, against British goods, and in regard to these it has been admittedly employed in order to exert pressure for political ends.

It is accepted that a boycott of this character and organised for this purpose will not be consistent with the participation of representatives of the Congress in a frank and friendly discussion of constitutional questions between representatives of British India, of the Indian States, and of His Majesty's Government and political parties in England, which the settlement is intended to secure. It is, therefore, agreed that the discontinuance of the Civil Disobedience movement connotes the definite discontinuance of the employment of the boycott of British commodities as a political weapon and that, in consequence, those who have given up, during a time of political excitement, the sale or purchase of British goods must be left free without any form of restraint to change their attitude if they so desire.

(7) In regard to the methods employed in furtherance of the replacement of non-Indian by Indian goods or against the consumption

or intoxicating liquor and drugs, resort will not be had to methods coming within the category of picketing, except within the limits permitted by the ordinary law. Such picketing shall be unaggressive and it shall not involve coercion, intimidation, restraint, hostile demonstration, obstruction to the public, or any offence under the ordinary law. If and when any of these methods is employed in any place, the practice of picketing in that place will be suspended.

(8) Mr. Gandhi has drawn the attention of Government to specific allegations against the conduct of the Police, and represented the desirability of a public enquiry into them. In the present circumstances, Government see great difficulty in this course and feel that it must inevitably lead to charges and counter-charges, and so militate against the re-establishment of peace. Having regard to these considerations, Mr. Gandhi agreed not to press the matter.

(9) The action that Government will take on the discontinuance of the Civil Disobedience movement is stated in the following paragraphs :

(10) Ordinances promulgated in connection with the Civil Disobedience movement will be withdrawn.

Ordinance No. 1 of 1931 relating to the Terrorist Movement does not come within the scope of the provision.

(11) Notifications declaring associations unlawful under the Criminal Law Amendment Act of 1908 will be withdrawn, provided that the Notifications were made in connection with the Civil Disobedience movement.

The notifications recently issued by the Burma Government under the Criminal Law Amendment Act do not come within the scope of the provision.

(12) (i) Pending prosecutions will be withdrawn if they have been filed in connection with the Civil Disobedience movement and relate to offences which do not involve violence other than technical violence, or incitement to such violence.

(ii) The same principles will apply to proceedings under the security provisions of the Criminal Procedure Code.

(iii) Where a Local Government has moved any High Court or has initiated proceedings under the Legal Practitioners, in connection with the Civil Disobedience movement, it will make application to the Court concerned for permission to withdraw such proceedings, provided that the alleged conduct of the person concerned does not relate to violence or incitement to violence.

(iv) Prosecutions, if any, against soldiers and police involving disobedience of orders will not come within the scope of this provision.

(13) (i) Those prisoners will be released who are undergoing imprisonment in connection with the Civil Disobedience movement for offences which did not involve violence, other than technical violence, or incitement to such violence.

(ii) If any prisoner who comes within the scope of (i) above has been also sentenced for a jail offence, not involving violence, or other than technical violence, incitement to such violence, the latter sentence also will be remitted, or if a prosecution relating to an offence of this character is pending against such a prisoner, it will be withdrawn.

(iii) Soldiers and Police convicted of offences involving disobedience of orders—in the very few cases that have occurred—will not come within the scope of the amnesty.

(14) Fines which have not been realised will be remitted. Where an order for the forfeiture of security has been made under the security provisions of the Criminal Procedure Code, and the security has not been realised, it will be similarly remitted.

Fines which have been realised and securities forfeited and realised under any law will not be returned.

(15) Additional Police imposed in connection with the Civil Disobedience movement at the expense of the inhabitants of a particular area will be withdrawn at the discretion of Local Governments. Local Governments will not refund any money, not in excess of the actual cost, that has been realised, but they will remit any sum that has not been realised.

(16) (a) Moveable property, which is not an illegal possession and which has been seized in connection with the Civil Disobedience movement under the Ordinance or the provisions of the Criminal Law, will be returned, if it is still in the possession of Government.

(b) Moveable property forfeited or attached in connection with the realization of land revenue or other dues will be returned, unless the Collector of the district has reason to believe that the defaulter will contumaciously refuse to pay the dues recoverable from him within a reasonable period. In deciding what is a reasonable period, special regard will be paid to cases in which the defaulters, while willing to pay, genuinely require time for the purpose, and if necessary, the revenue will be suspended in accordance with the ordinary principles of land revenue administration.

(c) Compensation will not be given for deterioration.

(d) Where moveable property has been sold or otherwise finally disposed of by Government, compensation will not be given and the sale proceeds will not be returned, except in so far as they are in excess of legal dues for which the property may have been sold.

(e) It will be open to any person to seek any legal remedy he may have on the ground that the attachment or seizure of property was not in accordance with the law.

(17) (a) Immoveable property of which possession has been taken under Ordinance IX of 1930 will be returned in accordance with the provisions of the Ordinance.

(b) Land and other immovable property in the possession of Government, which has been forfeited or attached in connection with the realization of land revenue or other dues, will be returned unless the Collector of the District has reason to believe that the defaulter will contumaciously refuse to pay the dues recoverable from him within a reasonable period. In deciding what is a reasonable period special regard will be paid to cases in which the defaulter, while willing to pay, genuinely requires time for the purpose, and if necessary the revenue will be suspended in accordance with the ordinary principles of Land Revenue administration.

(c) Where immovable property has been sold to third parties, the transaction must be regarded as final, so far as Government are concerned.

Note :— Mr. Gandhi has represented to Government that according to his information and belief some at least of these sales have been unlawful and unjust. Government, on the information before them, cannot accept this contention.

(d) It will be open to any person to seek any legal remedy on the ground that the seizure or attachment of property was not in accordance with the law.

(18) Government believe that there have been very few cases in which the realization of dues has not been made in accordance with the provisions of the law. In order to meet such cases, if any, Local Governments will issue instructions to District Officers to have prompt enquiry made into specific complaint of this nature, and to give redress without delay if illegality is established.

(19) Where the posts rendered vacant by resignations have been permanently filled, Government will not be able to reinstate the late

incumbents. Other cases of resignation will be considered on their merits by Local Governments who will pursue a liberal policy in regard to the re-appointment of Government servants and village officials who apply for reinstatement.

(20) Government are unable to condone breaches of the existing law relating to the Salt administration, nor are they able in the present financial conditions of the country to make substantial modifications in the Salt Acts.

For the sake, however, of giving relief to certain of the poorer classes, they are prepared to extend their administrative provisions, on lines already prevailing in certain places, in order to permit local residents in villages immediately adjoining areas where salt can be collected or made, to such villages, but not for sale to, or trading with, individuals living outside them.

(21) In the event of Congress failing to give full effect to the obligations of this settlement, Government will take such action as may in consequence become necessary for the protection of the public and individuals and the due observance of law and order.

Sd /- H. W. Emerson,
Secretary to the Government of India."

Bibliography

Primary Sources

Home Political, 1924-31.

Home Department (Judicial), 1929-31.

Debates, House of Commons, 1924-31.

Debates, House of Lords, 1924-31.

Debates, Legislative Assembly, 1924-31.

Debates, Punjab Legislative Council, 1924-31.

Published and Unpublished Reports, Documents and Proceedings

The Collected Works of Mahatma Gandhi, Volumes covering the period 1925-31.

Delhi Assembly Bomb Case and Judgment. These documents are available in National Archives of India.

Lahore Conspiracy Case and Judgment. These documents are available in National Archives of India.

The Punjab Jail Enquiry Committee Report, 1929.

Reports of the Sessions of the Indian National Congress, 1929 and 1931.

Selected Works of Jawaharlal Nehru, S. Gopal, (ed.), Vols. III & IV.

Private Papers

All India Congress Committee Papers, 1923-31

Bhagat Singh's Diary

Halifax Papers

Jawaharlal Nehru Papers

M.K. Gandhi Papers

Motilal Nehru Papers

Newspapers and Periodicals
The Amrita Bazar Patrika
Bengal Past and Present
The Hindu
The Hindustan Times
The Hitavada
Indian Review
The Leader
Modern Review
The Pioneer
Punjab Past and Present
The Searchlight
The Times of India
The Tribune
Young India

Oral History Interviews
These recorded interviews are available in Nehru Memorial Museum Interview with and Library, Teen Murti House, New Delhi.
Transcripts of Chhabil Das
Transcripts of Durga Das Khanna
Transcripts of Feroze Chand
Transcripts of Jai Dev Gupta
Transcripts of Manmathnath Gupta
Transcripts of M.D. Thapar

Secondary Works
Ahmed, Muzaffar, *The Communist Party of India and its Formation Abroad,* Calcutta, 1961.
Ali, Mohamed, *My Life a Fragment,* Lahore, 1944.
Baker, Dudley, Grivas: *Patriot of a Terrorist,* London, 1959.
Bakshi, S.R., Simon Commission and Indian Nationalism, Delhi, 1977.
Bipan Chandra, *Rise and Growth of Economic Nationalism in India,* New Delhi, 1966.
. . . . . .; *Nationalism and Colonialism in Modern India,* New Delhi, 1979.
Bandopadhyaya, Jayantanuja, *Indian Nationalism versus International Communism,* Calcutta, 1966.
Banerjee, Kalyan Kumar, *Indian Freedom Movement: Revolutionaries in America,* Calcutta, 1969.

Besant, Annie, *India: Bond or Free,* Adyar, 1939.
Bose, A.C., *The Indian Revolutionaries Abroad, 1905-22,* Patna, 1977.
Bose, S.C., *The Indian Struggle, 1920-42,* New York, 1964.
Brockway, A.F., *The Indian Crisis,* London, 1930.
Buch, M.A., *Rise and Growth of Indian Militant Nationalism,* Bombay, 1940.
Caveeshar, S.S., *India's Fight for Freedom,* Lahore, 1936.
Chakravarty, Chandra, *New India,* Calcutta, 1951.
Chatterjee, Jogesh, *The Search of Freedom,* Calcutta, 1967.
Chintamani, C.Y., *Indian Politics Since the Mutiny,* Allahabad, 1947.
Chirol, Valentine, *Indian Unrest,* London, 1910.
Coupland, R., *The Constitutional Problem of India,* Madras, 1934.
Craddock, Reginald, *The Dilemma in India,* London, 1929.
Crozier, Brian, *The Rebels,* London, 1960.
Das, C.R., *India for Indians,* Madras, 1921.
Das, R.P., *The Impact of the Russo-Japanese (1950) War on Indian Politics,* Delhi, 1966.
Deol, Gurdev Singh, *Shaeed Bhagat Singh: A Biography,* Patiala, 1969.
Fischer, Louis, *The Soviets in World Affairs,* London, 1930.
Fraser, Andrew, *Among Indian Rajahs and Ryots,* London, 1911.
Gandhi, M.K., *Autobiography,* Ahmedabad, 1963.
Garnett, David, *The Golden Eco.,* London, 1936.
Ghosh, Ajoy, *Bhagat Singh and His Comrades,* Bombay, 1945.
Ghosh, Kali Charan, *The Roel of Honour: Anecdotes of Indian Martyrs,* Calcutta, 1965.
Gokhale, G.K., *Speeches,* Madras, 1916.
Gopal, S., *Jawaharlal Nehru: A Biography, Vol. 1,* 1889-1947, London, 1975.
Gupta, Manmathnath, *They Lived Dangerously,* Delhi, 1969.
. . . . . .; *Bhagat Singh and His Times,* Delhi, 1977.
Griffiths, P.J., *The British Impact on India,* London, 1965.
Halifax, *The Earl of, Fullness of Days,* London, 1957.
Hoyland, John S., *The Case for India,* London, 1929.
Hyndman, H.M., *The Awakening of Asia,* London, 1919.
Irwin, Lord, *Indian Problems,* London, 1932.
Iyer, C.S. Ranga, *India in the Crucible,* London, 1928.
Kaye, Cecil, *Communism in India,* Delhi, 1926.
Kenworthy, J.M., *India: A Warning,* London, 1931.
Kohn, Hans, *A History of Nationalism in East,* New York, 1929.

Majumdar, R.C., *History of the Freedom Movement in India,* Vol. II, Calcutta, 1963.

Mehrotra, S.R., *India and the Commonwealth, 1885-1929,* London, 1965.

. . . . . .: *Towards Indian Freedom and Partition,* New Delhi, 1979.

Meston, Lord, *India and the Empire,* London, 1924.

Moraes, Frank, *Jawaharlal Nehru,* Bombay, 1957.

Nehru, Jawaharlal, *An Autobiography,* Delhi, 1962.

Pal, B.C., *Nationality and Empire,* Calcutta, 1916.

Pande, B.N., *Nehru,* Delhi, 1977.

Parmanand, Bhai, *The Story of My Life,* Lahore, 1934.

Payne, Robert, *Red Storm Over Asia,* New York, 1951.

Prabodh Chadra, *Sixty Years of Congress,* Lahore, 1964.

Pratap, Raja Mahendra, *My Life Story of Fifty-five Years,* Delhi, 1947.

Rai, Lajpat, *Young India,* Lahore, 1927.

Sandhu, Virendra, *Shaheed Bhagat Singh,* Delhi, 1974.

Sanyal, Jatindra Nath, *Sardar Bhagat Singh,* Allahabad, 1931.

Sarkar, Sumit, *The Swadeshi Movement in Bengal, 1903-08,* New Delhi, 1973.

Shastri, Bal Hardas, *India's Armed Struggle for Freedom,* Poona, 1958.

Durlab Singh, *Famous Letters and Ultimatums to the British Government,* Lahore, 1944.

Sitaramayya, B. Pattabhi, *The History of the Indian National Congress,* Vol. I, Bombay, 1946.

Tara Chand, *History of the Freedom Movement in India,* Vols. II and III, Delhi, 1967, 1972.

Thakur, Gopal, *Bhagat Singh: The Man and His Ideas,* New Delhi, 1962.

Woodruff, Philip, *The Men who Ruled India,* London, 1954.

Woolacot, J.E., *India on Trial,* London, 1929.

INDEX

A

Aga Khan, 63
All India Congress Committee, 67
Ajit Singh, Sardar (Uncle of Bhagat Singh), 12, 31 ff,
Allahabad, 76, 175
Amar Kaur, 39
Amba Prasad, 75
Amritsar, 12, 21, 173
Andaman Islands, 119, 175
Ansari, M.A., 244, 247
Arjun Singh, 34, 37
Arora, Sant Ram, 21
Asaf Ali, 102
Arya Samaj, its social activities, 17
Azad, Chandra Shekhar, 15, 92, 99, 117, 133, 221
Azad, Prithvi Singh, 133

B

Belgaum Congress, Gandhiji presided in 1924, 84
Besant, Annie, 173
Bhakana, Sohan Singh, 133
Bhargava, Gopi Chand, the first Premier in East Punjab, 13
Bihar, 112
Bishen Dass, 21
Bismal, Ram Prasad, 28, 159
Bombay, 160
Bose, Rash Behari, 46
Bose, S.C., 114, 180, 192 ff, 202; Bose and Calcutta Congress, 1928, 233; his speech at Karachi, 248 ff,
Buddh and Buddhism, 199

C

Calcutta, 72, 76, 89, 90, 111, 175
Canada, 174
Caveeshar, Sardul Singh, 46
Chamanlal, Diwan, 97, 106
Chandragupta, 56
Chatterjee, Jogesh Chandra, 15, 28
Chattar Singh, 129
Chattopadhyaya, B., 115
Chauri, Chaura, 15-16
Chelmsford, Lord, 160
Chhabil Das, 20-22
China, 24
Christ, 199
Churchill, Winston, 198
Civil Disobedience Movement, 206, 212
Comrades, (List of) 221 ff
CPI, 135
Congress Working Committee, 237
Criminal Law Amendment Act, 21

D

Dandi March, 212
Dange, S.A., 23, 25
Das, D.P., 192 ff
Das, J.N., 12, 15, 111, 229, 235-36
Das, C.R., 24-25, 72
Das, S.R., 79, 107
Dayanand, Swami, 34
Dehradun, 76, 82
Delhi, 234
Delhi Pact, 195 ff, 243

Death and Reaction, 131
Dhingra, Madanlal, 159
Doveton, Captain, 182
Duni Chand, 137
Dutta, B.N., 23
Dutta, B.K., 12, 73, 100, 117, 230
Dutt, Rajni Palme, 70
Dyer, R.E.H., 178

E

Emerson, 194, 306
England, 25, 184
Edward, J.M., 49

F

Faridkot, 82
Flogging, 181

G

Gandhi, M.K., 11, 14-15, 53, 75, 79, 110, 112 191, 195 ff, 210 ff, 245 ff
Gandhi-Irwin Pact, 162, 256 ff
Ganges, 54
Garibaldi, 288
Gaya Prasad, 15
Ghadr Movement, 15, 175
Ghosh, Ajoy, 132 ff
Ghosh, K.C., 181
Gobind Singh, 288
Gulbarga, 76
Gupta, Jai Dev, 16, 51
Gupta, Manmathnath, 47, 59
Gujarat, 37
Gujranwala, 56
Gurdit Singh, 114

H

Haig, H.G., 28
Hansraj, 36
Hardinge Bomb Case, 15
Hardyal, 61, 174
Hasrat Mohani, 81
Hindu-Muslim Unity, 182
Hindustan Socialist Republican Association, 28, 126
Hong Kong, 175
Hunter Commission, 183

I

Indians abroad, 174 ff
Indian National Congress, 60 ff, 203
Indian Penal Code, 22
Irwin, Lord, 14, 161, 191, 214 ff, 244, 248
Ireland, 24

J

Jabalpur, 76
Jafri, Ali Sardar, 46
Jallianwala Bagh Tragedy, 26, 44
Jhelum, 37
Jai Gopal, 47
Jai Kaur, 80
Japan, 24
Jind, 82
Jinnah's speech, in Legislative Assembly of India, 269 ff
Josh, Sohan Singh, 47, 136
Jugal Kishore, 51

K

Kakori Case, 23, 207
Kangra, 37
Kanpur, 66, 133
Kapurthala, 82
Kashi Ram, Pandit, 174
Karachi Congress, 1931, 189, 212
Karnal, 22
Kasur, 182
Kidwai, Rafi Ahmed, 114
Kesar Singh, 174
Kitchlew, S.D., 177
Khan, Ajmal, 77
Khan, Ashfaqullah, 159
Kathmandu, 166
Khudi Ram, 130

Kishan Singh, 12, 27, 34 ff, 37, 65, 217, 297
Kirti Kisan Party, 25, 47
Kohat, 76
Kuljit Sehgal, 21
Kuka Movement, 165

L

Labour Party, 256
Lahore, 11, 12, 45, 47, 66, 175
Conspiracy Case, 15, 207, 228, 234
Lajpat Rai, 23, 31, 51, 77, 177, 202, 206, 234
Laxmi Chand, 22
Lenin, 115, 123
Liberals, 177
London, 70, 244
Lucknow 176, 90, 175
Ludhiana, 167
Lyallpur, 43, 56, 175

M

Mac Sweeney, 255
Madras, 159, 282
Majit, M.A., 24, 47
Malaviya, Madan Mohan, 100, 274
Malerkotla, 167
Mandalay, 37, 175
Marx, 73, 251
Maryada, 221
Meerut, 175
Midnapore, 244
Moonje, B.S., 103
Morley, John, 32

N

Nabha, 78
Nagpur, 76
Nankana Saheb, 82
Napoleon, 103
National martyrs, 159 ff
Naujwan Bharat Sabha, 11, 16-17, 19, 21-22, 26, 234
Nehru, Jawaharlal, 79, 114
Nehru, Motilal, 79, 80, 114, 126, 137, 243
Nepal, 34, 37
Noad, C., 261 ff
Non-Cooperation Movement, 15

O

Operation Hunger-strike, 118
Orissa, 182

P

Pande, Shivram, 40
Parmanand, Bhai, 53, 174
Patel, Sardar, 237
Parwati Devi, 53
Peasants and workers, 252
Penang, 175
Peshawar, 160
Pike, 277
Pratap, 114
Pritt, D.N., 137
Privy Council, 112, 137 ff
Public Safety Bill, 97
Punjab Kesari, 123

Q

Quran, 81

R

Ram Singh, Baba, 165
Ranjit Singh, Maharaja, 167
Raj Guru, 12, 14
Ram Chandra, 25
Ram Tirath, 69
Rawalpindi, 32, 56
Round Table Conference, 123, 163, 242-43
Roy, M.N., 46, 115
Reading, Lord, 78
Revolutionaries (List of) 112
Rowlatt Committee Report, 54
Rur Singh, 133
Russia, 122, 123, 250

S

Saha, Gopinath, 74
San Francisco, 174
Sanders, J.P., 12, 97
Sanyal, S.N., 28, 46
Sarabha, Kartar Singh, 12, 159
Satyapal, 11, 179
Savarkar, V.D., 172
Schuster, George, 99, 108
Sehgal, Kidar Nath, 23-25, 47
Shahjahanpur, 76
Shivaji, 88
Sholapur, 160
Shraddhanand, Swami, 36
Simon Commission, 25
Sinn Fein, 255-56
Singpore, 175
Sitamayya, 75
Sinha, Bejoy Kumar, 47
Skeen Committee, 282
Smedley, Agnes, 24
Spratt, Philip, 23
Sukhdev, 12, 14
Sunder Das, 21
Swaraj Party, 72

T

Tagore, Rabindranath, 112
Tandon, P.D., 183
Terry, Sgt., 101
Tewari, K.N., 47
Tilak, B.G., 69, 103
Tolstoy, Leo, 199
Tosha Maru, 175
Tribune, The, 183
Turkey, 24

U

Udham Singh, 185
United Provinces, 46, 169
United States of America, 133
Usman, Shaukat, 73

V

Vancouver, 174
Verdict, 121 ff
Verma, Shiv, 116
Vidarbha, 37
Vidyavati, 38, 43
Vidyarathi, G.S., 110
Vidyalankar, Jai Chand, 54
Vivekanand, Swami, 69
Vohra, B., 15, 224

W

Washington, 288
Waterloo, 38
Wellingdon, Lord, 160
Women revolutionaries, 231
Wylie, W. Curzon, 171-72

Y

Yashpal, 15, 35-36, 40

Z

Zulu War, 184